"Janice Lynch maintained strong trust in God
in the face of loss and betrayal in her marriage.
I pray her story will encourage many others."
—*Joshua Harris*
Pastor, Covenant Life Church, Maryland

"Janice's story
is a testimony to the faithfulness of God
in an otherwise impossibly painful situation.
Page after page, the message is so clear and real:
We can trust the Lord through everything
and come out victorious.
Even though it was so different
from my own terribly difficult situation—
the same principles apply and are a huge help to me.
Thank you, Janice!"
—*Sheila Brown*
President, Maryland Chapter,
Aglow International

"Your story is so powerful.
It fills me with faith and trust in God."
—*Dr. Nancy Lawless, MD, Maryland*

"We need to have more books on the shelf
that tell the intimate story of how God works
through hardship in real people's lives –
this is one such book!"
—*Sandy Dufrin, Michigan*
Author, He Gives and He Takes Away

When God
is
Faithful

And Your Husband Isn't

by Janice Porter Lynch

SEVEN KEYS TO VICTORY OVER ANY CRISIS

When God is Faithful, And Your Husband Isn't
Seven Keys To Victory Over Any Crisis
by Janice Porter Lynch

Printed in the United States of America

ISBN 9781613795545

Unless otherwise indicated, Bible quotations are taken from The HOLY BIBLE, NEW INTERNATIONAL VERSION®. Copyright © 1973, 1978, 1984 by Biblica. Used by permission of Zondervan; and The King James Version (KJV).

Copy Editor: Aimee Lynch
Field Editor: Jim Kochenburger
A heartfelt thanks to numerous others
who gave input and feedback including David Fourney,
Carol Trebes, and Chris McSweeney.
Interior Graphics: Jessica Lynch, Kimberly Fourney
Cover Design: Rebecca Darling

Author Website: www.WhenGodisFaithful.com

Disclaimer:
Most names and some
irrelevant details
have been changed.

www.xulonpress.com

Dedication

To God Who Is My Help

*And to all those whom God used
as His personal hands to serve me,
His arms to hold me,
His feet to go for me,
and His mouth to encourage and to pray.
I am so grateful.
Thank you.*

My Prayer for You... Love, Janice

Dear God,

Reach each person who reads this story.
And please bring the ones
who need to hear its message.

I ask that You would open up
each one's understanding
and draw their heart to You.

Build their faith.

Let these words
make a significant difference
in each life.

And let each person discover
a depth in their relationship with You
that they never knew was possible.

Bless them in every way, Lord.

In Jesus' Name, Amen.

Table of Contents

My Prayer for You..ix

Prologue: The Day the World Became a Different Place......................xiii

I Thessalonians 5:16-18 xv

  1. My Prince Charming...17

  2. First Glimpses of California 25

  3. The Fingerprints of God 35

  4. The List...47

  5. New Arrival, New Hope 55

  6. Tremors of an Earthquake...59

  7. But God Sees 65

  8. A Stranger in My Bed 79

  9. What Happened Next...87

 10. Hard Steps...105

 11. Kirk's Decision 113

 12. As a Shepherd, He Leads 119

 13. Preparation for the Worst, Hoping for the Best 129

 14. The Escape 139

 15. In My Parents' Home 147

 16. Divine Direction 155

 17. The Retreat...161

 18. Road Trip 167

19. The Return 175

20. Adjustment.. 181

21. How Odd it Feels 189

22. Walking it Out.. 195

23. Fear in the Night 201

24. Another Attack 207

25. Prejudice 215

26. God Leads Again 223

27. Kirk's Agitation.. 229

28. God Convicts Me 231

29. More Steps in the Journey 237

30. A Sacrifice of Praise... 245

31. A Plan and a Future.. 251

32. The Court Trial... 259

33. The Choice to Praise 267

34. The Next Step Begins 271

35. Still Praying for Kirk 275

36. A Question That Would Pop Up 283

37. The Agreement.. 289

38. More Angels Sent by Him 295

39. A Chapter Closing.. 303

Believe 313

Seven Keys to Victory Over Any Crisis..................... 315

Author Bio 323

The Day the World Became a Different Place

I froze. My newborn baby son, who had filled his tummy with breast milk, also lay halted, unmoving. Fast asleep once more, with breath as soft and quiet as warm mist, he lay face turned toward mine on my chest.

His little arms covered in blue terrycloth rested like cooked spaghetti on his petite belly. The slight smell of dried, soured milk on his sleeper wafted upwards, but no one noticed.

Darkness still held the approaching day captive and barred the windows to the small office. I sat cross-legged at my husband's desk in a rolling swivel chair, the cluttered room illuminated only in part by the short desk lamp. Shadows stalked the corners and drew on the walls in the predawn hour.

Holding the baby in the crutch of my left arm, and my husband's pager which I'd been tinkering with in my right hand, I stared at it, unblinking, not daring to move, hardly daring to breathe.

But somehow I did take another breath. Slowly, I allowed the air to enter and to exit through my opened mouth as the words on the pager's screen scrolled over and over again, and marched defiantly before my bright hazel eyes in their single-lined demonstration.

Did I dare to comprehend the meaning of the words jeering and mocking me from the device no bigger than the palm of my hand?

I drank in this one last moment as my two small daughters and my husband slept in bedrooms across the hall. I drank in the last inch of a journey where nothing significantly bad or tragic had ever happened to me before. I drank it in because I knew that when I took my next step, it meant crossing over a bridge and into a world that I would never, ever have expected to enter.

So I continued to sit, still, stunned, and stationary.

It was then that the ticking clock on the wall beckoned to me, demanding my attention: 5:30 AM. It was time. It was time for me to move. I stood up.

Now, I knew. Now I knew for certain.

It was predawn, early Saturday morning, in Hillside, California, July 10, 1999.

~~~

"Be joyful always;
pray continually;
give thanks in all circumstances,
for this is God's will for you
in Christ Jesus."
I Thessalonians 5:16-18

~~~

1

My Prince Charming

My earliest teenage recollection is dreaming of myself growing up and married to my wonderful Prince Charming – dreaming that I lived happily ever after, in fact, with three small children and a brick house in the suburbs with large climbing trees in the front and back yards.

It was during my preteen growth spurt at my home on the East Coast with my mother, father, and my little brother, Michael, two years younger.

My girlfriends recall this vividly as we had many conversations locked behind closed doors inside my enormous, pink bedroom on the upper floor of our home in the late afternoons following long, tiring days at school.

Giggly young girls, our ideas of true love splashed over, spilling into piles of laughter, and sometimes even turning into more contemplative discussion and sharing in those early formative years.

At one time I'd come upon a book in the local library, quite by accident, on one of those weekly excursions carried out to expand my brother's and my own horizons of the world.

I read the words of romantic love with great interest and intrigue, except in my imagination it was my own destiny that I observed – almost certainly with no thought of practical constraints.

I experienced the future with my husband inside my head long before its arrival:

My family, friends, and relatives stood on the sidelines in awe and respect – the next generation had succeeded.

A magnificent union between my husband and myself with our children, well-behaved, obedient, and adorable - bore witness to the badge of success we would wear.

The expressions the onlookers wore on their faces said it all: never had any family been more blessed on the crust of this planet.

"Such wisdom and success at their youthful ages!" one in the group spoke loud enough for all to hear, marvel, and admire.

Little did I know that when I did at last meet my Prince Charming, a hidden time bomb in his soul, not yet detected nor diffused, ticked away, moment-by-moment, unchecked, toward the destruction that would one day unleash itself within the sacred womb of our marriage.

When that time came, perhaps because my confidence in the solemn vows of marriage had been so deep, perhaps because of my innocence or naiveté, perhaps because I'd lived the good life up until then and thought the best of those I knew, the force of the nauseating reality bewildered and surprised me like none other. It was an unforeseen possibility for my life, nor could it have been in the thoughts of any of those who knew us.

The sting was astonishing, like surgery without the help of anesthesia, like bleeding with no end. It was the most terrible pain I had ever known in my entire cheerful life. But it was only my own pain for a short time.

When the news of what had taken place spread to others, my heart was not the only one to be broken. Even worse, the multiple ramifications for my beloved children became increasingly apparent in my mind.

I cannot remember exactly what the weather was like outside that day, or what events topped the local news, but I do remember being astounded that I could still live and breathe and move when my beloved husband had simply, suddenly, and stoically walked out that door and closed it, leaving me all at once by myself in the home that we had made together; alone with the responsibility of caring for two preschoolers and our infant son, and wondering *what in the world happened?*

~~~

We'd been married nine years and Kirk had moved us from one city to the next whenever a better job opportunity came along. Three thousand miles across the country in Northern California, 707 Strawberry Lane was address number seven in less than a decade, and the furthest we'd been from family and friends.

As usual, a stream of overtime at Kirk's work descended on our lives. I don't know when it was that I had grown used to Kirk's sporadic hours that had begun early on in his career of servicing hospital equipment.

The only thought I remember with precision was the one that I repeated aloud to myself on trying occasions: "Kirk provides well for our family and he works very hard. I will support him by having fresh meals ready for him, cleaned and ironed clothes, listening to him, conversing with him, and, most of all, *by not complaining*."

Kirk himself was always ready to fix what was broken, find what was lost, or listen to the antics of his children. Kirk had an engaging way with people, and this quality had attracted me from the beginning.

But the most important characteristic of Kirk was this: Kirk was a Christian. We'd met in the summer after our college graduations while being trained in a school to serve as youth ministers in the church.

Whenever a twinge of longing or doubt struggled to arise about his long hours away, I comforted myself with this: Kirk worshipped the Lord with his guitar when he put the kids to bed, Kirk had a Bible, Kirk tithed, and Kirk brought us to church on Sundays.

Sometimes, when Kirk was alone at the computer monitor, his eyes glazed and his lips curled upward slightly with an unusual kind of grin. He answered interruptions with an abrupt curtness and lacked the patience he normally demonstrated.

Flash! It was like being in a dark room when the bright light of a camera goes off and your eyes just barely adjust to make out a few images that disappear just as suddenly. Like this, Kirk appeared to return quickly to normal. It was easy to explain away any inconsistencies. It was easy to believe his excuses when I did question him.

I remember the brief prickles of foreboding that something was not altogether quite right, the split-second of uncertainty, and, mostly, I remember the happy life that I led.

While there was sometimes, briefly, a hint of something that did not make sense, more often than not I remained occupied in the delightful tasks of living that took up my time: serving my husband, exploring the wonders of the California coast as a family, weekly ballroom dancing classes and date nights with Kirk, putting my children to bed, changing diapers, decorating my home, hosting our church's women's Bible study, playgroups, and beginning the homeschool education that we'd prayed about and that I'd especially felt convicted in my heart to pursue.

In many ways, God protected me until exactly the right moment for me to know about the double-life that my husband was leading behind my unsuspicious, unsuspecting eyes.

How can someone who has made such a godly commitment leave his wife and children?

I don't know. Until that time, it was a scenario that I had never considered possible.

~~~

From the beginning, excitement filled my heart every time I viewed or even thought about Kirk Tufton Lynch.

Built slightly taller than myself, the same fair skin of the Irish with a top of dark brown hair like my own, *I saw my own self in his reflection.* Not only in physique, but he matched my 'jar is half full' perspective, enjoyment of others, and enthusiasm. Again, he was *like me.*

Meeting in the same summer camp, or, in actuality, it was a ten-week, all-day, intensive business training school for those applying for the position of youth director in one of many small, local churches, Kirk and I shared the same goals: to make a huge difference in the lives of teenagers with the gospel.

Spiritually speaking, I met Kirk at a time when he was full of passion for the Lord. His conversion had been not that long before, while in his later years of college. There, because of his involvement in campus ministry, he had been recruited by an organization looking for youth director potential.

Taken with this new direction for ministry after college graduation, he'd put aside engineering plans for the short term in order to focus on the difference he could make in a youth's life.

I, sensing the same direction, and carrying many wonderful memories of my growing-up experience under my own church's youth ministry program, wholeheartedly committed to the like-task presented us.

We were both 22 years old, he just a few weeks older than myself.

Even though the days of that summer were long, and homework was required of each of us in the evening, Kirk and I both made our early morning individual time with the Lord a priority. Kirk rose early to sing and to worship the Lord for up to an hour on his guitar – by the time he arrived for our classes, the sweet aroma of God's presence accompanied him. I was smitten.

It happened at the zoo. Our group of forty had opted to take a Saturday tour on one of our first and only days off, but the rest had left Kirk and me in the distance because we'd both had so much to say about the bat exhibit.

And then there was the elephant ride. That is what we wandered up to next. Sitting side-by-side atop that huge animal as it lumbered us around the yard, my heart fluttered. Kirk's jokes were so funny, his words so interesting, his manners so thoughtful and caring.

And so the summer went on growing warmer and hotter with each progressing day. By the end I had been certain: I wanted to marry Kirk Tufton Lynch. I'd met no other like him in all my short life.

That was when we'd received the bad news. It was after our summer graduations from the business school and it was time to receive our assignments and invitations to interview with a local church.

I struggled to hold back tears that morning in August as I walked down the street from my host family's home to meet up with my ride to the school. At 10:00 AM, I had an appointment with the couple who had originally interviewed me and would place me with a church.

I had reason to believe that we would be offered assignments very far away from one another due to the territories of our different recruiters. I just knew it.

I felt ripped apart inside as I contemplated two years of separation across many, many miles. We were not ready to get married yet – it was still too soon, and we both desired to fulfill our calls to youth ministry.

That is when the jogger intersected my path and paused, moving his feet in place. The middle-aged man with gray hair, shorts, and a sweat towel asked me, "How are you today?"

"Terrible," I replied, eyes tearing. "You see," I told this unlikely stranger while standing at the corner and gesturing with my hands, "Today I will find out that I have been offered an assignment far away from the man I love."

The jogger looked into my face. "God is in charge," he said, "and God knows what He is doing." With those simple words, he'd jogged away. Stunned, I took hope in the reminder that God did know what He was doing.

What followed were two years of great happiness even with the long distance. Kirk was the one with whom I talked on the phone every day. He was the one who wrote me letters and expressed his thoughts. I'd never forget his list of *100 Reasons Why I Love You.*

We completed Christian couples' workbooks over the phone and discussed the aspects of our relationship as guided in our studies.

And then, one day when I'd least expected it, because, after all, Kirk lived over 500 miles away, there'd been a knock at my apartment door.

I didn't even look through the peephole to see who it was because I'd been expecting some other friends to pick me up for a Valentine's Day dessert outing.

And there he was. Kirk, clothed in a smashing black tuxedo with a red cummerbund. Kirk, with shiny black shoes and kneeling in front of me, taking my hand, and saying those words I'd so longed to hear: "Janice, I love you. Will you marry me?" He had driven ten straight hours to the tuxedo rental store in town without stopping one time.

"Oh, yes! Yes, Kirk. Yes." I breathed and danced and spun in his arms as he held me tight, lifted me off my feet, and turned me in the air. Dinner with wine. And then the many happy phone calls.

The marriage had taken place after the completion of our two-year contracts at our churches. The reception happened at a mansion back home, adorned with bouquets and arches of balloons, fancy hors d'oeuvres, piano accompaniment, and a walking barbershop quartet wading through the patios and flower gardens.

Family and friends traveled for miles to take part in the important ceremony. It was a most treasured day.

We married, then honeymooned, then settled down in a city in Florida. God provided.

Kirk landed an exciting medical engineering job even though the odds had been stacked against him. I began a career in social work. We traded in our first 325-square-foot rental apartment for our first single family home on Sunnyside Court.

We attended church, we had godly friends, and we had no television for a year while instead we spent part of each day singing and worshipping the Lord together.

Memories. Yes, special memories. Friday nights at Ryan's Steakhouse. The day I found out my grandfather had died and Kirk held me and he cried also, even though it was *my* grandfather. Team teaching Sunday School. Our first married Christmas eating pizza for dinner in the surprising warmth at the beach. The cockroaches, and then the fleas we'd tackled and conquered in our first home, and the long, black snake in the garage.

We laughed and we played and it was fun.

It turned out that Kirk was a whole lot brighter and more talented than I could ever have imagined. Kirk fixed anything broken in our house or in our car. Eager companies offered him employment to come and work for them.

Kirk, I thought, was pretty amazing.

After only two years, we moved from Florida to North Carolina.

But here Kirk's hours were crazy. His meager pay had doubled, but his new female boss remained unsympathetic and unrelenting. It was not uncommon for Kirk to work thirty-six hours straight because of the high demands of keeping hospital equipment up and running.

It was also here that he had just one co-worker – the co-worker whom, it turned out, was attracted to the strip clubs located outside the town. I never considered that Kirk would stop there, and I felt sorry for his co-worker's wife because I knew that her husband did.

After two more years, one more apartment, one beautifully custom-built house, and our first precious baby girl, Kirk accepted a job offer in another city in North Carolina. Here, it was promised, the hours would be better. And they were, in a way.

In the newest city in North Carolina, Kirk worked daytime hours one week and then nights the next. His hours were consistent but still difficult due to the constant shift.

Still, we made time for family fun. On the weekends, Kirk drove us to Bluegrass festivals big and small.

We lived in a town of missionaries and our friends were good ones. We had another beautiful daughter, and then came the fantastic job offer from California only six years after we'd first been married.

Kirk interviewed. And, Kirk took it.

Little did I know what the next chapter in our lives would hold.

2

First Glimpses of California

July 1996

"Babe!" Kirk shouted to me almost giddy with excitement from the tip on the mountain rise where he stood. I sat and waited with baby Meaghan in the car. "Babe, *you've got* to see this!"

We'd pulled over along the curvy, windy roadside to where water trickled over a rock about the size of a bassinet. It spurted out of a natural spring.

Having been raised in suburbia on the East Coast, it was surprising that *just anybody* could stop here and collect some drinking water from a natural spring. I'd only ever seen spring water sold at the grocery store.

The mountain breeze tenderly combed my hair as I climbed out of the rental car and unhitched our four-month-old from her carseat in the back. My husband scrambled back down to me to take hold of my hand and pulled me along up to the rise to where he'd been standing.

I caught my breath when the scene came into view. Layers and layers of mountain ridges covered in trees, and beyond this, the Pacific Ocean, frothy and wild. *How could I have not known before how beautiful Northern California is?*

"Babe," he said, holding me around the waist, standing behind me, and squeezing me tight, "There are so many spectacular places here, and I can't wait to show you them all!"

Being three thousand miles away from family and friends and relocating to a whole different world was as breath-taking as the view. But with my much-loved husband's strong arms around me and his familiar aftershave lingering in the air, I felt safe and secure.

I looked forward to our new home in California and hoped for better hours at his new workplace.

~~~

California, except for being far away from our relatives, seemed like a dream. Every day was sunny and one could count on it. Every day was comfortable, mild, and pleasant – out with all our heavy winter clothes needed back East.

That is why the hills outside the city 'beamed with gold,' our realtor tried to persuade us. "No, they are not brown," she corrected, "they are golden," she insisted, nodding again at the barren land.

Kirk and I eyed each other and smiled in amusement, observing her face, unmoved. Kirk sat sideways in the front seat with his back to the door of the car so that he could hold my hand where I sat in the back beside our tiny little girls in their carseats. Our hands exchanged the three short squeezes that we knew stood for the words, *I love you.*

And the realtor drove us on, continuing to expound on the golden hills of Northern California located outside of the city.

Soon giant, white bodies came into view with only three spiked ends on the wheel, some spinning, some still. Others were shorter, with a stick pointing up, and oval-bended ends on each side, spinning like tops side-to-side.

Against the brown dirt landscape, it was eerie – I felt like I was on the set for Star Wars. "What are those things?" I asked Kirk.

"Probably the largest windmill farm in the entire world," he responded. This was the Altamont Pass.

Things in California were so different. This land had so many surprises in store.

The windmills were not the only unique objects in the California north. There were also the trees: the huge, monstrous, big-enough-to-fit-inside-of Sequoias. Visits to the national park, Muir Woods, became a regular favorite family outing.

And California quickly filled with friends.

From the outset, Kirk had settled us into a local church of about 500, only blocks from our home. Here we were soon taken under wing by the main church secretary, Emilie, because she had drawn my name from a hat for the annual secret sister program.

Donald and Debbie, the assistant pastor and his wife, along with their two young children, also became fast friends.

I'd discovered the local Women's Aglow chapter before we'd even moved from the temporary suites that Kirk's company had provided and into our new home in Hillside.

In addition, a new preschool playgroup was quickly formed with our two small daughters. Mothers of Preschoolers (MOPS) meetings began, as well as weekly church Bible studies.

Promise Keepers, a praying men's group that met early before work, asked Kirk to join. Though he'd been part of this organization before we'd moved, Kirk declined. "Because," he said, "I have to work at those times."

~~~

Late June, 1998

It was late in the afternoon and I read a book while laying down on our bed for few moments. The girls, ages four and two, still napped and Kirk would be home from work soon.

Rays of setting sun penetrated through the sliding glass doors of our bedroom, warming me like a blanket.

In moments, the front door opened and closed, my dark-haired husband strode into our bedroom, gave me a kiss, and then turned to undo his tie, hanging it on the rack in the closet.

That's when he made his remarkable statement:

"You know what, Babe?" he waited for me to look directly into his face, "I think I'm ready to have another baby."

I stared back at Kirk, trying hard not to miss the words that he was saying.

My mind flipped back through the pages in time to when we were living across the country on the East Coast, to the birth of our second child over two years before. I'd laid in the hospital bed waiting to hold my precious second daughter right after she'd been delivered, but the team of specialists still checked her lungs.

I'd become a Christian at the age of fifteen, but it had certainly not been often that I'd heard the Holy Spirit speak to me in such a clear, distinct, obvious voice. But, as I'd laid there, He'd done just that.

The next time it will be David Michael, I'd heard from an inward depth as clear and understandable as could be.

At first, I'd rejoiced. But then I began to wonder. Why would God speak these words to me? After all, I was not disappointed at all to have a second daughter. I'd not preferred either a boy or a girl for my next child.

27

Feeling that my husband should know what the Holy Spirit had spoken so precisely, I'd shared the words and the experience with Kirk after we'd returned home.

His only response had been, "Two children are enough." He made the statement, turned, walked out of our bedroom, and closed the door as he left the house for work.

Surprised by his curt response, I began to adjust to this new information. Previously, we'd both talked about having more. *Maybe*, I'd concluded, this was the reason why God had spoken to me – to reassure me that I would have another child.

I was to find that these eight words would indeed be extremely comforting – but not for the reasons I had suspected.

Now here in California, two years later, I continued to gawk at my husband, my mouth falling open.

"Yes, I *really am* ready to have another one," he repeated to my hushed, shocked face. Then, he turned to walk back down the hallway into his office.

Astounded at his change of heart, I continued to rest on the bed, not moving a muscle.

Joy gradually began from the tips of my toes and I wiggled them. The tingling sensation climbed all the way up to my mouth. *"Wow, God,"* I prayed, beginning to feel quivers of excitement, *"Thank You, God! Thank You!"*

~~~

Late Night, August, 1998

I lay in the bed by myself, waiting. The girls had been asleep in their room for hours. Dozing off did not seem probable, no matter how hard I tried to do so. I could not, because Kirk had not returned home yet.

It was a Friday night and he'd had an office party. I looked at the digital clock. It read 12:01 AM. *Where could Kirk be? How late could this party go?*

I recalled a recent one that I'd been invited to also: Kirk's boss had taken those in his department and their significant others out 'to the finest food in San Francisco.' Afterwards, a surprise limousine pulled up for our party of fourteen and we'd toured the city at night. It stopped in front of a theatre, and inside we were treated to a performance of *The Phantom of the Opera*. Spectacular evening.

But Kirk had said it was just a casual outing tonight with co-workers at a local restaurant.

Rolling over, I grabbed the phone on the night table by my side of the bed. I punched in the numbers again, paging Kirk. I'd already tried three times. *Why had he not answered?* The room remained silent.

Scenes of an ugly car accident entered my mind. Was Kirk alright? What if I were left a widow? And then, what if I found out that I was also carrying Kirk's third child? How would I break the news to the girls? Would the police be the ones to call me instead of Kirk?

"Oh God!" I pled aloud. "Please protect Kirk. Please help him to be alright. Please let him phone me and tell me that everything is okay." News headlines flashed in my mind: *Engineer Drives Off Cliff – Doesn't See Side of the Road.*

Anger rose in me. If he is fine and he just didn't bother to call me! In every minute that lapsed, I waffled between anger and fear. "Oh God! You see where Kirk is – please tell him to phone me."

I tried to sleep more. I tossed, I turned. I kept opening my eyes, and seeing the red numbers on the clock: *12:13 AM; 12:17AM; 1:20 AM; 2:10 AM; 2:55 AM.*

I missed Kirk's arms around me. I missed the way he always held me as I slept.

I was so tired but I punched the redial button of the phone that I now slept with, and tried paging Kirk, again.

3:03 AM. I heard a vehicle outside. I heard the key in the door. I lifted my head now, fully alert. I heard Kirk shuffle down the long hallway into our bedroom. He walked with slow steps.

"Hi," he whispered, "I was trying not to wake you."

Sitting upright in bed and flipping on the lamp, I exclaimed, "Trying not to wake me?!!" I raised my voice, "Where have you been?!! Why have you not answered my pages?" Mad and relieved all at once, tears sprinkled my cheeks.

Kirk looked at the floor. "I'm sorry," he said, speaking softly. "I guess that I just shouldn't go to parties after work."

"I'm so mad at you!" I cried. "I think you should just stay away!"

Without hurrying, Kirk changed his clothes. "You don't really want that, do you?" Kirk asked.

"No!" I admitted, punctuating the word, still angry, but more relieved that he was now home safe.

He crawled into bed.

Reluctantly, with mixed feelings, I draped my arm over his chest and I placed my nose up against his shoulder. I relaxed now. As I fell asleep, did he sniffle? His breathing seemed different. His chest rose and fell. Did I feel a tremor? Could it be that he wiped his eyes? I was so tired and I felt so groggy. It was so late.

Very soon it was morning.

~~~

Late September, 1998

The two lines really did turn pink. I kept looking at the stick. And they'd done it right away. I kept looking at the stick. Pink.

"Babe!" I called to Kirk, my voice rising even though it was early and the girls still slept.

It took only a moment for him to stride the few steps from his home office to where I stood in front of our vanity, wearing fuzzy rose slippers and matching bathrobe.

I still stared at the two pink lines that had appeared on the stick. "I'm pregnant," I breathed. "Kirk! We're pregnant!" I said, looking up and reaching over to embrace my husband.

"Wow," Kirk answered, standing there, surprised. "That was fast." Kirk gave a smile and returned to his office.

~~~

A family meeting was soon called in the hallway outside of Kirk's office. Nicole and Meaghan stood before us waiting for us to say something.

"Guess what girls?" I said, bouncing in place. "We are going to have a baby!"

Matching my excitement, four-year-old Nicole jumped and flew to my side. "I know what the baby is going to be, Mommy! It is going to be a boy! Last night I asked God for a baby brother!" She beamed, all thirty-nine inches of her radiating.

Yes, I pondered her words in my heart. How interesting that God had given her that desire and that prayer. I couldn't help but remember the words again from over two-and-a-half years before – *The next time it will be David Michael.*

~~~

Handpicked friends from the Lord are like a bouquet of flowers on the table enhancing the décor, adding sweet aroma, and boasting a pretty picture to be thankful for every time they come into view.

So it was with Kayla and Ginny. Since we'd moved to California two years before, they'd been a part of the scenery, planted in my life specifically by Him.

I'd met them at Women's Aglow – a monthly gathering of Christian women.

Kayla, fair-skinned, strawberry-blonde, and tall, young mother of seven, and now our president. And Ginny, who mirrored both my short, dark brunette hair and stature, still yet to have children, and now in charge of leading Aglow's worship.

Meeting on Wednesdays during my daughters' naptimes, the Lord's presence enveloped us as we worshipped Him and prayed together. We'd seen God answer significant prayers of business opportunities in both Kayla and Ginny's lives, and both Kayla and I were able to get into homes which had seemed far out of reach.

Often God gave us words or pictures to share with one another as we interceded. Refreshed, we left our meetings amazed and rejuvenated at all that the Lord had done during our time.

During today's prayer time, Kayla began to intercede for Kirk who was scheduled to go away on an upcoming business trip that weekend. "And please God," she prayed, "help Kirk to make right choices while he is away on this trip. Let him not turn to the right or to the left, or have anything to do with any other woman."

"Where did that come from, Kayla?" I asked, opening my eyes and looking at her.

"I don't know, I don't know," she said, flustered a bit. "I know that Kirk is nothing like that. I just felt led to pray that way."

That seemed out of the blue, I thought, not taking the idea seriously at all.

~~~

It was a Monday night in the middle of January and I'd set up a baby-sitter for the girls. Kirk drove us to the annual Young Life fundraiser banquet on the outskirts of town just like we'd done the year before.

Dressed couples and people of different generations dined at round tables decked out in tablecloths and fancy place settings. The meal finished, Kirk and I turned our chairs to face the platform where the speaker would soon address us.

I felt the baby kick. It was my 23rd week of pregnancy.

"Kirk," I pulled his hand over to rest on my protruding womb. "Feel the baby moving?" I looked into my husband's face, excited.

He smiled back briefly, but his hand did not linger.

~~~

February, 1999

It was the morning after Nicole's 5th birthday party – one with a clown theme. Some guests had spent the night. Brother and sister, Derrick and Donna, the children of one of our pastors, lay in sleeping bags in the living room along with our own children, beginning to wake up to the aroma of the steamy, hot pancakes. Their parents would be by soon to pick them up for church.

"Kirk, I love this," I smiled from the kitchen, happy to flip another pancake onto the stack growing high on the plate.

"What?" he asked, looking up at me from the old, blue couch.

"Just, everybody being here, you know. All of us having so much fun together. I love living just blocks from the church so that we're so convenient for everyone to pick up and drop off. Maybe we should have an Everyone-Is-Welcome-For-A-Pancake-Breakfast-Party more often! What d'ya think?" I asked, taking a short break from the hot griddle to bounce over to him, belly growing, pancake flipper in hand, to plant a firm kiss on Kirk's lips.

Kirk turned to help Meaghan with the bow on the back of her dress. Then the doorbell rang.

~~~

Each year Hillside hosted a large home show at the fairgrounds with many vendors sporting their goods. At this fair, Kirk and I had met a man working a machine that could do amazing crafts. It was a scrollsaw. With it one could cut not only wood, but also glass and coins, and, it seemed, any other material imaginable into fine and detailed shapes and sizes.

The demonstration, which I'd seen the previous couple of years, always thrilled me. *Oh, what I could make with that machine!*

The only problem was the price: $1500.

In our marriage, I'd always managed the finances because my father had trained me to do so and because I liked it. Kirk was happy to let me have the job.

This year, I felt we could squeeze out the money for the scrollsaw. After all, normally we were so careful and frugal with our finances. We'd even waited six months when we were first married to get our first real bed, just so we could avoid the debt.

"Kirk," I asked one day, "do you think I might be able to buy the scrollsaw this year?" I guessed he would be agreeable because he'd spent money on his fiddle and on lessons, and now we still had money available. I was already dreaming of all the crafts I would make and sell.

"What?" Kirk asked, looking up from his desk. "Don't you think it's too expensive?"

I felt surprised by his hesitancy. It wasn't like him. I explained all the reasons why I thought it was a great idea.

Reluctantly, he'd agreed. But I still hadn't made the purchase. I had the phone number of the dealer and could call him anytime, but I felt a restraint inside of me that kept me from doing so.

So it was that one day while I was driving around doing the errands and still praying about it, that I had an inspiration. *Why not give away the $1500 to God instead of purchasing the scrollsaw?* The more I thought about doing this, the more filled with joy I became.

"Kirk," I came to his office that evening, "Kirk, I've been thinking about the scrollsaw thing."

He looked up at me from his computer. "I've been thinking that I'd like to give the $1500 I was going to spend on the scrollsaw to God instead."

"What?!" Kirk asked, scrunching his face together more than I'd ever seen. "What do you mean?" he said, giving me his full attention and looking straight at me.

"Well," I tried to explain, "I know you said that I could spend the money, and I'm grateful. But I just feel restrained from doing so whenever I pray about it. But when I think about giving it away to God, I get filled with joy, you know?"

Kirk looked at me with unbelief, then turned back to his computer. "Do what you want with the money."

"Okay," I said, turning back into the hallway, relieved and excited.

Little did I know at the time that God knew something about my life that I would have never expected.

~~~

> *"Give, and it will be given to you.*
> *A good measure, pressed down,*
> *shaken together and running over,*
> *will be poured into your lap.*
> *For with the measure you use,*
> *it will be measured to you."*
> Luke 6:38

~~~

I remember it so clearly because it was so unusual.

It happened as I walked the hallway down into our bedroom, located at the back of our house. The girls were napping in the afternoon and I was tiptoeing softly, trying to accomplish as much work as possible.

"Will you serve me, even if Kirk does not?" The Holy Spirit whispered inside of me, with precise clarity.

Baffled, I thought *that was a strange question.* But, I wanted to give the Lord an answer.

"Lord," I said quietly, "I will, if You will help me."

I still thought the idea was surprising as I reached the night table.

Picking up my Bible, I sat down on the edge of the bed, and fingered through it. Maybe the Lord just wanted me to get back into regular quiet times, I thought. I'd been trying to hold back, not wanting to outrun my husband. I had wanted him to take the lead.

Now I breathed in deeply because I felt the release to enjoy Him. I sat down and read the Word all afternoon.

I didn't know it then, but I had an especially great need to be anchored in the truths of God's Word.

3

The Fingerprints of God

I f you'd been the oft-referred-to, fly-on-the-wall at our Women's Aglow spring retreat, you'd have seen over one hundred women from local chapters in the area joining together for a special time in the Lord.

Kirk had agreed to watch Nicole and Meaghan so that I could attend. In fact, he'd seemed eager to do so.

This year the speaker was named Ms. Irma, a former politician for nearly twenty years, but now, later in life, a prophetic minister.

I sat next to Ginny in a folding chair along the aisle on the right side of the room about halfway from the front. I was in my 26th week of pregnancy. My protruding tummy caused some discomfort, but I ignored that right now.

It was late in the afternoon on Saturday, and we attended the optional afternoon ministry meeting with many others.

The assembly of women gave themselves to prayer and enjoyed the presence of the Lord following the intense worship period. Ladies lined up in the front to be prayed for by the prayer teams, and others sat in their seats or kneeled on the floor, individually seeking the Lord. The five musicians played in harmony, setting the tone for the continued worship.

Ginny and I sat on our chairs quietly enjoying the faith-filled environment. Ms. Irma, the speaker, began to walk up and down the center of the aisle passing us and, at times, pointing for different ladies in the room to stand up for prayer and prophecy as she felt the Holy Spirit lead her.

Then, to my surprise, instead of passing by us again, she stopped by my folding chair and motioned for me to stand up so that she could pray for me. My heart began to pound at being in the spotlight like this, though it seemed others were mostly distracted by their own prayers.

More surprising yet were the tears that this tall woman minister began to cry over me, "He just loves you so much," she insisted. She pulled me to herself and continued to speak as she literally wept. "You are His precious, precious, precious, treasured possession. He just loves you so much," she repeated over again and again. Standing higher than I, her tears mingled in my hair. I noticed that she didn't cry like that over anybody else.

Out of the speaker's embrace and her tears, I sat back down beside my friend. Ginny nudged me and I turned my head to look at her, shrugging my shoulders while I did.

"Janice!" Ginny exclaimed, wide-eyed, "What was that about?!"

"I don't know," I answered her, wondering about it just as much myself. I mean, I knew that God loved me.

I wondered about it the rest of the day and later at home that night as I shared the experience with Kirk while we lay chatting in bed. Still resonating with the joy and the warmness I felt from the afternoon meeting, I wriggled Kirk's feet with my own and reminded him again of how much God loved me, laughing.

"That's great, Babe." His voice was sincere and even glad. He'd had an especially happy day, too, he'd said.

"And you know, Kirk," I remembered aloud, "Treasure has always been such a keyword for me. Remember me telling you about how I buried treasure every summer at our beach home and then tried to dig it up when we came back the next year?"

Not quite ready to find sleep, I basked in the quietness of the night as I felt again the words and the experience of God's special dose of love for me. Eventually, I did sleep, wrapped up in God's peace and embrace until morning.

But I had not been privy to exactly why Kirk had been so entertained during his day. He'd not shared with me all his details or the secret which kept him grinning in the dark.

~~~

"For you are a people holy to the LORD your God.
The LORD your God has chosen you
out of all the peoples on the face of the earth
to be his people, his treasured possession."
Deuteronomy 7:6

~~~

The digital clock read 7:30 AM. That was when I heard three-year-old Meaghan call me from her bed.

"Honey, I'll be there in a minute," I answered her, lifting myself up on my arms to a sitting position, then opening my eyes.

That is when the room spun. It turned in circles. Like being on an upside-down rollercoaster. I shut my eyes tight and firm.

Were we having an earthquake? I considered, because after all, we did live in California. But, I reasoned, I did not hear any noises like that of picture frames falling off the walls, or things sliding off bookshelves. There were no crashes and no bangs.

I opened my eyes again. The room began to spin again. I quickly closed my eyes shut again.

My mind recalled the term, 'vertigo,' and I knew this must be it.

I found that I could get up and feel my way down the familiar hallway as long as I kept my eyes shut safely behind closed lids. I pictured the geography of our home and made it to the girls' room.

After a few minutes on the old, blue couch in the living room, while sitting straight up, the world righted itself and turned back to the way it should be.

That was disconcerting, I thought. Experiencing one's world turned upside-down sure was kind of jolting.

~~~

"God is our refuge and strength,
an ever-present help in trouble.
Therefore we will not fear, though the earth give way
and the mountains fall into the heart of the sea,"
Psalm 46:1-2

~~~

I should just sleep and forget about it, I thought. Everything was surely alright. But no, Kirk had said he would always answer my page and he should have been home by now. He had said so.

The baby, who had been moving inside me earlier, now rested quietly within. Again, my daughters had been asleep for hours.

Why did he not answer my page?

Kirk had phoned and asked me if I wanted to meet him with the girls at the outlet mall for dinner. We had done that several times before.

But it had already been a long day for us, and my preschoolers were in more need of a regular bedtime than a late night out – especially with a homeschool field trip scheduled early the next morning. So this time I'd decided it was best that we stay home.

Kirk, however, decided he'd work late, and "get caught up."

And now, at 11:00 PM, *where was he?* He knew how upset I'd been the last time when he didn't check in and when he didn't answer his pages.

The what-ifs began to play like a theatrical production on the stage of my mind. Before I could control it, I began to cry into my pillow to muffle the sound and to keep from waking the girls.

I know, I thought, sitting up all at once. I'd call the security at his work and ask them to check on him. My friend's husband did security work and I knew that it was generally boring work, sitting around just passing the time.

I looked at the digital clock: 12:30 AM.

"Hello," I phoned the 24-hour answering service at Kirk's work. This time instead of giving them a message to type into Kirk's pager, I had them transfer me to the security office on his complex.

"Hello, security?" I inquired. "Would you check on my husband, Kirk Lynch? He was supposed to be home hours ago and I am really worried about him. He was working late. Could you ask him to phone me?"

Waiting, waiting, waiting. Trying to rest. Tears.

1:30 AM. The phone rang. "Hello, ma'am. This is security. We located your husband. We told him to call you."

"Where was he?" I asked, relieved, embarrassed.

"He's going to phone you, ma'am," the voice on the other end evaded my question.

2:00 AM. The phone rang. Grabbing it as fast as possible, half asleep, but more awake, I leaned over to speak into the receiver, "Kirk! Where have you been? I've been paging you all night and it's so late! Why did you do this to me again?" I cried, frustrated, angry, and yet relieved.

"My pager must not have been getting reception," Kirk excused himself. "I got locked out of the building, and then locked out of my truck."

"What? How? What did you do? I'm so sorry, Babe!" I sat up in bed once more, leaning my back against the pillows, my fiery emotions melting into compassion. "I phoned security. I've been so worried! It's so late and way past when you said you'd be home," I explained.

"Babe," Kirk said, sounding almost mad and even like he clenched his jaw, "Listen to me: Do not ever call security on me again."

Puzzled, I wondered why I was the one that felt chagrined when Kirk had not called or come home on time?

As I rested on my bed, I thought, what would I do way out here in California if something happened to Kirk?

Thirty minutes later Kirk stepped softly into the room after using the kid's bathroom down the hall. He crept into bed.

But instead of holding me all night long while we slept like I was accustomed to, he kept to his side of the bed.

~~~

Saturday, April 17, 1999

It was an enormous feeling of possibility when Kirk offered to take the little ones with him to the mall the next day for an outing.

So many tasks begged my attention before the new baby arrived only two months away. So I fed my family, bid them each a grand time, and turned my attention to attack the first of many projects without interruption.

How kind, I thought, of Kirk to provide this respite for me when so often I had no breaks from the care of the children. Especially with all the overtime recently.

When everyone arrived home several hours later, the girls bounded into the back bedroom and found me sorting the laundry. "Mommy! Mommy! Guess what?" The girls began.

"We met Daddy's friend, Leanne, at the mall today," said Nicole.

"While we were at the Froggie Park," added Meaghan.

"Kirk?" I asked him later while he worked at his computer, "Who is this person that the girls said they met at the mall today? Someone named Leanne?"

"Oh, just a co-worker. We ran into her while we were at the playland in the mall," he said, not even looking away from his monitor.

"Really? You mean she was all the way out here in Hillside from over the mountain?" I said. "That's strange."

Kirk did not answer.

But, I reasoned, I often ran into people that I knew whenever I went out. Kirk didn't seem to portray anything out of the ordinary and so I soon forgot about it, too.

~~~

Giving a skip, even with my enlarging belly, I went to check on Kirk.

He was always working on some project or another. If it wasn't one of the cars, it was breaking up the concrete in the driveway with a jackhammer. And if it wasn't the driveway, it was installing decorative columns on our porch. And if it wasn't that, it was digging up all the nasty old carpet, and so on.

Just as I'd thought, I found him in the garage. He was painting the door of a cabinet for our bathroom.

My ears met with loud, unrecognizable raucous music blaring from the CD player. "Hey, what happened to the bluegrass?" I asked. "And some of those words! What are you listening to?" I demanded.

"Babe," he called, sidestepping my questions and glancing at me in the doorway, "The shelves and closet in our bathroom need painted."

"They do?" I asked carelessly, distracted by feeling my round, hard belly, and the baby who had just kicked me on the left side. Tired, we'd all awoken early for the family tour at the hospital aimed at older siblings expecting the arrival of a new baby.

"I'll give you a brush and open the can," he said, unusually insistent that I join his world of handyman work.

"Okay, but do you think it will be alright for the baby? I mean, the paint fumes?" I questioned. It was my third pregnancy and so it was my third set of nine months of abstaining from raw cookie dough, cake mix, and brownie batter in order to be healthy for the baby.

"It'll be fine," he answered quickly, leading the way back into the house and down the hallway to the bathroom where he set down the full can of paint, handed me a brush, and retreated.

"Well, Lord," I prayed at the same time as I picked up a wet brush, "Here I am. Help me to do a good job. Help the baby to be protected." I added a fan for ventilation.

As I worked, I began to sing a new song to God about how good He had been to me. I was so grateful for a husband who could be so gifted at fixing things around the house.

"Sometimes though," I said as I talked to the Lord, "I just wish we could spend more time just enjoying being together." But there were always so many projects that needed to be done in the fixer-upper house we had bought because it had been in our price range.

Then, looking down at the clock, I quickened my pace, noticing that the girls would be up again soon from their naps.

~~~

I didn't notice it at first. I never drove Kirk's truck which was a stick-shift with only a front seat, and which he parked on the far right side of our mostly cemented front yard.

But one day I drew closer for some reason, and I noticed that the front fender was missing. Then, I saw that there were also marks, scratches, and small dents around the front.

"Kirk?!" I ran inside, alarmed, finding him at work on the computer in the home office, "What happened to the truck?!"

"Oh," he seemed unconcerned, "It was nothing. It happened awhile ago."

"Nothing?!" My voice rose, "There's damage! What about our car insurance? What will they say?" I asked, unsatisfied with his response.

"It was just a small fender-bender," Kirk answered, "We decided not to file claims and take care of it ourselves."

Though I pressed Kirk for more details, he gave none. Because Kirk could fix almost everything and planned to take care of it himself, I dropped the matter.

But, I wondered, especially much later on, *what was the real story behind Kirk's fender-bender?*

~~~

April 1999

"But why are you accepting this job change?" I wanted to know. "What are the advantages?"

"It's just a good career step." Kirk said, offering no other explanation, and not sitting down to discuss it.

"How?" I asked. "You said there is no pay raise, no move up, no more cell phone so that we can keep talking on your long ride home, and not near as much flexibility in being able to work from home. In fact, you say they won't even give you a guarantee of working at home at all. How can you give all that up? I don't understand."

"I'm not leaving the company. And I probably won't have to go on as many overnight last-minute business trips. I'm going to take it." Kirk said, avoiding every one of my questions and walking down the hallway to his office, leaving me standing in the living room by myself.

I was puzzled. Before this, Kirk had always discussed decisions with me and wanted my input. I wasn't accustomed to him just making an announcement of a major change.

But I believed the best about Kirk. He was providing for us and working hard. If he really wanted to change positions, who was I to stand in his way?

I buckled myself in to support Kirk. I knew that a new job meant another learning curve and a period of time for him to readjust to the different requirements.

As the future unfolded I was to wonder, *had he really wanted this job change? Or was there really a whole lot more to this tale as well?*

~~~

"You're home early!" I exclaimed as Kirk walked through the door of our bedroom at four in the afternoon. "What a treat to have you home early for a change," I said, all smiles, and greeting him with a kiss.

"I had the best time this afternoon, Babe!" Kirk gushed as he hung up his work clothes in the closet. "I took off work early. And there was this air show nearby. And a friend and I sat on the hood of the truck and just watched it! It was INCREDIBLE!" Kirk exclaimed, strangely excited. "I just had such a good time," Kirk still grinned, looking at me.

"Well that's good, Babe, I'm glad you had so much fun." I replied, somewhat perplexed at his exceeding excitement.

"I did, Babe, it was great!" he repeated, still standing there in front of his closet, a wide smile stretched all the way across his face.

"Well, who did you go with?" I asked from where I now sat down on the edge of the bed.

"Oh, just someone from work," he shrugged and began to turn away toward the direction of the long bedroom hallway. "Hey," he paused, "when do you think you'll book some plane tickets to go out and see your parents this summer?"

"Well, what is your schedule like?" I asked, standing up now. "Because you know that we'd all like you to join us for part of the time. Do you think you can make it during the family beach week again at the end of August?"

"You know," Kirk said walking away now, "I just don't see how I'll be able to get the time off work this summer with starting up in a new department and all," he looked at me for a moment from the hallway before disappearing into his office.

"Oh," I was disappointed. "Well, honey," I called out to him, "I just haven't had peace about purchasing those tickets yet. I'm just not sure exactly when to go. I'll keep praying about it," I promised from our bedroom where I put away his clean socks.

"Well," Kirk concluded our conversation with an odd firmness, "I think you should figure it out soon." His voice trailed off as he turned his attention to that which was in his office.

~~~

May 1999

It was a night when Kirk had worked at home during the day and we all sat around the kitchen table for dinner.

Three-year-old Meaghan rearranged her fork and her plate. Nicole, five, sat quietly across from her, patient. Kirk resided at the far end, and I, across from him, nearest to the stove.

The smell of homemade baked chicken wafted up from the platter in the center. A bowl of green beans and a plate of sliced tomatoes stood by its side. We all said our family grace and began to pass the dishes to fill our plates.

Realizing that the baked potatoes were still in the oven, I rose from my chair and pulled another bowl from the cabinet to hold them. "You know, Babe," I began, first noting the empty walls in our eat-in kitchen just begging to be decorated with the new blue-and-white-checkered wallpaper I'd purchased, "I just love living in California."

My thoughts flew to the fun that Mom and I had had going to the Ladies Tea at our church earlier in the month while my parents had been visiting. And Nicole's swimming lessons, right around the corner, which could be walked to. And our preschool playgroup where recently we'd had so much fun decorating our friend's front door with flowers, ribbons, bows, and candy for her birthday.

"It's just amazing how God has knit us in so quickly to so many special people's lives in such a short time, don't you think?" I asked, smiling at the blessings as I thought of them.

Kirk chewed his chicken, but nodded up at me, then added, "Yes, I think I have decided to stay in California permanently."

"Really?" I asked, caught off-guard, remembering that we'd talked before about moving back East someday, to be nearer to my family.

Kirk nodded affirmatively and wiped his fingers on his napkin.

"You know," I said, considering, "I was thinking about all the moves we've made since we've been married. I think you actually enjoyed all those times when you got offered a new job and decided to move on," I said innocently, pausing, and wrinkling my brow as I thought about it even more. "You know," I continued, "I think you liked dropping the bombshell on your previous bosses when you told them that you were leaving and knew how much you'd be missed. Don't you think?" I asked Kirk, laughing at the idea as I pictured him meeting with one of his many previous bosses.

Kirk looked at me from behind his next chicken leg, kind of funny-like, with his eyes wider than usual, but shook his head, denying it.

"Now come on," I said feeling certain that I was on to something. "Once you made your decision, you never did look back," I finished, finally taking my seat and passing the bowl of baked potatoes in Nicole's direction. "I've never known you to change your mind," I repeated, proud of the man who had steered us to such a wonderful life in California.

Kirk dropped his fork.

"I'll get you another one," I jumped first to move toward the silverware drawer, pleased to find a way to serve him.

"No, I'll get it," Kirk took two long steps into the kitchen and retrieved his own fork out of the drawer.

"Well, okay," I said, "I just thought that since I was closer..."

Dinner continued as it routinely did with Kirk asking the girls about what they did during the day and with each one giving him a bubbly rundown.

Finishing first, I got up and began to work on the dishes. I looked over at Kirk, still seated across the table from where I'd been. He held his pager up in front of his face, strangely captivated by it. He had that unusual grin on his face. He looked at whatever was on the pager for a long minute.

"What's that?" I asked. "Something important?"

"Oh, it's nothing," Kirk said, depositing the pager back into his shirt pocket. "I have some work in the office I haven't finished up yet," he said, excusing himself.

"Okay," I called after him, "but can you help me by putting the girls to bed tonight?" I asked.

"Of course," he answered, already down the hall, "just call me when they're ready."

~~~

Actually, Kirk often put the girls to bed when he was home in time. He played his fiddle or his guitar or even his banjo for a long, long time. In fact, it seemed to be getting longer every night.

Tonight, as I heard him go into the girls' room, turn off their light, and begin the routine of playing his music and singing his familiar songs, often

Christian lyrics, I decided to join them. Lately, he'd sing to the girls until they were both fast asleep.

I'd always wanted to marry someone who could play the guitar like Kirk had grown to do over the years since I'd met him. Again, I felt so blessed.

Donning my pajamas as quickly as I could with the almost full-term baby in my womb, I brushed and flossed my teeth. I was tired.

With my slippers on, I entered the girls' bedroom, coming in with a bright shaft of light. Kirk did not look up but kept playing on the strings.

I climbed awkwardly into Nicole's larger bed and lay down beside her, my belly resting sideways on the bed, giving some comfort to the weight of it, and placed my left arm around her. I was looking forward to lying there, in the midst of my family, with Kirk playing his bluegrass-style music.

Just as soon as I'd settled in, Kirk abruptly stopped his playing and his singing. Instead, he held the guitar straight up and down, supported on the floor.

"Daddy!" the girls cried together. "More! Daddy! More!"

"Yes! More, Babe!" I added with enthusiasm. "Encore!"

"Not tonight, girls," he said with decisiveness, standing up in the dark and then leaving the room.

Everyone lay there disappointed by his early and abrupt departure. I pulled myself up and spent a few moments praying with each of my daughters, and then kissed them both goodnight on their foreheads.

~~~

"Babe," I said, entering Kirk's office where he'd gone after leaving the girls' bedroom. "What's the matter? Why did you leave so suddenly? All the other nights you've been in there singing and playing your guitar until even after the girls were long asleep."

I leaned my back against the doorframe for support. "Babe," I asked, trying to get him to open up with the peculiar way he'd been acting, "Don't you love me anymore?"

"Of course I love you," Kirk said, "look at all the work I do for you around the house."

I couldn't argue. Kirk was always doing things that blessed us.

4

The List

May 21, 1999

It was Friday evening.

I'd gotten the girls to bed early and entered our bedroom to get some rest myself. We'd had a homeschool field trip with our co-op that day at The FlowerSpot Nursery, and tomorrow I was scheduled to go to an all-day seminar titled *How to Homeschool: The Beginning Years*.

I paused in front of the mirror over our vanity. My belly had grown. I was beginning to wear some of my larger-sized maternity clothes and the baby was due in only three or four weeks. Oh, I thought, I just can't wait to give birth to this sweet baby and get my body back. Maybe then life will get back to normal.

Somehow I felt unconnected to Kirk. Like I could not get his attention. Like he was distracted. It seemed he'd been this way off and on since... maybe April? Maybe since his job had changed?

I felt like I was swimming against a strong current and he was moving off in a different direction. I couldn't seem to reach him.

While I continued to stare in the mirror at my oversized figure, I bit my lower lip and thought. It's a good thing that I don't depend on Kirk to pump up my ego or to make me feel better when I look so stretched out and awkward these days. At thirty-six weeks, I was nearing that point where I was so uncomfortable that I was looking forward to that day of labor and birth.

"God," I said, "I thank You that *You think* that I look beautiful, especially in this late season of my pregnancy."

~~~

I stopped by Kirk's office, viewed a blank monitor that he'd been staring at for some reason, and informed him that I was going to bed. "Have to be up early tomorrow for the seminar. The girls are in bed," I said, beginning to leave and return back down the hallway to get some sleep.

"What time are you leaving in the morning?" Kirk called out before I got any further, and now looked up at me through the doorway.

Recognizing that he seemed to want to talk, I leaned against the doorframe of the office, supporting the weight of the moving baby inside, and wearing my rosy bathrobe that Kirk had purchased for me at Christmas.

We chit-chatted for awhile about the details of the next day. I was just glad that he was talking to me like normal again.

But then Kirk said some things to me that made me feel like one does when a tire suddenly goes flat while they're just going along minding their own business, simply driving their car down the road, doing their regular every day errands – and then, kaboom – blowout!

"I don't think I'm happy anymore," Kirk spoke up, in the middle of our conversation about the week's schedule.

My eyebrows dipped and I responded, "Why not, Babe?" I asked, with concern. It was not like Kirk to say something like this. And, as far as I could see, our lives were filled with happy things.

"I've changed. It's me, not you," Kirk qualified. "There's just not a lot that we can do together anymore," he answered, eyeing me.

I stared at Kirk's face, wondering if I had missed something. "Well, what kind of things do you mean?" I finally asked, bewildered, feeling supported only by the wall behind me.

"You don't like to do the things that I want to do. And that's okay," he said, tilting back in his office chair with his two feet on the floor beneath his desk. "I don't expect you to," he added, looking down, hands on his lap.

"What things?" I asked, startled, staring at him, wondering what in the world Kirk was talking about, and standing up straight now.

"I mean," Kirk said, "you can't watch the kind of movies with me that I want to watch. And, I'd like someone to go to bars with me, and drink, and dance." Kirk paused, looking at me again, challenging me. "And, I don't know if I love you anymore," Kirk ended.

Hadn't Kirk just told me the other day that he did love me?

Kirk shared the finer details about exactly what he meant by the activities that he now wanted to do. In fact, what he said he really wanted to do did indeed go clearly against God's boundaries for those who are Christians. Unquestionably.

Silence followed these shocking declarations. I felt sick, achy, suddenly alone, and turned upside-down.

I paused to think before I spoke, and then I began slowly. "Well, you're right. We cannot do those kinds of things together. But, there are a lot of other things we can do. I know that sometimes people change over time. But we are married. We need to find those things that we can do together." I stated my words to him clearly, logically, level-headed, looking directly at him.

My heart pounded faster and faster inside my chest with each sentence. I wondered if he could hear it.

As I stood there waiting for him to respond, my mind reverted back to our discussions in the early days when I'd first known Kirk and about how love was a choice, not a feeling. My mind reverted back to our courtship days, and to when we'd planned with two other couples to lead marriage seminars with the business training we'd all received as we trained for youth ministry. My mind reverted back to men that Kirk had once reached out to in order to help them to make wise decisions for their wives and families.

"Kirk," I suggested without moving, "maybe we need marriage counseling or something. Love is a choice, Babe, not a feeling – you know that. It's a commitment. And, *I love you*. God is big enough to put a spark back into our marriage. He can do it."

Funny, I felt certain that I loved him even as he sat there saying those strange, outrageous, and unfamiliar statements to me.

Kirk only nodded, closing our conversation, and turned back to his computer monitor.

~~~

I don't know how I did it without tripping, but I managed to get down the hallway and to the bed. I took a deep breath sitting on the edge, and I felt my bulky, unvalued body.

I held out both my hands in front of me and I noticed they were shaking.

What was Kirk missing that he needed? Was I not giving him enough attention? Had I gotten too immersed in homeschooling? Was Kirk unhappy due to his new work situation? Was he depressed, or tired from doing all the work at the office and then having to work on the home projects?

I could not figure out what the problem could be. I felt bewildered and alarmed. I mean, I had felt happy, *until this moment,* and I loved Kirk.

I'd been so tired, but now I did not feel like I could sleep. When I lay back into the bed, the mattress felt bumpy and uncomfortable.

Fear tried to take my face in its hands like a mother does with her small child. Fear tried to force my eyes to focus on terrible possibilities. My baby was due in three short weeks. I felt suddenly very alone in my marriage, far away in California.

Fear tried to push me around, push me to the ground and stand over me to shout words of hopelessness and despair – what-ifs and worst-case scenarios. It was like a rushing tide swirling around my feet, attempting to knock me over, to carry me out to sea.

But God. God drew faith and hope from the well that He had dug deep in me over the years – from my salvation in Jesus through the Cross, then to the nuggets I had gleaned from the countless Bible Studies where I'd meditated on His Word, the quiet times, and all the Bible verses which I'd memorized.

I found that I was tethered to His love and that speaking words of faith and truth aloud had a stabilizing effect.

God could do all things. God had a plan. God saw. God knew. God was already at work. God loved me.

I sought God in earnest for our marriage as I lay in our bed. And, I made a vow that night: For every day up until I gave birth, I would do something extra special just for Kirk and for our marriage, to show him just how much I really did care.

I began to make a mental list as I fell asleep:

- I'd hire a regular babysitter again for our weekly date night – saving money was not the priority right now.
- I'd get some of Kirk's favorite candies to leave by his bedside.
- I'd look for some books on amazon.com to give me more ideas.
- I'd do some special clothes shopping.
- I'd see if Ginny's new friend who worked for Glamour Shots could give me some extra-special make-up tips.

Finally, I fell asleep. Kirk had still not come to bed.

~~~

Down the road, I wondered if Kirk had hoped that I would be the one to get highly offended, or terribly angry, or to be greatly disturbed enough to be the one to reject him first.

I only know that God shielded me and held me up, and gave me supernatural grace to respond to Kirk with a gentle answer.

It was not time yet for me to know what might seem obvious in retrospect.

~~~

"O LORD, you have searched me
and you know me.
You know when I sit and when I rise;
you perceive my thoughts from afar.
You discern my going out and my lying down;
you are familiar with all my ways."
Psalm 139: 1-3

~~~

In Robert Louis Stevenson's classic novella, Dr. Jekyll is the friendly man whom everybody likes – whom everybody sees. He holds a respectable job and he does respectable things. But at night, when nobody watches, he chooses to drink an evil potion and to do evil deeds under the alias of Mr. Hyde.

Over time, Dr. Jekyll does not need to take the potion for his wicked side to emerge – the wicked becomes greater than the good and it begins to take over.

The next morning, Kirk acted like the conversation had never taken place. In fact, the tension seemed to have disappeared. He was cheerful, friendly, and he seemed normal again.

Perhaps things were moving in a better direction since we'd talked openly. Perhaps he'd just needed to vent those random ideas. Perhaps the situation was not really as bad as it had seemed the night before. I held hope.

Regardless, I shifted into full gear and began my pursuit to make Kirk happy – to shake off whatever encumbered him, to get my old, loving, cheerful, and connected Kirk back again like before.

Before all else, I prayed, often, and with earnestness. I read God's Word to find footholds on which to secure my faith.

I ignored the budget and drove to the mall. In the home section of a department store, I purchased tall candles, romantic-looking vases, flowers, and frames. As a final touch of décor, I discovered a large wall-hanging of a knight-in-shining-armor who lay dazed and falling off his horse because he was so enraptured by his fair maiden.

Returning home, I compiled all I'd bought into a tender, tasteful romantic display in our bedroom before Kirk returned home from work.

It wasn't long before I heard the engine of Kirk's truck pull up before dinner. Excited, I flew to meet him at the door and pulled him down the hallway and back to the bedroom to see. With my arms around his waist I asked, "Do you like it, Babe?"

Kirk stood there, quiet, looking up and down at the new items in our bedroom.

"Do you see that knight falling off his horse for his maiden?" I asked. He nodded.

"Well, that's going to be the way you feel about me again someday, Babe." I said with confidence, kissing him on his cheek. Fresh in my memory were his own passionate kisses for me that I'd experienced from him not all that long ago.

"Hhhhm, nice." Kirk said, as he walked out of the room and back down the hallway to his office.

I sat down, disappointed, but not undetermined.

And, I talked to God about it some more.

~~~

Kirk did not bring up what had been talked about. Things seemed like they were getting better.

Maybe it had really been nothing after all. Maybe I had imagined it.

Mostly, Dr. Jekyll appeared in our house and the days were busy and full. It appeared that I had a willing partner in our marriage and in our family life.

I easily forgot again about an unseen, underlying, Mr. Hyde.

~~~

June 1, 1999

A middle-aged woman with reddish-gray, frizzy, shoulder-length hair crossed our cement driveway and appeared at the doorstep with two empty trays, a roller, and a can of wallpaper paste.

Intercepting her before she reached for the doorbell and awakened the girls from their naps, I led her inside. We talked in hushed tones.

"Oh, yeah," Ruby exclaimed with her raspy voice when she entered the family room adjacent to the eat-in kitchen, "this shouldn't be too hard of a job."

"Do you think we can get it done before Kirk gets home in a few hours?" I asked. "He'll probably be working late tonight." *I prayed he would be working late tonight* – I wanted so much to surprise him with a job well done.

Kirk would not be able to get to the wallpaper anytime soon. He had his hand in so many other house projects, such as getting the baby's room finished.

"Well, we can try our best," Ruby offered.

~~~

It was 10:00 PM before we finished. The girls were back in bed for the night.

Ruby and I stood back to admire our work. It really looked nice. "Ruby," I said, "It looks beautiful! Thank you so much for helping me with this!"

"It does look nice," she agreed, smiling, too. We both turned toward the front door as we heard the click of the knob.

"Kirk!" I cried, "Look what we did! Ruby helped me. Do you like it?" I ran over to stand beside him in the entryway as he took in the new kitchen scene highlighted by the fresh, whimsical, blue-and-white-check-ered wallpaper.

"Nice!" he said, standing in the entryway and looking at our work from a distance with a broad smile. "It looks really nice. Why, look at that."

Ruby patted my shoulder and left.

"Kirk, I was so worried that you would get here while we were still in the middle of it, and I wanted to surprise you!" I explained, putting both arms around his waist, and again, turning my head toward the eat-in kitchen to take in the view of finished work with great satisfaction. "I prayed that you would be late," I laughed.

Kirk stood there looking at the wallpaper for another few seconds, nodding his head up and down. Then he left my side to walk back to his office, briefcase in hand.

What I didn't know at the time was this: Kirk had been late because he'd been conducting some financial business. And he'd not been conducting it just by himself.

~~~

The phone rang, interrupting sleep.

Drowsy, I turned over from laying beside Kirk in our bed to answer it. "Hello?" Click. The phone rang again – I answered it again. "Hello?" Click.

"There's no one there," I relayed to Kirk. "That's strange, Babe, it's happened before," I said.

I looked at the clock – time to get the children up and ready for church. Tired and almost due with the baby, I still lay in bed, but moved back closer to Kirk to enjoy his warmth.

"I'm not going to church," Kirk said, eyes still closed, facing the wall.

"What?" I asked.

"I'm not going to church." Kirk repeated, eyes shut, "I have a headache."

Irritation rose in me and I sat up, fully awakened. "But, I need your help," I protested. "Do you know how hard it is to get everybody up and out of the house by myself? And then to get them settled into their Sunday School classes and then to sit alone in church?"

I paused and then realized more, "Last week, you stayed home with a headache, too! And when we all came back to nurse you, we found you up and about and acting like you felt fine!"

"I'm not going to church today," Kirk repeated flatly.

I rolled out of bed, my feet landing on the floor. Maybe Kirk was not really over his out-of-character behavior as I'd hoped. I certainly could not figure it out. He'd been acting so normal lately, and now this.

My stomach felt queasy even though I'd barely experienced any morning sickness in any of my three pregnancies.

I began to get the kids and myself ready for church. Kirk did not move to help.

5

New Arrival, New Hope

June 11, 1999

I lay close beside Kirk, his arm around my shoulders, both of us still talking in bed early in the morning.

"So, when do you think the baby will come?" Kirk asked, mirroring my wish that it be soon.

"Well, I don't know, Nicole and Meaghan both came at least a couple days early," I calculated. "So it should be any day now, especially since I lost the plug two weeks ago."

After awhile Kirk got out of bed and dressed for the day. I lay still, not moving from the bed, running over the list in my mind of what needed to be done today. Besides the homeschool co-op meeting, I needed to get the guest bedroom all set up for Mom and Dad who had plane tickets to fly into town the next day. They had plans to stay all the way through the end of June, for the next three weeks.

I heard Kirk's truck door slam outside. The motor started, the gas revved, and he left for work. After about twenty more minutes of resting, I decided it was also time for me to get my shower. Feeling heavy and tired, I began to pull myself up.

It was then that I felt the swift, warm water begin to flow and I knew that this was to be the baby's birthday!

Reaching for the phone, I paged Kirk, trying to catch him before he got too far along the way over the mountain to work.

After paging him, I phoned Emilie down the street who planned to help out with the girls. I reached Suzy, also from church, who had a daughter

Nicole's age, and who was in place to drive me the forty-five minutes or so to Almond Creek if Kirk did not respond to my page.

In a matter of minutes, even though it was still early in the morning, a little party of excited people gathered in our foyer: myself, five-year-old Nicole, three-year-old Meaghan, Emilie, and Suzy.

"Should I drive you now?" Suzy asked, looking at her watch.

"Well, let's just give Kirk a few more minutes in case he got my page in time," I said, knowing that Kirk would want to drive me if at all possible. Just then, the front door opened and Kirk walked in.

"Hello, everyone!" Kirk said, all smiles. "Is this a party? Are you having the baby, Babe?" he asked, red in the face and out of breath.

"Yes! My water broke, but the contractions haven't begun yet," I explained, standing in the hallway.

"Well, let's get you to the hospital," he said, smiling wider. We both hugged and kissed Nicole and Meaghan.

Emilie and Suzy still stood in the doorway as we left, discussing details, mapping out the day, and planning how to best care for the girls.

On the way to the hospital the contractions began. I patted my belly, talked to the baby, and reported to Kirk when they occurred.

I felt bathed in gratefulness for my husband by my side, and for my faithful and kind friends caring for our daughters since our own families lived so far away.

~~~

Driving into the hospital entrance at Almond Creek, Kirk helped me out of the car and into a waiting wheelchair before he went and parked. Pushed inside, I filled out paperwork before being given a small room within which to wait on an examining table.

"So," a male nurse came in and began, "on a scale of 1-10, 10 being the worst, how bad is the pain that you are in now?"

"I would say a '7,' because I want an epidural right now!" I instructed. I hated pain of any sort.

A balding doctor entered the room, with whom I was not familiar. "Hhhmmm," he informed me after having me lay down for the examination, "your cervix is not dilated enough. I'm going to put you on some Pitocin."

"I know," I said, "that's the way it always happens." A room assignment was issued and the waiting began.

The contractions grew stronger in a short period of time with the Pitocin. Soon I experienced the same repeated scenario of the baby I was delivering having meconium. The nurse set up a cleansing system for the baby before giving me my requested epidural. It turned out there was a queue of other delivering mothers and only one anesthesiologist to go around.

Shorter than either of my previous deliveries, it was only about four hours before the baby's head emerged. Kirk stood by the doctor at the bottom of the bed. "Push, Babe, you have to do it, so just do it." Kirk said, matter-of-factly, vacant of tones of pampering or tenderness in his voice.

But I did not really notice.

Later, I remembered the contrast, the way he'd encouraged me in the past with much more gentleness and care.

When the baby came through, I was grateful because it was the easiest labor I'd experienced. Such a feeling of joy, relief, and happiness flooded me to be on the other end of this pregnancy.

It was a boy! It seemed an amazing miracle that a boy person could be growing inside of me all these months.

My mind returned again to the words that God had spoken to me just after Meaghan's birth: *The next time it will be David Michael.* And I knew, like each child, that this one was no mere coincidence.

Kirk watched baby David as the team of technicians cleaned his lungs from any remnants of meconium. I noticed tears in Kirk's eyes as he viewed his son for the very first time.

Lying quietly, I praised God and waited for Kirk to carry the beautiful boy bundle over to me to be admired and nursed.

Everything seemed so wonderful and so perfect.

~~~

Left alone with one nurse, I felt glad that Kirk accompanied our son to his physical.

It was then that the nurse sighed and began to complain. "I'm supposed to be off," she stated. "This is not my job," she added, eyeing me, and all the work that I required.

I felt a twinge of guilt at being an inconvenience, and at a loss to help her because I couldn't move after just giving birth and receiving stitches.

"Oh," I drew her out, "you're not happy today?"

Before long, she'd shared with me about how she was a single mom, raising a daughter alone, divorced, and actually did not live too far from us in Hillside.

Later, much later, after Kirk had disappeared for quite a long time, he brought me a bouquet of flowers to celebrate the baby's arrival.

The flowers shone with beauty, care, and thoughtfulness.

I shared the details about the nurse with him. "How awful that must be!" I told him about her situation, "How terrible to be divorced and to have to raise her child alone."

That afternoon I spent some time praying for her.

Little did I know then, that I, too, would desperately need the prayers of others all too soon.

~~~

June 1999

Mom and Dad arrived the day after David's birth. Emilie from church, and Ginny and Kayla, my Aglow prayer partners, and Hannah from pre-school playgroup, were among the many special friends who stopped by for a look at the baby and an encouraging word or a gift.

Mostly, everyone sat in the family room on the old blue couch or the blue rocking-glider, visiting and counting little fingers and tiny toes, and flashing pictures on cameras.

Kirk was there, too. But he mostly stayed in his office.

6

Tremors of an Earthquake

W hy was Kirk always in front of that computer monitor even after work hours? I wondered a few nights later around midnight as I lay in bed without him. Why did the screen only show icons whenever I tried to catch a glimpse of what he was doing?

Rolling out of the bed, I tiptoed down the hall toward the office. In silence, I slipped into the room where Kirk sat in front of the monitor. My eyes focused on its sideways image.

Startled, I thought I'd seen the words *Jacuzzi bathtub* in an opened e-mail. It closed before I could be sure and Kirk glanced my way.

"Babe?" I demanded. "What was that all about? Why is your co-worker and roommate for your business trip this weekend talking about Jacuzzi bathtubs?" I knew from what Kirk had said that this man led an ungodly lifestyle.

"What?!" Kirk replied, incredulous. "Our company pays for us to have separate rooms." Kirk looked at my concerned face and laughed aloud. Then he laughed some more and he obviously regarded me as getting things really mixed up.

I felt relieved that the first dark questions I'd jumped to had been false, but something was still not quite right.

Perplexed, I returned to bed.

~~~

Big purchases were never made without discussing it together. That's why I phoned Kirk from the mall that afternoon in late June.

I'd met with one of Nordstrom's personal shoppers because I'd wanted to enhance my wardrobe after the baby's birth. She'd done better than I'd expected in finding me stylish new outfits.

"What do you think, Babe?" I said, while sitting in front of the desk in the office of my personal shopper. "It's all so expensive. Should I wait?"

"Buy it all, Babe." Kirk answered. "You deserve it."

"Are you sure about that?" I asked, standing up.

"Yes. Just go ahead and get it all," he repeated.

~~~

"Girls," I began as I sat on their pink-carpeted bedroom floor before turning out the lights, "what did you do with your daddy today while I was out shopping?"

"Oh, Mommy," they both cried while they climbed from their beds and into my lap. Nicole began, "Daddy is always on the telephone or at the computer behind the locked door when you're not home."

"He doesn't play with us when you're away," added Meaghan.

That's strange, I thought. That didn't sound like something I'd expect of Kirk.

~~~

Thursday, June 17, 1999

Our ballroom dancing classes had concluded part way through the pregnancy. So now, a dinner date often took its place.

Tonight I could not remember the last time I'd had to fill my car with gas by myself. Thankfulness washed over me as Kirk jumped out of the car to do just that on the way to our date night dinner out.

Not only was I thankful to not be the one to hop out of the car and to fill up the tank, but I was also thankful for the wonderful feeling of security that I had in being married to Kirk. I shot up prayers for the handful that I knew who still longed for marriage and for taking a Christian vow with someone that would not be broken.

When Kirk climbed back into the car, I shared these reasons why I was grateful for him, hoping to encourage him.

We ended up at the Macaroni Grill. Kirk said he'd been there with someone from work.

There was this mysterious, unnamed, 'someone from work' who kept popping up in his conversation. Was it that same 'someone' whom Kirk had said knew the name of the picture now on our bedroom wall depicting a knight falling off his horse for his fair maiden?

As we walked toward the restaurant, Kirk reached back and took my hand. "See?" he said, turning toward me as he led us through the door, "Isn't it good that I'm holding your hand?"

That was a strange comment, I thought, not knowing what to say. I followed Kirk to the welcoming hostess.

Though the restaurant was dark, large pots boasting greenery and walls of reds and oranges highlighted our trail to the table. We were seated in the center of the stylish room that reeked of strong Italian spices.

I tried to hear what Kirk had just spoken to the waitress. Loud music emanating from speakers and full tables of people talking and laughing made it difficult to make out the words. But for the first time that I'd been out with Kirk since our engagement, I realized that he had ordered alcohol.

Not that I was against a glass of wine over dinner, I'd just never seen Kirk make that choice before.

~~~

Thursday, June 24, 1999

Mom and Dad came and went on day trips from our California home while still on their extended stay to see their new grandson. The next week for our date night, Mom and Dad stayed at home with all three children and we didn't have to hire our babysitter.

Kirk took us to Ruby Tuesday. This time, he strode quickly, growing far ahead of me as he walked to the door of the restaurant. I ran to catch up with him just inside.

Seated at a table whose odor hinted that it had been freshly wiped, this time the atmosphere was quiet, the tables surrounding us empty of people, and the music soft in the background. It was still early in the evening since Kirk had worked from home that day.

I studied the menu but could not decide between two entrées. The waitress stood ready and Kirk ordered so I chose quickly, still not sure.

When our food arrived, I looked over at Kirk's plate and wanted to try what he had, but his mood of silence warned me not to ask.

Kirk did not talk, and he kept his eyes on his food which disappeared in large mouthfuls.

"Do you want dessert?" he asked, at last looking up.

The exquisite desserts looked too big. I was too full for one of those. "Why don't we stop by McDonald's for something smaller on the way home?" I suggested. "Also, Babe, you know that I brought this couples' Bible study and discussion book for us to go through – maybe we could do the first chapter while we're there?"

"Okay," Kirk signaled for the check, and paid the bill.

Happy to be wearing one of my new outfits, I smiled, feeling confident, even pretty. I prayed and hoped that Kirk and I could get connected with this new couples' book I'd located at the Christian bookstore.

At McDonald's, even though the aroma was of french fries, we each ordered a hot fudge sundae and took a booth, sitting across from one another. I placed the book I'd brought for couples on top of the table where it sat in full view, but unopened, ignored.

In the middle of the room sat a loud group of four middle-aged women at a table. It was not hard to overhear their spicy conversation or their noisy laughter. Each one of them took turns and named their favorite movie actor or TV celebrity with whom they dreamed of being with.

I looked at the hands of those I could see – wedding rings – they were married women.

Kirk looked from me to them. "I find that attractive in a woman," he said. "I mean, what those ladies are talking about."

Dumbfounded, I only gazed back at him and my stomach knotted. "Just so you know," I looked straight back into Kirk's face. "You're the only one that I think about in that way."

Kirk stood up and said, "I'm finished."

Both of us tossed mostly uneaten sundaes into the wastebasket.

I followed after Kirk, who was already out the door.

~~~

Saturday, July 3, 1999

The house now lay emptier, quieter, cooler, early in the morning, and the children still slept.

I patted my tummy. It was amazing how it'd felt like I'd been carrying that baby forever. But now, I missed the thrill of a little one inside of me, kicking and moving.

I'd climbed back into bed after saying goodbye to my parents, whom Kirk was driving to the airport to catch their early morning flight back to the East Coast.

Paula's birthday had already come and gone, but today Hannah & I had plans to surprise her with a celebration. Paula, a mom from our preschool playgroup, just thought we were meeting for lunch at Mimi's Cafe. Candy, who had recently moved to Santa Cruz, was driving in, too.

Hearing the baby begin to cry, I pulled myself up and out of bed. Soon the girls were awake. We all got fed, dressed, and ready for our day. Now it was 11:00 AM – the time I was supposed to leave.

Where was Kirk?

Candy arrived before long, smiling, welcoming, open arms, happy to meet the newest member of our family, David Michael. She'd come here first so that we could drive together to the restaurant.

The digital clock on the stove read 11:30. Still no sign of Kirk.

I paged him once more. It was noon before he called.

"Where are you?" I asked, exasperated and embarrassed because he was now messing up other people's plans as well. "Candy has been here for an hour and Hannah and Paula have been waiting for me at the restaurant this whole time!" I fumed. We had gone over the schedule more than once before he'd left to take Mom and Dad to the airport.

"I'll be there soon," was all Kirk said, offering no explanation.

Twenty minutes later, the sound of Kirk's white truck pulling into our driveway bid me look out the window. He zipped into the house, greeting Candy.

"*Where were you?*" I demanded again, standing in the foyer, trying not to get too upset in front of our company, trying not to cry.

"Do you want me to help you get David into the car?" Kirk answered.

"Where were you?" I asked again.

"Look," Kirk said, "you're late, so do you want to talk about this right now?"

Looking back at Candy, I agreed. It was time for Candy and me to go.

My friends were gracious about the inconvenience. Soon, the whole incident was swallowed up and forgotten about in our laughter and fun girl-time at Mimi's Café.

~~~

Sunday, July 4, 1999

It had not been easy to get everybody out the door and into church that morning, but finally we'd made it.

With the girls deposited in their Sunday School classrooms, Kirk and I now sat together in one of the pews in the middle of the church. I pulled out our checkbook from my purse so that Kirk could write our tithe check.

My heart warmed as first Hannah and Henry, and then Paula, and then Emilie and her husband all took seats surrounding us with their smiles, hellos, and hugs from all sides. I felt surrounded by love and care.

The baby sat at our feet sleeping in his carseat.

Sitting next to Kirk with his arm slipped around me, everything seemed so right again.

During the sermon, Kirk only focused on David Michael as the baby snoozed. I noticed tears welling in his eyes, and looked up to see that Emilie had also noticed Kirk's absorption in his new baby son.

After all, I thought, it was his only son.

But that wasn't the issue that brought tears to Kirk's eyes.

7

But God Sees

Monday Evening, July 5, 1999

I felt unsettled and troubled. Something seemed very wrong.
Cross-legged, I sat on the far left end of the old blue couch in our now repainted living room, next to the garage door.

Nicole, Meaghan, and newborn David Michael were safely tucked under their light summer blankets, asleep in their beds. It was still too early for me to go to bed, only 8:00 PM.

The heat of summer moved in and out through open windows, though the air temperature was comfortable due to its lack of humidity.

Dinner dishes awaited me in the sink and released the aroma of homemade lasagna still stuck on plates from the adjoining kitchen. I was thankful that the meal had been brought to us as one of those given after the birth of a baby so I'd not had to cook.

Kirk had mandatory time off from work this entire week. It was the week in July every year that all employees did not work in order for the company to save money.

Not typical for me, I found I could not contain the tears that leaked downward, sliding, slowly, steadily, one drop at a time. And, while not knowing what else to do, I continued to just sit there.

Now and then, I snatched a tissue from the box I'd brought to my side, and the pile of crumpled white climbed higher and higher above my rose slippers on the floor in front of me.

Kirk passed by me yet another time.

His thick, dirty work shoes traversed from inside the garage door to down the hallway to our now unoccupied guest bedroom, also the baby's room. Kirk continued his project, unmoved by my crying, still in the process of completing the remodeling work on outlets and light switches.

Now the clomping dirty shoes stopped in front of me.

From my view of the beige, carpeted floor, I saw Kirk's hairy legs, black knee-high men's socks and old work shoes, now standing still. "Why are you crying?" he demanded, at last, with a tone of annoyance, irritation.

"I don't know," I answered, new tears joining old ones, now overflowing. I squinted from the bright light behind him coming from the kitchen when I looked up into Kirk's cross face.

"I just don't know what is wrong, Babe. But I know that there is something terribly, terribly wrong. I don't know what it is," I said, helplessly. I pulled another tissue from the box, blew my nose, and tossed it on top of the pile covering my slippers.

The shoes carried him away again, and he slipped outside into the garage. Unfamiliar, unsynchronized music blared at my neck for brief moments before the door closed.

A minute later, Kirk came back inside and walked with a tool in his hand down the hallway.

Anger began to rise inside of me at his lack of concern. Getting up with a jerk and scattering the pile of tissues, I decided to go down the hallway and have a discussion with Kirk.

Seated on a short stool in the empty room, Kirk changed the outlet covers with a screwdriver.

"Kirk," I tested, standing in the doorway, "I guess I'll go out to Borders to hang out for a change of pace – they're open late and the kids are all in bed."

"Okay," he agreed immediately, without even looking up.

Additional anger rose in me at his indifference and I cried out, "Don't you even care? I mean, I keep going out of my way to serve you – and I dress especially for you – and I do everything I can think of for you! Don't you even care about me?" I asked, exhausted from already having cried so much.

Now he looked up and turned his eyes toward me readily. He looked like he was almost glad that I'd asked that question. "I don't think I love you anymore, Janice."

Startled at his solemn, flat words, I stepped back to steady myself against the doorframe. All I could think was *he never uses my real name. He always calls me, 'Babe.'*

"What do you mean you don't love me anymore?" I asked, standing there now with a feeling of dread rising. "I mean, how can you stop loving somebody? That's impossible. Can you stop loving your mom, or your dad, or your best friend?"

Kirk returned to the outlet with his screwdriver and replied, "I just don't think that I do. I think I'm ripe to have an affair."

I continued to stand there, not comprehending. "Well, maybe we need some marriage counseling," I said.

He looked at me coldly, disappointed. "Well," he added, "I'm not the same person I used to be. I've changed. We don't have anything in common anymore," he offered, sounding vaguely reminiscent of that previous conversation we'd had awhile before.

Kirk continued using the screwdriver without looking at me.

"Well," I said evenly, "sometimes people change over time, but we are married and we have three children and we need to work this out. And *I do* love you, Kirk."

He looked sullen and continued his work. Kirk did not seem happy about my love for him. It seemed like he wanted me to fight with him. It seemed... like he wanted me to say that I agreed with him that we were incompatible.

After a long minute or two, I retreated to our bedroom and sat down on the edge of our green, wrought-iron, canopy bed.

I took a deep breath and I prayed aloud, "Well, God. Kirk doesn't think that he loves me anymore. But, I know that *You do*! You love me more than I can imagine! You know when I sit down and when I get up and what I am thinking like it says in Psalm 139. You love me, God!" I declared and I cried and the tears slid down my cheeks all at the same time.

Hearing the words of truth brought definition to my world and I clung to God's words of love for me.

~~~

Kirk worked late that night. I went to bed early. My head ached from all the crying. And I knew the baby would wake me in a just a few hours.

Later on, Kirk crawled into our bed and woke me slightly as he curled his body around mine and draped his left arm over my side. Wrapped in his arms and feeling his breath on the back of my neck, I rested in his crevice all night long. Again, I realized how long it had been since we'd slept close like this, something that used to be so ordinary.

Now I felt comforted again. Hope eased into my heart. But I was so, *so* confused by the way Kirk treated me. Maybe, maybe, maybe though, everything would really be okay now, I hoped.

I did not know it then, but this would be the last time that I ever felt the comfort and warmth of Kirk's closeness.

~~~

Tuesday, July 6, 1999

In the morning, I woke up and heard Kirk shaving at the sink. Sleepy, but encouraged and comforted by Kirk's embrace all night long, I walked down the hall and put my arms around his waist and gave a kiss to his shoulder. "So," I asked, "where do you want to go on our date night tonight?"

His body turned rigid, unresponsive, stiffening. The reflection of his eyes in the mirror bore into mine from underneath his white foam-covered face. Looking at me stonily, penetrating, he answered, "We're not going on a date night."

Stunned at his response, I released my grip from around his waist, let my arms drop, and took a step back. Just then I heard one of the girls calling so I turned toward the door, feeling confused, puzzled, and disorientated once again.

What was the matter with Kirk? I wondered. He had just held me in his arms through the night, but now his eyes looked vacant and icy. I'd never seen such a cold, cold look before.

I shivered even though it was summer and the air was warm.

Inhaling slowly, I called out to God under my breath and answered the duties in our home with three small children that awaited me and kept me busy, and demanded my constant attention.

~~~

If we were to return to the time when I was seventeen years old, just two years after I'd become a Christian, one would see that God had peppered my life with at least four significant, godly mentors. All these were caring Christian adults who took a great deal of time to listen to me and to pour God's Word into my life and to teach me His ways.

The one I phoned to talk to today was Miriam. It did not matter at all that it had been a long time since we'd spoken.

"Miriam," I began right away, using hushed, serious tones as the children played in the living room down the hall and as Kirk kept his dental appointment. "I think there is something wrong. I think there is something wrong... with... my marriage." I swallowed hard. That had been so difficult to say.

"Oh, no," she responded, quietly, from across the country after I'd shared with her the little bit that I knew to tell her. "Do you think, Janice, that it is possible that there is someone else?"

"Certainly not!" I answered emphatically and sat down on the floor in the hallway. "Not Kirk. He would never do something like that!"

Then she began to pray. Miriam was no stranger to prayer. Together, we approached the throne of God boldly and asked Him for His divine help, wisdom, revelation, and timing.

Miriam would keep praying and listening to the Holy Spirit.

~~~

In times like this, as always, it is very important to choose carefully the words that come out of one's mouth.

In fact, how one first reacts to a crisis situation – whether by faith or by fear – will often begin the snowball that picks up speed as it goes down the proverbial mountain. The Bible says, "Do not fear (Is. 41:13)." And even Jesus said to his disciples *before His own crucifixion*, "Do not let your hearts be troubled (John 14:1)."

"But, God knows!" I called aloud, looking up toward heaven and declaring this several times as I walked up and down the narrow hallway after having prayed with Miriam. "I might not know what is going on, but You do, Lord Jesus. You know. You've seen everything that has happened. And in Your timing, I will know, too. So I praise You that You are taking care of me and helping me. I praise You!!!"

I continued to declare what was true and to pray aloud even as my small children kept at their play without noticing my dilemma.

I did not stop declaring God's promises aloud directly from His Word as I changed the diapers, fed the children, and cleaned the house. I sang His Word, and I danced as I sang, and I played with the children. It was the truth and the promises from God's Word that I clung to.

As I heard the Bible verses aloud, ones which I'd memorized long ago, my courage grew and fear retreated.

I felt the Holy Spirit strong within me.

~~~

Yes, something was seriously wrong, I thought more about it while I stood at the sink with the water running, loading the cups with sticky orange juice residue. I just really didn't understand what it could be.

But it was now obvious to me that my much-loved husband and I needed marriage help, and I was going to ask for it. I'll go to church, I thought, to see what kind of counseling would be available when I talked to a pastor.

It was then that Kirk walked through the door and closed it behind him as he returned from his dental appointment.

"Hey, Babe," I greeted him from the kitchen. "The girls are in their naps, so can I go out and run some errands?"

~~~

Emilie, seated at the main desk, looked up at me as I entered the large church office. Two or three others also worked at desks or talked on phones. I drew close to the counter where she stood to join me by a large vase of flowers, and said, almost whispering, "I think I need to talk to a pastor."

Emilie led me into a side room with the copier machines, away from everyone else.

"Do you mind if I ask why?" she inquired, standing in front of me while I, exhausted, sat down in the only chair in the narrow room with the carseat holding baby David parked at my feet. "Is there some kind of a problem?"

"Yes, I mean, probably not that bad. I don't know." I stumbled over my words and I looked at the floor and then back at her. "It's Kirk... our marriage."

"You and Kirk?" she asked, her voice rising in alarm. "But, you and Kirk... you're such a wonderful couple..." Her eyebrows turned down and a look of concern spread across her motherly face.

"I know," I countered, crossing my arms over my chest, struggling at having to share the information, "but he is saying bizarre stuff – like... that he doesn't love me."

"Do you think there is someone else involved?" Emilie's eyes began to brim with tears now and she held fast her gaze.

I looked away from her, down at the floor again, then at the wall. The tears were catching and beginning to brim into my own eyes, too.

"Of course not," I stated vigorously, gesturing. "Kirk would never do something like that." But my words sounded hollow.

Still, I believed them.

But now Emilie was the second person that had asked me that astonishing question. The idea was absurd. Kirk was 'my Precious Babe,' after all.

"No, of course not," I repeated, "he knows better than that." I assured myself, and Emilie, too.

"Well, good. I read there is a better chance of mending a marriage when there is no one else involved." Emilie turned toward the door to check for a pastor, closing it behind her. But she turned to me and instructed before it clicked shut, "You stay in here and wait."

I pushed away a couple of new tear escapees on my cheek, irritated by them.

After a few long moments, the door swung open again, "Pastor Logan's not here," Emilie said, referring to the senior pastor whom I'd asked to speak with. "But Pastor Donald is," she continued, "and I know he'd like to speak with you. I'll wait in here by you until he is ready," she said.

Then she prayed aloud for me and for Kirk, and for our marriage. I knew that she would continue to do so.

~~~

Pastor Donald sat behind his large desk in an office decorated with a potted silk tree in the corner. The aroma of coffee lingered in from the main office. Blonde hair, blue eyes, tall, he motioned for me to sit in the chair pulled up for me by the side of his desk.

I sat down with carseat and sleeping baby again by my feet. Suddenly I felt my hands begin to tremble and my heart beat through my chest.

Meeting with Pastor Donald under these circumstances seemed so foreign compared to the fellowship Kirk and I had experienced with him and his wife, Debbie, in their home for Thanksgiving, or on that couples' date to see a show in 'The City' and eat at the famous garlic restaurant, *The Stinking Rose*.

Pastor Donald and his wife were our friends, and their kids were buddies with ours. They'd reached out and cared for us when we'd moved to California three years before.

It was awkward to introduce the subject. Blood rushed to my cheeks but I concentrated on what I had to do. I felt embarrassed, so embarrassed, but I brushed that aside because I knew that Kirk and I needed help, it seemed, in the desperate sort of way.

I shared everything that I possibly thought might open up and solve the mystery.

Then Pastor Donald tilted his head to one side and asked that terrible question – the same one that I'd been asked now twice already in the same day: "Do you think there could be somebody else?"

Again, adamantly, I straightened myself in my chair and rejected this idea. I could not conceive of it. I mean, we'd never fought or anything.

But it did trouble me that Pastor Donald was the third person whom I'd talked to that day who had asked me that identical question.

I went home and made dinner. As I sat across the table from Kirk while he ate, I wondered, *what was going on in his mind?*

~~~

Wednesday, July 7, 1999

Kirk drove our family car, the red Ford Taurus, and I sat in the passenger's seat with all three children buckled in their carseats in the back.

Mandatory time off for the week of July 4th meant we'd scheduled a family picnic on the coast, just one hour away. Hoping that getting Kirk away from his computer and from the unending remodeling projects would help us, I'd packed the trunk with our lunches and planned the kids' naptimes around our outing.

But Kirk was fidgety. He would not maintain eye contact with me and he appeared angry under the surface. We drove along with barely any words until we reached one of many public beaches which we'd visited before.

As we unfastened seatbelts and stood outside the car, the girls jumped up and down in the parking lot. The wind smelled of sea salt and blew hair in our faces and made it hard to hear one another.

Grabbing the picnic food and blankets from the car, and holding hands with the children, we all managed to scale down the steep incline to the beach below, even with the carseat.

The wind picked up speed down by the surf and we each cowered from the flying sand by eating low to the ground on our blanket. Conversation was blown away by the same fierce wind that peppered our food and stung our eyes with the sand.

Nicole and Meaghan cried with dismay. I comforted infant David by cradling him close to my chest under his blanket, nursing him, and turning my back against the wind to protect him.

I had a deep awareness inside that I dare not say a word or voice any complaints.

All of a sudden, Kirk jumped to his feet and shouted at me through the wind, "I'm leaving!" He grabbed a few items and a child's hand and walked on ahead. I worked hard and struggled to get the rest of us and the rest of our stuff back up the hill and to the parking lot.

Back in the car, Kirk decided that a picnic in the woods would be a better choice. With Kirk at the wheel, he set his jaw and seemed determined to get to our new destination in top speed.

He hurried us around twisting, curving mountain roads winding up and around and down and back upwards again. I wondered if I would be sick to my stomach, but I felt constrained to not say a word. I silently prayed and called out to God.

We arrived at a wooded park full of huge trees, trails, picnic groves, and only a little bit of wind. As we ate our lunch at the picnic table, Kirk never looked at me or even spoke to me. Instead, he engaged our daughters in playful conversation.

I wondered if I were invisible.

"Let's take a walk, girls!" Kirk announced with the last bite of his sandwich and they followed him, skipping.

He ran ahead of them, turning back and calling for them to catch up. Sometimes he stopped to explain the different trees and plants that they came across with an unusual, heightened enthusiasm.

I was left in the distance.

Finding a huge, fallen Redwood tree around a bend, he climbed up to its highest point, about twelve feet or more off the ground, where the humongous tree's roots stuck out into the air. He called to Nicole and Meaghan, "Come up here with me, girls!"

"No, Daddy, it's too high," they both said.

"You can do it girls, I really want you to try," Kirk persuaded them.

Slowly, one-by-one, our preschool-aged girls joined him 12-15 feet off the ground.

Cringing, I watched them and I knew what might happen if they were to fall off that tree. But I sensed strongly that I had better not say a word. So I stood underneath, brow crinkled, and praying hard instead.

One of the girls did lose her footing, but Kirk caught her just in time. "Let's go down, Daddy!" she cried, looking up at him.

In only a few minutes we were back in the car and Kirk had us zipping along down the mountainous, winding roads. A passing car honked in protest of Kirk's acceleration and because of his crossing over the middle line of the road. Kirk snapped at one of the girls when they issued a complaint.

I knew that I knew that I knew that I had better not say a word.

At last we arrived home.

"I have to check my e-mail to see if there's something important from work," Kirk stated with curtness, and he left me standing outside our home with our three small children and a car to unpack.

~~~

Thursday, July 8, 1999

It was not accidental that I suggested to the girls how much fun it would be if their daddy might take them to the park the next morning.

Living only a few short blocks from the Hillside Children's Park made the outing a regular activity. And so, with some reluctance, Kirk left his computer and set out with the two cheerful girls ready for the swings and the slides.

I had some investigating to do and only a little bit of time while they'd be out.

Trying not to tremble and looking back over my shoulder while I stood outside by the white truck, I checked a third time to make sure that Kirk had turned the corner with the kids.

The front fender still needed work, and when I peered inside the driver's window, I could see a handful of papers on the passenger's seat and some crumpled bags from fast food on the floor. It was unlocked, so I opened the door. The smell of half-eaten hamburger met me.

With shaking hands, I assured myself that Kirk was at the park now. I looked up the street again just to make sure.

Reaching across the driver's side, I turned over a piece of lined notebook paper with two words written across the top: 'Dear Sweetie.' That was when my heart plunged.

My mind flashed back to all the letters that Kirk had once written to me daily during our long engagement – ones which had been titled in the same way. But Kirk had not written me any of those kinds of notes in recent days.

I found nothing else, put everything back the way I found it, and hurried inside the house.

Next, I went to Kirk's office and rummaged through the wallet that he'd placed on the bookshelf. Inside, I found one credit card that was not ours – one that I did not recognize. Well, I thought, it could be a card that his work issued to him.

I fumbled and fumbled with Kirk's pager. I could not figure out how to work all the controls. But I did find a current message which read: Call Leanne.

Leanne? I wondered. Hadn't the children talked about meeting 'Daddy's friend, Leanne,' at the mall awhile back? I remembered he'd said it was just a co-worker that he'd happened to run into 'by chance.'

But my heart raced and my stomach did somersaults and at the same time I felt like I was sinking below sea level.

I phoned Miriam. "Miriam," I cried when she immediately picked up, "I think Kirk might be having an affair." I related all the information about the few scant clues I'd managed to collect, keeping watch out the window. David slept in the bassinet in our bedroom. "I am just bursting with wanting to shout and scream and confront Kirk with what I've found!" I cried out.

"No." Miriam warned me, "You cannot do that yet. You don't have enough evidence. He could explain all those things away, easily. You still don't really know anything. You have to wait until God gives you enough facts so that you know for certain."

"But, Miriam," I answered, "how can I keep quiet about this? How can I just not say anything?"

"I'll pray for you, Janice. I'll pray that God puts a guard on the door of your lips, and He will help you. Just don't say anything until it's the right time, okay?" she asked again.

"Okay," I agreed, and Miriam prayed for me.

~~~

As soon as I hung up the phone with Miriam, I felt scared, like I was too close to the edge of a cliff. *But God.* I turned to His Word:

> *"The LORD is my light and my salvation—*
> *whom shall I fear?*
> *The LORD is the stronghold of my life—*
> *of whom shall I be afraid?*
> *When evil men advance against me*
> *to devour my flesh,*
> *when my enemies and my foes attack me,*
> *they will stumble and fall.*
> *Though an army besiege me, my heart will not fear;*

though war break out against me,
even then will I be confident."
Psalm 27:1-3

~~~

Because I knew that God was with me,
my confidence grew.
Because I knew that Jesus loved me,
my confidence grew.
Because I knew that He could see every detail
about what was happening, even when I could not,
my confidence grew.
Because I knew that there is always victory in store
for a child of the King in the end,
I had confidence.

~~~

So I declared aloud the promises of God, and my ears heard myself speak them. I repeated God's promises again and again with strong conviction in my voice, no matter what I felt on the inside.

I held close to Psalm 37:23 (KJV) which I'd hidden in my heart as a teen in a song which I now remembered and I sang aloud.

~~~

I prayed aloud, "Lord, You are the One in charge OF WHEN I get the information that I need."

I began to thank God for all that He was doing to help me. And I thanked Him for Who He Is and I thought aloud about God's wonderful character.

As I stayed before the Lord clinging to Him, His Presence enveloped me, comforted me, flowed through me, and even brought to me, surprisingly, joy!

~~~

By the time Kirk returned with the girls, the courage and the faith inside of me were flowing strong. I greeted him with a heartfelt, friendly, smiling welcome.

"I've got to do some errands now," Kirk said, and he turned away to walk out the front door and left in his white truck.

~~~

"Therefore we will not fear,
though the earth give way
and the mountains fall
into the heart of the sea,"
Psalm 46:2

~~~

8

A Stranger in My Bed

That night, I lay beside a man whom I did not know. Someone whom I now suspected of grave wrong-doing. Someone whom I now had serious doubts of being at all trustworthy.

It was me that hugged the edge of the bed, wanting to be as far away from Kirk as possible. I fell in and out of sleep as my mind searched over the day's events backwards and forwards, looking for further clues that I may have missed as to what could possibly be going on.

My thoughts of Kirk felt numb, frozen, and bewildered. I hardly dared to move in my bed. I hardly dared to breathe as I slept beside this new stranger. I did not know what to expect next.

At the same time, I felt certain of this: God was in charge. The situation was submitted to Him. And, I had a deep awareness of God's care by His closeness and presence.

Jesus, I was certain, would be the One to decide when I would find out what I needed to know.

~~~

Friday, July 9, 1999

Kirk had agreed to babysit. I was scheduled to attend the first of a two-day homeschool seminar for beginners with my co-op teaching friend, Frankie.

Getting out of bed before daybreak from my restless, disturbing night, I nursed David and packed up the diaper bag. I still needed to locate some directions on the Internet and to check the gas in the car.

It was an all-day seminar about an hour away, and it began bright and early at 8:00 AM.

I phoned Frankie while standing by the washing machine in the privacy of the garage and explained that I needed to drive separately. With reluctance, I shared that there was something wrong. "Something," I said, "is going on that seems to be serious and I don't know if I will need to cut out early, or leave suddenly."

"Maybe it's not as bad as you're thinking," she tried to encourage me.

"I hope you're right," I said, doubtful.

I checked on the girls. Both were sound asleep in their separate beds in the corner bedroom that they shared. They looked so precious, so innocent. I prayed for them and kissed them goodbye, not waking them.

I approached Kirk who lay in bed, too, down at the end of the hallway.

"Bye, Babe," he mumbled to me and rolled away with his eyes still closed as I approached.

I wondered if I should return early and see if there was anything important to see. Everything, however, appeared so normal right now.

~~~

Getting lost was a familiar experience for me, but this time I actually found the address the first time. After parking, I gathered my water bottle, purse, and notetaking supplies, and, of course, baby David in his carseat along with the diaper bag. I managed to carry it all across the lot and into the church building.

I joined the line of ladies formed behind a table in order to sign in. Frankie found me in the lobby, "Goooood morning, Janice! I see you made it here on time!" She presented me with a large welcoming embrace and a huge smile.

"And how is little David doing this morning?" she peeked under the blanket that I had on top of the carseat. "Cute as a button!" she pronounced.

Taking seats beside one another in the conference room, we placed a sleeping David between us. This would be a rigorous two-day course on how to teach one's child to spell, read, and write.

I heard the laughter and exclamations of other women greeting one another in happy reunion as they arrived. Coffee brewed in the corner, and its aroma spread by the various cups that traveled with it around the room sent out a comforting fragrance in all directions. More ladies filtered in. It was almost time to begin.

"So, how are you today?" Frankie turned and looked at me.

"Well, so far, so good. But I think something is very wrong." I told her, wiping wisps of hair away from my eyes. I explained the unsettling information that I had found the day before, and the terrible sense of trepidation I felt.

"It's going to be okay," Frankie said, squeezing my arm. "Maybe it's just not what it seems and there's actually nothing to get upset about."

"Maybe," I faltered, hoping that she was right, but I felt a deep feeling of dread delivering strong doubts. Just then, the speaker stood up at the mike and welcomed us to the seminar.

It was the strangest experience. My eyes faced the speaker, and my ears listened, and my mind thrilled with the new information which I could apply to our homeschool. At the same time, my heart felt like a heavy weight which was threatening to drown.

My thoughts kept returning to the situation at home, and all the baffling questions and mystery that surrounded it. Before I could stop it, tears began to fall down my cheeks. Frustrated that I lacked control over them, I found that I needed a tissue.

Frankie, realizing this, handed me a box of them from somewhere. She then helped me to turn my pages and to keep my place while many more tears slid down my cheeks. Grief swelled up in me like a huge wave and escaped one drop at a time, through salty tears.

But I kept listening to the speaker. *This is so odd,* I thought. Then it was break time.

"Are you going to be okay?" Frankie turned her face to look at mine.

"Yes," I said, blowing my nose into another tissue. "But, all I can do is wonder what is going on at home. I wonder if I should leave early."

Before I could decide to do anything different, the speaker began the session again. The next part continued in the same vein as the first with me both listening and crying simultaneously, and Frankie helping me to turn pages.

Lunch time arrived.

Others went to find fast food, but Frankie and I took our bag lunches up the stairs of the host church to find a quiet, empty Sunday School room.

After awhile of chewing at my dry and tasteless sandwich in silence, and sitting on a cold metal child's chair, I noticed that Frankie looked up at me from the floor where she sat. I heard her words, "What can I do to help you? I'm not a crier – I'm sorry, but is there anything I can do to help?"

"Oh, Frankie, I'm not a crier either, I understand. But all I can do is cry!" I wiped yet another tear from my face. "Maybe you can let me borrow your cell phone so that I can call my friend, Miriam, and give her an update. I know that she is praying and waiting to hear from me."

"Of course! Talk as long as you want. Here, I'll go downstairs and give you some privacy." Frankie left, carrying the baby in my sling.

The seminar lasted for the rest of the day. It ended at 5:00 PM. Sometimes the tears petered out for awhile. But mostly they continued to drain without a sound.

At one point, I remembered that I needed to get something from the car. I returned back through the parking lot with the tears still streaming. People passed me, and I kept my head up, nodding a greeting to them. The strangers just nodded back, looking puzzled, but continued on their way.

~~~

I may have arrived at the seminar without getting lost, but when Frankie and I tried to follow each other home in our separate cars, we got turned around again and again. Motions and gestures could not be understood using only rearview mirrors. We drove in circles.

At last we stopped at a gas station to get directions. But then one of us blocked the other from getting gas and we found our cars stuck in a lane facing each another. It was just so funny that we both laughed and laughed and laughed.

The hilarity of it all ushered in release and relief and refreshment, and, for a few minutes, forgetfulness. For a moment, I could not recollect the pain that I knew.

But soon I pulled into our driveway at 707 Strawberry Lane, and I wondered what I would find when I walked inside the front door.

~~~

"Record my lament; list my tears on your scroll
are they not in your record?"
Psalm 56:8

~~~

I did not go inside immediately because I was scared.

For a few moments I just sat inside the car, looking at the house from the driveway to see if anything unusual stood out. Nothing did.

Pulling David, who still rested in his carseat out of the car and grabbing his diaper bag, I made myself walk up to the front door of our house. I could see the lights on inside. Taking a deep breath and saying a prayer, I unlocked our door.

Kirk's upbeat, familiar bluegrass music was the first sound to fill my ears as I stepped inside. Walking further into the entryway and setting David down, I looked into our family room.

"Mommy!" Meaghan chimed from where she climbed on Kirk's legs. He lay stretched out on the old blue couch toying with a small piece of unrecognizable machinery.

"Hi, Babe!" Kirk called to me, looking up, and smiling. I noticed that Nicole sat at the kitchen table still eating her supper.

"How did everything go today?" I asked, moving tentatively inside to take a closer look.

"Great! Some women from your Mothers of Hillside group brought us a meal. It was really good. The leftovers are on the table." Kirk answered, cheerful.

Oh yes, I remembered. My parents had only left last week after being here for the first three weeks after David had been born. The meals had just begun to be scheduled from different groups who brought them after the birth of a newborn. It was a relief to not have to try to figure out what to have for dinner.

"What did you and the girls do today?" I asked softly, spent, sitting down in the kitchen next to Nicole. I was hungry.

"Oh, we just went to the playground and then I worked in the garage while the girls played outside on their trikes," Kirk answered, putting his project on the floor and lifting up a squealing Meaghan in the air with his legs.

"Well, I'm exhausted," I said. "Do you mind if I just eat and go to bed?" I spooned some casserole onto a paper plate. I'd have to be up a couple times for David, and then ready again early in the morning for the seminar.

"Sure, Babe, I'll put the girls to bed," he said, continuing again to work with the metal parts in his hands and not looking up.

Everything appeared alright. Maybe it really was all just my imagination. Maybe there was nothing wrong. Maybe I shouldn't have gone in to talk to the pastor and told Miriam and Emilie and Frankie that there might be a problem.

I was too tired to think. I felt confused. One minute Kirk was stony, icy, withdrawn, and the next he was cheery, happy, helpful.

~~~

"Before they call I will answer;
while they are still speaking I will hear."
Isaiah 65:24

~~~

Saturday, July 10, 1999

It was still dark when I heard the baby crying for me to nurse him for the second time that night. I turned over to view the digital clock: 5:00 AM. Still another half hour I could have slept before having to get up. Perhaps he would fall back to sleep for a few more minutes. But no, his cries were getting louder, more insistent.

Kirk did not move but lay still, sleeping underneath our blanket with his back to me.

Swinging my feet over the side of the bed, I grabbed my bathrobe and put it on. I stumbled down the hallway in the dark to David's bedroom. Though the girls' room was right next door to his, they also did not stir. How could they sleep through this noise? How could somebody so small make this much noise?

All that I had been so blissfully unconscious of only a few seconds before returned to my thoughts. The questions swarmed back like flies buzzing around a dish of spoiled food. *What was terribly wrong with our marriage? With Kirk?* I wished that I could awaken from this dream, this nightmare, and have things go back to the happy normal as they had always been.

Lifting the baby from his crib, I decided that as long as I was up, I might as well nurse him in the office, just in case I might find whatever it was that I was looking for.

What that was, I did not know.

I walked the few steps across the hall, and settled into the chair at the office desk. It was awkward for nursing a baby, but at least I could look through the papers and whatever else was nearby.

A giant collage of paperwork, trays, pens, and cords covered the floor, metal file cabinets, and Kirk's large mahogany desk. Kirk's laptop was on top of it all, closed. Beside it lay keys, change, and Kirk's pager.

I picked up his pager again. I had tried to fiddle with it several times before, looking for clues. I couldn't figure out how to get any information out of it. I pushed the same old buttons, went through the same old cycles, which revealed nothing new.

David finished nursing on one side. I turned him to nurse on the other.

Lately, I recalled, I had noticed Kirk staring at his pager. He didn't just stare at it, he'd grin at it. When I'd asked why, or what he was reading on it, he'd brushed my questions aside.

I picked up the pager again. I prayed. I hoped that I could figure it out. Somehow, I did.

Typed text from a saved memory bank began to roll across the one-line screen.

I froze. The moment stood still. I felt myself barely breathe as I recognized that I had finally found what I'd been looking for.

I sat there, motionless, unable to release any muscle from its current position. Baby David had fallen asleep, so he did not move either.

Stunned, I knew. Now I knew that my life would never be the same.

With the inadvertent push of a button, I had entered into a new reality.

In that second, my innocence had crumbled, and my naiveté vanished. Pollution filled the air of the happy world I lived in, and there was no way of avoiding its fumes.

Kirk was committing adultery.

~~~

"'For I know the plans I have for you,"
declares the LORD,
"plans to prosper you and not to harm you,
plans to give you hope and a future.'"
Jeremiah 29:11

~~~

9

What Happened Next

I stood up.

It was a declaration. It was a charge to the battle line. Not against a person, but against an unseen, invisible enemy coming against our marriage.

Moving slowly, purposely, stepping gingerly and softly, I walked through the doorway and into the hall. I stopped, bit my lip, and realized that I would need the telephone. I would take both telephones, just in case. I clutched the one from the office under my arm which held the baby, but I needed the one by our bed.

It would not do if the phone rang and Kirk answered it. Or, if he picked it up for some reason, and he realized too early that I knew.

The hallway stretched out before me, longer than I remembered. I jiggled the baby in my left arm gently and turned on the bathroom fan for white noise.

Stepping on the wooden floor boards where they were less likely to creak, I returned to our bedroom where, at long last, I reached the telephone on my night table. Grabbing it in my free hand, I made my way back down the hall, past the girls sound asleep in their beds, through the family room and out into the garage where I stood in front of the washer and dryer.

My mind raced. 5:30 AM. That meant it was 8:30 AM on the East Coast. I phoned Miriam.

"What are you going to do now?" she asked.

"I'm going to confront him," I said, unhesitating, jiggling the baby. "It's time. It's God's timing. I could not figure out that pager until this morning."

"I'll be praying," Miriam said.

"But, I don't want to do it alone," I said, shifting the baby on my hip. "I need somebody to help me because Kirk has been acting too unpredictable. It scares me.

"I am going to call one of our pastors. He and his wife are our friends. I'm going to call Pastor Donald because I just talked to him about all this earlier this week."

I took another long breath as I stood in the garage and dialed the home number for Pastor Donald. I glanced at my watch: 5:50 AM.

After three rings, I heard a groggy voice. It was Debbie's voice.

"Debbie? Debbie? This is Janice. I need to talk to Pastor Donald. Kirk is having an affair. I just found out. I need Donald to come over here and talk to us."

"What?" I could hear her disorientation. "What?" she repeated. "The phone is not working in our bedroom – I don't know how I heard it."

She didn't seem to be aware of my conversation with her husband from earlier in the week.

"I'll call you back in a few minutes, Janice," she said.

Waiting and walking, the baby and I made circles in the garage. I dared not sit on the steps because David might wake up.

I counted every second before the phone rang only a minute later. It was Pastor Donald's voice on the other end when I picked up immediately.

"Janice, what's happened?" he asked.

I explained.

"Hold on." I heard talking back and forth between Pastor Donald and Debbie. "I'll call you back in a few minutes."

The phone rang, and this time it was Debbie on the other end.

"Janice, Donald phoned Daniel, an elder from church. He lives down the street from you. He will pick him up and then they will come over to talk with you and Kirk. How about I take the girls to play with Donna and Derrick?"

"Okay," I answered, "I'll wake them up and tell them it's a surprise playdate."

"I'll be there at 7:00 AM," said Debbie. That would give me thirty minutes.

I still had some time. I phoned Miriam to tell her the plan. I called Rosie, another one of those few significant Christian mentors from my early teenage years. She would be on her knees praying, too.

I phoned Ginny, my prayer partner in Hillside. Still half asleep, she got up to pray. Kayla, my other Hillside prayer partner did not answer the phone. I phoned Frankie. Everybody I talked to said they would pray. I knew that they would.

~~~

Clothes for the day? I had to get dressed, I realized. Opening up the dryer, I found some clothes not yet folded that I could wear. I managed to change slowly, carefully, one arm and one leg at a time, while still holding the baby who continued to doze because of his full tummy.

I opened the door and peeked inside the house. I listened: no noises except for the hum of the refrigerator. The house slept soundly. "Oh God," I prayed quietly, but aloud. "Thank You for Your timing. Thank You for showing me what I need to know. Thank You for caring for me."

Adrenaline pumped through me and I had more energy than I should have had after being up so early the previous two days, and with a baby nursing in the middle of the night.

Shadows and darkness still hung on the walls inside, but the daylight was beginning to move in and I could now see.

The baby slept on my arm and I ached with the weight of carrying him for so long. I dared not put him in the crib as he might be stirred and awaken.

I knelt down beside five-year-old Nicole. "Nicole," I whispered. "Nicole, guess what, sweetie? You're going to Donna's house to play."

Nicole opened her eyes, yawned, and looked at me still mostly asleep. I pulled off her nightie as easily and gently as I could with one hand and passed her a play dress to put on.

As she began to dress, I approached three-year-old Meaghan and patted her shoulder. "Honeybun, time to wake up. You get to go to Donna and Derrick's to play."

She frowned, then smiled, then sat up, and began to change her clothes right away with what help I could give her.

"Okay, go use the bathroom," I said, whispering to them both. "Try to be quiet so we don't wake up Daddy. Your friends will be here soon."

My heart beat louder when they stood at the sink and washed their hands. I hoped it would not awaken Kirk.

The baby still slept on my left arm, heavy, but comforting.

From behind the curtain in the family room, I saw the wine-colored van pull up. They parked on the street so as not to make noise in the driveway right outside the front door of our house.

I brought the girls out on the porch and prevented any doors from banging. Soon five-year-old, blonde-haired Donna, hopping beside her mother, said a cheery 'hello' in her high little voice as they joined us on our porch.

Debbie took both my girls' hands in her own. She leaned forward and whispered in my ear, "Donald will be here soon – he went to pick up Daniel."

I watched them all climb into the vehicle, shut the door, and drive away. I breathed a sigh of relief that the girls were safely out of the house and being cared for.

~~~

Not knowing how Kirk would react, nor the full details of what Kirk was involved in, I hid the keys to his white truck and to my red Ford Taurus deep inside a kitchen cabinet by the soup cans. I also hid his shoes in the pantry.

Keeping vigilance near the family room window, I watched for Pastor Donald and the elder, Daniel, before they might knock at the door. Kirk still slept in our back bedroom and baby David still hung sound asleep and well-fed, resting on my left arm.

It was only a few more minutes before two men parked a little white car out on the street. With Bibles under their arms, they walked up to our door, talking together with words that I could not discern.

I did not know Daniel. He was middle-aged, but not old. Mostly bald, salt-and-pepper hair graced both sides of his head. He wore glasses and dressed casual but neat.

When they entered, Pastor Donald made the introductions, talking in a low voice. The two men looked at me, and I at them. "Tell Daniel what has happened, Janice."

I did.

"What do you want us to do?" Pastor Donald asked.

"I want you to talk to him and I want to find out what is going on. I want to reconcile our marriage," I said.

They both nodded.

"And I know that this is God's timing because I've been praying that God would show me what I needed to know at just the right time. I've been searching for answers, and this morning I was finally able to find some. I know that it was no coincidence that I discovered the message on the pager when I did."

"Let's pray together first," Pastor Donald said.

With solemn, sad, serious eyes we all held hands, standing in a circle and facing one another. We bowed our heads and asked God to intervene. Opening our eyes, we looked at each other. *7:30 AM*. It was time.

Pastor Donald and Daniel waited in the family room while I went to get Kirk.

~~~

I walked down the long hallway into our bedroom. Kirk still stretched out on the bed, his breathing deep, his mouth open.

"Babe," I shook his shoulder with my right hand, standing over him. "Babe," he really was sound asleep.

"Whar? Whut?" his eyes remained closed.

"Kirk," I said, as I stood at our bed. "Listen to me. I'm not going to the homeschool seminar today."

"What?" he groaned and rolled away from me.

He seemed more annoyed than anything. Maybe he'd had plans.

He blinked open his eyes, but he looked at the ceiling instead of at me.

"Kirk, the girls are out of the house," I paused, and then continued, "I know that you're having an affair. Pastor Donald and an elder from our church are waiting in our family room to help us and to talk about it."

Now his eyes opened wide and big. He sat up in bed instantly, looking fully alert, giving me his attention. "I'm not having an affair," he denied and he shook his head.

Looking at him steadily, evenly, understanding that this was no game we were playing, I stated, "I know that you are."

I stared at the stranger in my bed, at one time my knight-in-shining-armor.

"Would you like to take a shower and get dressed?" I asked, breaking the silence when he did not speak.

"Yeah," he mumbled, shuffling with the blankets.

I began my walk back down the aisle, the hallway of our bedroom. I left the room.

Kirk locked the door.

~~~

Kirk did not come out.

Using a long, thin rod that I kept in the office for locked doors, I unlatched our bedroom door from the outside, and entered the room.

At the end of our bedroom hallway, Kirk sat on our wrought-iron, green-canopy bed, fully dressed in jeans and white t-shirt, his back against a pillow, and his legs stretched out before him, one ankle crossed over the top of the other.

"How did you know that I was having an affair?" he asked, with an unusual gleam in his eyes and a sort of unholy smirk on his lips.

"It's not important how I know." I countered, and then persisted, "Come on, Pastor Donald and a man from our church, an elder named Daniel, are waiting for us."

"I won't talk to them." Kirk stated in a flat voice, unmoving.

"You won't?" I asked, dumbfounded, surprised, standing in the bedroom hallway. "But... why not? Pastor Donald's our friend. We need help."

"I'll talk to you. But not to them. Tell them to leave." Kirk said in a firm voice, still not moving his position.

I stood still, looking at him because I did not think it wise to be there in the house by myself with Kirk.

"We'll go out to a restaurant," he said.

My mind raced. What would I do now when he would not let someone help? Was it safe for me to be around him? I felt like I could not be sure of what he might do, what he might say, or what was really going on. I really had no idea what to expect from Kirk.

It was a feeling that I was to become familiar with: the scary, insecure feeling of a man who once knew me intimately, who once protected me, cared for me, romanced me, treated me generously and kindly – now a man that I realized I did not know, that I could not trust, one who was, in fact, playing the role of an adversary.

Disappointed and not knowing what would happen now, I returned to convey the message to Pastor Donald and Daniel. They left.

I dug out car keys from the pantry and retrieved the baby who was now asleep in his carseat. Grabbing him and the diaper bag, I found Kirk waiting outside in the red Ford Taurus wearing some older, worn-out shoes on his feet that he must've found in the back of his closet.

I handed him the keys. He started the ignition. It was 8:30 AM.

Pastor Donald and Daniel were nowhere to be seen, but I learned later that they watched from a distance.

~~~

The air in the car added to the dampness of the day. Cold, stale moisture hung between us like a curtain.

92

Pulling out into the street, Kirk only looked ahead at the road.

"Who is Leanne?" I asked, turning my head from the street to face Kirk.

"You mean Lana? Just somebody from work," he said, still focusing on the road. "It happened only once. A one-night stand."

I fell silent and looked at my hands on my lap, absorbing what he'd told me. Waves of shock collided into my heart as Kirk, my beloved husband, confirmed that he had been with another woman.

"What are you going to do now?" Kirk asked, insistent.

"What do you mean 'What am I going to do now?'" I responded, now staring back at the road.

"I mean, what kind of job are you going to get?" he questioned me, even briefly turning his head toward me.

"What kind of job am I going to get?" I repeated, bewildered, still thinking about our marriage and how to put it all back together.

"Yes, you could do daycare in the home – a friend of mine does that," he announced, driving.

What was he talking about? What happened to us working this out? I did not move and only felt numb.

"You really should be reading books about this," he pressed now, still only viewing the road and not me.

"Books about what?" I wanted to know, wondering how it was that I could even breathe now. I looked down at my clamped hands again.

"Books about getting divorced," he said. "There are a lot of good ones out there, you know. I've been reading some," he informed me.

"We're Christians, Kirk. We need to work this out. We have a family," I reminded him, now turning to him.

"Lots of Christians get divorced every day, Janice," he said, now firmer. "People do it all the time." He looked directly at me.

My chest tightened again as he called me by my first name and I only viewed the windshield. The breath had been knocked out of me. I had nothing to say. He had obviously been thinking about this before now. *Divorce was not a word in my vocabulary. Why was it in his?*

I prayed silently, imploring God and the hosts of heaven to intervene. I sat still, and I felt God's presence and His grip around me. At the same time, I also sensed that I was in enemy territory.

The conversation stopped as Kirk pulled into the parking lot of the family restaurant, Baker's Square.

~~~

It was a local family restaurant – but one like Denny's, or IHOP. The flagrant smells of bacon and sausage and eggs met us at the door.

Mid-morning on a Saturday had filled up the tables with couples, friends, and retirees enjoying some chit-chat along with the breakfast bar. Glasses clinked, kids asked for more water, and the chatter of friends filled the air. Waitresses made their way from one table to the next.

Kirk got right to the point: "Two," he stated to the hostess, giving her a quick nod of his head. Kirk took the carseat from my hand where the baby slept unaware, and I trailed him and the baby from behind while he followed the waitress to the back.

We passed thrcc tables where I spotted people that we knew. They smiled, they grinned, they congratulated us on our baby, our third, our newborn son. Kirk moved quickly, passing by all of them.

A weak obligatory image of a smile crossed over my lips, but I did not linger either. I clung to the diaper bag to make sure that I still had it. I felt like I was marching down to receive a sentence.

The friends we passed probably thought I was tired. *If only they knew what was happening,* I thought.

A small table for two was empty in the middle of the back dining room. The others surrounding it were filled. We sat down. The waitress handed each of us a menu with a cheery 'hello,' and she left.

No talking took place at our table while we looked over our menus.

The whole thing was too big for me to comprehend.

I was stunned. I felt restrained from reacting, from jumping up and screaming. I felt strangely calm. I felt the prayers steadying me from the handful who did know, and who interceded.

Though it seemed like my view of this situation was blocked and that I could only see the tiniest part of the scene which was taking place in my life, I somehow remembered *the One who did know* all the mystifying facts. I took comfort in this truth. I felt Him overshadowing me. I silently offered thanks. I felt His hold on the inside of me – and I was surprisingly peaceful.

"Are you ready?" asked the waitress, interrupting our silence.

"Yes." Kirk spoke up first, and ordered quickly.

Scanning the menu that I had looked at but not seen, I hastily decided what I would order, too.

The waitress left again. She smiled at us in her hustle and bustle, as if everything were just ordinary, as if my world were not falling apart as we sat at her table, as if we were just more customers with happy lives.

"Well?" I looked at Kirk, waiting for an explanation, some information, something.

"I've been thinking about leaving you for a long time," he said, meeting my eyes.

"You have?" I couldn't imagine. I stared at him. Wasn't he there on the day we took our vows and signed our marriage license? Didn't we have three children, one only four weeks old?

Baby David stirred. I rocked him with my foot. My heart now felt like it had been squeezed, but in a very bad way.

"Well what are you going to do now?" I asked, unblinking.

"I'm going to leave you," he said, handing me his verdict and setting down his glass of water.

"When?" I couldn't believe the words that I was hearing and my heart beat hard in my chest.

"Right now. Today." he answered, "As soon as we get back to the house." He looked at me.

Could others hear this conversation? People were so close in this crowded restaurant. Were they witnessing my world crumbling? I dared not look around to see if anybody had overheard what my husband had just told me.

I know that I asked why. I know that he evaded my questions.

I know that I tried to reason with him. I know that it was like trying to reason with a man who was not there.

It was like the man I had loved had already moved out. He was not willing to discuss a change of plans. He had made up his mind.

Pushing aside his mostly untouched plate, he said, "I'm not hungry. Let's leave."

~~~

"But, God says,
'Never will I leave you;
never will I forsake you.'"
Hebrews 13:5

~~~

It took a couple minutes to latch in the baby's carseat and to buckle in ourselves.

"Why are you doing this?" I asked, frustrated that I could not make him change his mind, frustrated that I could not reach him, and frustrated that he would not even give me the chance for a true discussion.

"I'm just not happy," he said, keeping his eyes on the road once again.

"Why not?" I asked, looking at him.

He paused, and then answered, still keeping his eyes on the road, "Because you don't want to have a horse ranch."

"What?! You have never, ever talked about wanting a horse ranch." I said incredulously looking at the dashboard.

Not even an ounce of logic. It was ridiculous. He was leaving me because I did not want to have a horse ranch? He'd even mentioned long ago that it was his sister who especially loved horses, and not him.

"Janice," Kirk stated, still driving, "I can divorce you – and I will."

It was hard to believe that the sounds my ears interpreted were words that my husband actually said. Were his words distorted? Was he speaking a foreign language? I stared ahead at the road.

"Just think of the great experience this will be for our kids. They'll be exposed to so many different things in two homes," Kirk looked at me again.

"What?!" I said, astonished once more at his logic, or lack of it.

Hillside only spanned two miles from one end to the other. Soon we were home. Kirk maneuvered the car into our short front yard made up of mostly cement, and moved the car into park with a jolt.

He exited. He went inside. He did not look back.

~~~

Sitting alone in the passenger's seat, I glanced into the back of the car where newborn baby David slept. I could not bring myself to leave the car, or to go inside the house to watch Kirk pack.

I spoke purposefully aloud: "God, I thank You that You are in charge. You have a plan and You promise that it is a good one. You have heard and seen all of this from the beginning to the end. I thank You that You are caring for me and directing my steps. In Jesus' Name. Amen."

Struggling to move myself over the console, I managed to get into the driver's seat without getting out of the car. Unblinking, I turned on the ignition and dazedly began to drive to our church, only a few blocks away.

Once again I was surprised that I could remember how to drive. Feeling like a robot, I backed out into the street and turned the corner.

My hands steered, and my foot pressed the accelerator and the brakes as needed. My senses numbed; smell and taste left me.

I wondered if anybody would be at the church on an early Saturday morning? Only a couple of cars were parked outside in the lot.

When I approached the office door, carrying David in his carseat, I could see a man, the senior pastor, inside.

He opened the door to let me in.

~~~

"Well," the middle-aged Pastor Logan remarked standing in front of me, crossing his arms and stroking his chin. "I hear from Pastor Donald that you and Kirk are having some difficulties."

"He left." I stated bluntly, standing there. "He is packing up right now to leave."

"He left?" the pastor repeated my words, his voice rising, his arms dropping to his sides.

"Yes, he says that he's 'not happy.'" I said, setting the heavy carseat down on the carpeted floor.

"What does that have to do with it?" Pastor Logan asked, obviously irritated now.

"That's exactly what I thought," I said, looking down. "There's another woman," I added, still looking down. "I just found out for sure this morning."

Now our eyes connected and we just stared at one another in silence, absorbing the seriousness of the situation. I felt humbled again, embarrassed, exposed.

The pastor seemed angered by Kirk's actions and made some comments under his breath.

"Well," the pastor said, "I'm due to conduct a wedding shortly. I have to go, but you can stay in my office for as long as you need." He pointed toward the back of the main office to his own.

"Is it alright if I call long-distance on the phone?" I asked, picking up David and his carseat once more.

"Certainly, and here is how it works." He walked back to his office, bade me to follow him, and then showed me how to work the phone system. "Help yourself to any of the refreshments on the table left over from our meeting this morning."

"Thanks," I said, "but I'm not hungry."

"Well, please, eat something." The pastor left.

~~~

I looked around the pastor's office.

A computer sat on a desk by the window with a phone on the right. A large, oval table graced the center of the room taking up most of the space. On it were donuts and Danishes, and a plate of cut-up fruits. Their scents permeated the room.

I walked over to the big office chair nearest the phone and set David's carseat down. He was beginning to turn his head from side-to-side, looking for his mid-morning meal. It had been several hours now since he had nursed.

Taking a seat, I pulled him up and out of the carseat and settled him under a blanket draped over my shoulder. He nursed with the full force of a newborn.

Maneuvering around in the swivel seat, I reached for the phone and dialed Miriam, and then Rosie. Each of them listened and I spent a lengthy time praying with them both. We stood on the promises in God's Word and we gave thanks and praise to God for showing me what was going on in His exact timing. I felt refreshed by their care, God's closeness, and by remembering His Word.

When I hung up the phone, David had unlatched and lay quietly dozing underneath the blanket. I lifted him up and gazed at his sweet, satisfied face.

He could not even hold his head up, nor could he open his little shut eyes. He was 'out' and I brought him close again for the necessary burping, and then, to hold him close to my heart.

I could have laid the baby back down in his carseat, but I held him instead, still taking in all his beautiful newborn features, amazed at each and every one and thanking God for them all, one at a time.

~~~

Outside the pastor's office, I heard some shuffling of feet. Looking up, Pastor Donald and the elder, Daniel, stood in the door of the senior pastor's office.

"May we come in and talk to you?" Daniel asked, waiting for my reply before he entered.

"Sure," I welcomed them, and adjusted the sleeping baby.

"We went back to try to talk to Kirk," he informed me as he pulled up a chair.

"Yes," Pastor Donald added, pulling up another chair. "We saw that he went into the house after you returned, and so we knocked and knocked but he did not answer the door. Then, after awhile, your neighbor with a missing front tooth approached us and began to ask us questions, so we thought it best that we leave."

"Yeah, I guess Kirk doesn't want to talk to anyone," I said, discouraged, quiet, looking back and forth between them sitting in the two chairs in front of me.

"Well," Daniel spoke up, "this is serious stuff. You have been married for how long?" he asked, looking straight at me.

"Nine years next month," I answered softly, feeling defeated.

"Yes, nine years is a long time to be a part of someone's life. And three children, including one infant. Marriage is not just something you walk away from. You've both invested so much. At least there should be counseling," Daniel pleaded, still connecting with my eyes.

"I totally agree," I said, wondering why he didn't know that I was in complete unison with him. "I believe that there should be reconciliation, too. But, Kirk does not seem to think so. And I've seen him walk away from major things before. Once he's made up his mind, he never looks back."

"But this is marriage," said Daniel, still looking at me. "One just doesn't walk away from a marriage. Won't you try to talk to him about it some more?"

"Yes, yes I will," I said. "I already have, but certainly, I'll try again." I wished they could both see how I'd tried to reason with him and how I'd been praying for that in earnest.

"Well," Pastor Donald said, now straightening up in his chair, "there are certain things that you should do to protect yourself," he continued. "I mean, financially. Just in case."

Those thoughts had already crossed my mind. "Yes," I agreed.

"It seems odd," asserted Daniel, "that you are not crying. It seems that a woman in your situation should be more upset."

Oh brother, I thought to myself. I remembered the day before when the tears had flowed all day long without my permission.

"Believe me," I said, growing tired of defending myself, "I think I cried them all out yesterday when they came nonstop. You should have seen me at the homeschool seminar. But today I can't cry. Today I have too much to do. Yesterday was my crying day."

They looked at me, silenced, not fully comprehending, their inquiry over.

"Would you like to come to dinner with some families from the church who are getting together tonight?" asked Daniel. "We're having a potluck, and we'd like for you and the children to join us. I'll stop by about 6:00 PM and you can follow me in your car."

"Okay," I agreed. It would be good to have a place to go for dinner that night.

"I'll drop off the girls from our house to eat with you there," Pastor Donald said. "Debbie will watch them until then."

"Okay," I said, relieved with the provision for the girls. That would give me time to run errands and to rest. I was feeling very tired.

We prayed together and exited the church. I headed to the bank.

~~~

It was as busy at the bank as it had been at the restaurant – a long line waited for the tellers. Walking past those in the queue, I took a chair to see one of the sales associates about my personal account information.

A well-dressed, smiling woman with long, thick brown hair signaled for me with her hand to sit down in her cubicle area while she finished a phone call.

I sat, subdued, with David in his carseat by my foot. He was awake, looking around at the new lights and sights.

At last she turned her attention to me. "How can I help you today?" she inquired with a broad smile.

I wondered how much to tell her. I decided to keep it private. I said, "I'd like to open up a new account."

"Okay," she said, glancing at me. She began to type on her keyboard. "Do you already have an account with us?"

"Yes, I'd like to open up one with only my name on it," I said with a quiet voice, my legs crossed. I looked at David, trying hard not to cry because the tears had begun to edge toward the surface.

"Oh, I see," she said, glancing at me again.

Another woman approached us and called out to the woman helping me, "Hello, Wanda," harnessing her attention.

"How's it going today, Mary?" my sales associate responded.

"Oh, not so good, Wanda. Today, my father-in-law passed away. It's a sad, sad day in our family," she relayed the information, standing there, tears in her eyes.

I sat motionless, but now my eyes welled up visibly with tears, too. Wanda looked back and forth from this woman to myself, both of us in tears.

"Oh," said Wanda, "I see that it is a sad, sad day for everybody."

The woman moved on. I decided to tell Wanda about how my husband had just left, and she helped me more accurately with my banking needs.

~~~

Outside, the local farmer's market across the street had been a favorite diversion for Ginny and me on early Saturday mornings. Beautiful bouquets of flowers, flats of strawberries, and signs of free samples caused me to pause. I dared not stop in today. I had too much to do.

Turning back toward my car, I unlocked it and secured David and his carseat back into place. I held my breath as I drove in the direction of our house, and my heart began to pound, not knowing what I would encounter when I arrived. As I drove, I declared aloud God's Word and God's promises to me.

I need not have been worried about what would happen if I saw Kirk. His white truck was not there.

~~~

Gingerly, I opened the front door. All the shades were drawn. I peered inside. All was quiet and empty and the lights were out. The cleaned dishes from the night before left no fresh smell of food to greet me.

I set David's carseat down with him in it, and I walked through the house, unsure of what I would see or discover.

From the entry foyer, I turned to the right to go down the hallway passing the baby's bedroom, and then the girls'. Nothing appeared any different. Turning left, I peered into the office on the right. His laptop was missing. I continued into the master bedroom and down its long hallway.

I looked into Kirk's closet across from the bed. Usually disorganized with ties and shirts hanging loosely on hooks and hangers, with some always fallen onto the floor, I saw instead that the closet was emptied and cleaned out. There was nothing left. Not even one single sock.

Picking up speed, I retraced my steps back down the hall to our master bathroom. His toothbrush, razor, and shaving cream were gone. My heart pounded. I went back to his office, and I noticed that Kirk's guitar was not in its spot.

I found my way to the old blue couch in the family room and collapsed, dazed with the reality of what was taking place.

~~~

No one was with me, except God. No one knew what I experienced or felt at that moment, except God.

I was alone, but it was a good aloneness because I felt God's sturdy presence.

It was a good pause because no sympathy poured out on me. I had no feeling of 'being sorry for myself,' no 'poor-me-syndrome,' which could kill instead of bring life.

It was just a small, needy me, and a big, generous God, together. And Him faithful, always.

After sitting for awhile in that stillness of feeling Him overshadow me, I began, again, to intercede for Kirk, and for our marriage.

~~~

"Be still, and know that I am God"
Psalm 46:10

~~~

Alone and nursing the baby once more, I began to look around at the condition of our home.

Remodeling projects only partially finished left clutter. A hole in the ceiling over the foyer where Kirk's foot had slipped through from the unfinished attic floor boards gaped at me. The fancy front door stood in place useable, but untrimmed. I remembered that the outlets in the baby's room were replaced but not all covered, unsafe.

The ring of the phone interrupted my thoughts. Hopping to answer it, I managed to keep the baby in place, nursing.

It was Kirk answering an earlier page I'd left.

He sounded dazed. "I'm just driving all around in circles and thinking," Kirk said. "I'm going to get a motel room."

"Please think about what you are doing, Kirk." I pled with him while I stood in the kitchen. "We have been married almost nine years now. We have three small children! You are really hurting me and all of us," I invited him to reconsider, speaking with emotion.

"Okay," he said, and he hung up the phone, still unwilling to enter into an actual conversation.

~~~

"Christ Jesus, who died—
more than that, who was raised to life—
is at the right hand of God
and is also interceding for us."
Romans 8:34:b

~~~

10

Hard Steps

Saturday Afternoon, July 10, 1999

It was the hardest phone call I ever made.

I prayed first. Then, standing in the cold kitchen, I began to push the buttons one-by-one, each of them sending out a beep as I pressed ten digits.

"Hello?" Mom answered, "Guess who just arrived? My cousin Shirley from Iowa – I haven't seen her in years!"

"Mom," I said, interrupting and getting straight to the point, aware that she could not be on the phone for long. "Kirk and I are having some marriage problems."

I heard the sound of her sucking in her breath.

"In fact," I leaned against the pantry door now, "Kirk left me today."

"Oh God!" My mother cried out in prayer.

"And, there is another woman involved," I said, finished, now leaning my head back on the pantry door, too.

Immediately she said, "Let's pray." She prayed a short heartfelt prayer, and we hung up to talk about it later.

After this, thoroughly exhausted, I fell into bed. David slept soundly in his bassinet beside me.

~~~

It was kind of them to invite me so I would not have to be alone.

Daniel, the elder, knocked on our door at 6:00 PM and I walked outside behind him to where I buckled David into our own car. Backing out onto the street behind Daniel's vehicle, I saw the waving neighborhood lady with the missing front tooth standing on her sidewalk, still curious to know what was happening. She gestured at me, beckoning, inquisitive. But I did not stop. Her shallow curiosity felt like a painful intrusion.

We turned right and then left onto some streets that I knew, and then onto some that I did not. Eventually we came to a stop less than a mile away.

Parallel parking was required and I managed to get in after a few tries. I unfastened David, and walked with him in one arm and his carseat hanging awkwardly on my other arm toward the floral garden near the front door opened for us.

Indoors it was a potluck-get-together with a handful of families from our church. The purpose had been to provide for a husband whose wife was out of town for the weekend. He was temporarily caring for four little ones on his own.

I put on a smile and did small chat. They had no idea, I thought, and neither did my little daughters who had now been dropped off by Pastor Donald.

Tired of meaningless conversation but glad to have the help of others with my small girls to get food on their plates, I found a quiet room with a couch where I could nurse David in semi-privacy.

Hearing all the talk and laughter from the kitchen, I only felt strangely cut off from everyone, alone, and apart in the den with the couch and the lights out. Numbness, weariness, and a feeling like I could only move in slow motion filtrated me.

The aroma of macaroni & cheese wafted into the room but I had no desire for it. I drank some water from a bottle to keep hydrated.

I looked at the face of my suckling baby. For him, I was grateful. He was a warm body who needed me to take care of him. His needy, constant presence, comforted me.

It felt so strange to be here without Kirk. It felt so strange to be alone, and it felt so strange to be in charge of all the kids by myself now, without his help.

I kept reminding myself by talking aloud of God's ordering of my steps, of God's perfect timing, and of God, who was The One in control.

It helped me to hear the words of faith gleaned from Bible verses and to meditate on them in my thoughts.

~~~

I stayed as long as I felt I had to, but the sun had already gone down when we left. The girls, tired and full, readily agreed to bedtime when our car pulled into the driveway. "Daddy," I explained when they asked, "still had to be away on business." They'd heard that before.

Finally in bed myself, I played a cassette tape of my prayers that I'd recorded earlier in the day, and I agreed with myself aloud in prayer.

As I drifted off to sleep, I thought about how *the real Kirk* would be appalled at what he was putting me through. *The real Kirk*, the one I had known, would never do this to me, or to anyone.

I felt emptied of my dignity, and of all else that I'd ever felt sure of. There was only one thing left: God.

I mumbled aloud to Him: "You have good plans for me, God. Plans to prosper me and to give me hope and a future. I love You, God."

And *I felt* God with me.

God's peace blanketed me and the children as He watched over us personally while we slept.

~~~

Sunday, July 11, 1999

The alarm clock awoke me because I had been sleeping so deeply, so soundly, like a baby myself on her own father's chest.

Even infant David in his bassinet had not stirred for his early morning feeding. A profound sense of peace and an unusual feeling of freedom lingered over me.

The worship music I'd left to play on repeat through the night, very softly, sifted into my consciousness, and I began to feel uplifted by the words. I began to join in with my own voice.

What day was this? I wondered, and then I began to remember, big-piece-by-big-piece, that Kirk had left me. Oh, to return to that state of unconsciousness that I'd just been in, to be so blissfully and peacefully unaware as I had been while I'd slept so deeply!

It felt heavy again, and just plain bad inside. I wondered, will I ever be free of this underlying achiness? Could things ever be right or happy again?

I did not stop to think about it long but began to declare aloud what I knew to be true:

"God, You can revive our marriage just like you did the valley of the dry bones in Ezekiel 37. You can do anything, God! Maybe Kirk and I will lead those marriage seminars someday – and have empathy like those who have been through the worst and lived to tell Your testimony of power and healing!"

I did not stop talking aloud to God, and I continued all morning to repeat His Words to Him. His strength welled up in me to give me the power to do so.

It was strange to think that I did not know where Kirk was, or what he was doing. So I prayed for him.

Soon I wondered: What should I do today? It was Sunday, so we would go to church, just like always. Elisabeth Elliot, a speaker I'd heard on the radio and one whom herself had experienced much hardship in life had this advice: 'Just do the next thing.' The next thing, then, was to go to church.

Amazed at how easily everybody got up, dressed, and fed, the girls and I stood ready to go when it was still too early to leave. Recently, it had always seemed like such a battle to get all of us ready to go to church. But there was freedom in this home now.

How unusual and unexpected, I thought.

Because we had a few extra minutes, I talked to the children about the Lord. I spoke to them about how He's our Savior and how He died on the cross for us because He loves us and wants to be in relationship with us. I talked about how He can forgive even the worst of sins.

No sin can separate us from God's love I told them. Jesus paid the price and wants us.

I taught the girls the song that Kirk had taught me about how Jesus paid a debt that He did not owe, and how I owed a debt that I could not pay.

The girls and I held hands to do a little dance while we sang and David watched us from his carseat, arms and feet moving, and his head turning up at us.

This, too, seemed so fresh. It had been a long time, I realized, since I had not felt a hidden, edgy, threatening restraint from talking freely about my Lord and Savior, Jesus Christ. I wondered when that tension had begun to take place in our home.

As we left, I thought, would Kirk return to the house while he knew we'd be at church? If so, what would he do, or take? Well, that's God's area to watch, I decided, and I left the praise and worship music running on repeat, but louder.

~~~

It was hard, but I got through all the motions at church. Most of the people did not know what had happened and I needed to exude cheerfulness. For the few that did know, I needed to shield the girls from anything that might accidentally be spoken or that would put concern in their hearts.

After all, Kirk would most likely return soon and then we could deal with this privately, without our wider circle of friends knowing all the details.

I did have to make arrangements with Angela, however. She had initiated a homeschool club at our church and there was a meeting scheduled for later that afternoon. She'd asked Kirk to lead the prayer. I had to find her and explain to her that Kirk was unavailable.

We returned home to an empty, untouched house. As I changed clothes and prepared for lunch, the worship songs uplifted me again, and the words of the music gave order to what thoughts were allowed in my head. It kept my imagination under control, and it helped me to speak words of faith aloud.

~~~

The children asked again about where their daddy was, and I continued to assure them about his being away on important business. All were still tired enough from the activities the day before that naptime came easily.

As soon as the children were fed and settled, I phoned Rosie from my bedroom. We spent an hour on the phone praying together. "Whew!" I thought, "That was some intercession time!" Greatly encouraged, I bathed in His presence afterwards by offering up praises to Him and sensing His closeness.

I had hope that Kirk would come around. I did not see how he could resist God's drawing him because of the seasoned prayer warriors that were on their knees interceding. I, myself, was in the throne room constantly.

~~~

To my great surprise, the phone rang and on the other end I heard Kirk's mother and father. "We were thinking of coming out for a visit," Kirk's dad told me, "to see the new baby, you know."

"Oh!" I said, shocked, sitting back down on the bed. They had not been out to see us in the three years since we'd moved. And to call now, today, at this moment.

"I'll tell Kirk you called," I assured them, but I hung up with unusual quickness before I might say anything else.

~~~

Next, it was my father who was on the other end of the line. "Janice, what's this I hear about you and Kirk?" Dad said with concern in his voice, all the way from the East Coast.

"He left," I informed Dad, lying there on the bed. "But we are doing fine, really," I attempted to reassure him.

"Tell me what happened," he asked.

I told him everything I knew so far.

Toward the end of our conversation, Dad said something that reached my heart: "Janice, you know that lately I've had some testing done and the doctor's reports have not been what I'd hoped for.

"Recently, I was just lying in bed feeling scared and lonely about it when your mother came and said this: 'Terry, I want you to know that we are in this together.'

"It made me feel much better when she said that.

"So I want to say to you, too, Janice: You are not alone. We are in this together. Alright?"

~~~

This time when the phone rang, it was Kirk.

His voice sounded quieter, maybe confused, weaker. He sounded broken. This gave me hope because maybe he was reconsidering his choices. Maybe all the prayers were having an impact on him.

"I've just been in a motel room, thinking," he said when I asked him what he'd been doing. "And I just drove around all yesterday," he added, "just thinking."

"Please consider what you are doing and what you could do instead," I pleaded, sitting up completely on the bed. "Please consider your children and how hard this would be for them," I continued. At those words, I even thought I heard him break up.

Then I told him the story that my Dad had just related to me, and I said: "Kirk, we are in this together. We can reconcile our marriage and we can work this out. It's the right thing to do and God will help us."

"I'll think about it," he said, and he hung up with a click when I would have talked longer.

~~~

Three-year-old Meaghan was the first to awaken from her nap and come down the hallway into my bedroom. Rubbing her eyes, she announced, matter-of-factly, in her little voice, "Mommy, I had a dream."

"What was it, honey?" I tried to be interested and put aside all that I'd been thinking about that afternoon, and the many conversations I'd had on the phone.

"We were at the mall with Daddy by the water fountain and Daddy was walking down the hallway with his friend from work named Leanne. They were kissing." Meaghan informed me while she spun on one foot on the wooden floor, having no idea of the dynamite in her words.

Shock filled my being and I caught my breath. My head spun as though I were experiencing vertigo as I realized that Kirk had already introduced the girls to this 'other woman.'

While I lay there, stunned, Meaghan noticed Kirk's empty closet.

"Mommy, why are all of Daddy's clothes missing?" she asked, climbing into his bare closet. She grinned and found that she could fit inside and even open and close the door. "Look, Mommy! We can play hide-and-seek!"

"Who is Leanne?" I asked Meaghan, breathless, remembering that Kirk had referred to his 'one-night stand' as being with a 'Lana.'

"Oh," Meaghan looked out at me, "someone like you."

I collapsed falling backwards against the pillows. The recent buoyancy and hope that I'd felt just a few seconds before drained away. I felt weak inside. It was the feeling of an explosion, like being knocked out by a physical blow in the stomach, a feeling that I would become all-too-familiar with.

"Where's Daddy, Mommy?" Meaghan looked into my face as she leaned her head playfully against the wall in the empty closet.

"Oh-oh," I stuttered, "you know that I told you he is away on business? But, you know what Meaghan?" I said, sitting up and remembering the afternoon prayer time and what I'd been meditating on in God's Word. "You can pray for your daddy, too, while he is away, okay?"

11

Kirk's Decision

Monday, July 12, 1999 Early AM

"Sorry to phone you so early," Ginny said when I picked up the receiver the next morning while already in the kitchen putting breakfast on the table for the girls.

"It's okay," I answered, pouring water from the pitcher into their little pink cups. "I'm up now so that I can get the girls to their Vacation Bible School on time."

"Well, I've got to come over there and pray with you," Ginny insisted. "I can't believe this has happened! Kirk? I just can't believe it, Janice. Never, ever, in a million years would I have thought that Kirk would do something like this – I mean, walk out and leave you and the kids."

"I know, Ginny, I never would've thought it and I'm the one married to him!" I said, now sitting down in a chair in the kitchen. "But I am hoping that he is reconsidering because he sounded broken when I talked to him on the phone yesterday."

I'd been over the conversation I'd had with Kirk again and again in my head.

"Why don't I come over today during the kids' naptime?" Ginny asked. "Would that be good for you?"

"Yes, Ginny, that would be great. Since they'll both have a lot of activity this morning, they'll be tired during their afternoon naptime. How about 2:30?" That settled, I hung up the phone.

~~~

It was only a few seconds before the phone rang again. Straightening up quickly in the hard wooden chair where I still sat in the kitchen, I realized it was Kirk's voice on the other end.

"Janice," Kirk began, his voice sounding cool and distant. "I am going to leave you. I am going to serve you papers. I have already met with a lawyer and had them prepared."

"But, Kirk," I started, "you can't just walk away from a marriage and three kids!"

"I can divorce you, and I will." he stated, his voice resolute, firm, unyielding.

"But, Kirk," I began again, losing my ground for the hope which I'd been standing on since yesterday's conversation when his tone had sounded so different. "Kirk, you need to pray about this – you need to think about this more – about what you're doing – about what this means."

Sidestepping my words, he asked, "Are the girls there?"

"They're in the bathtub so I can't hand them the telephone," I answered. It was true – their playful shrieks at one another from their bubble bath reached down the hallway and into the kitchen. David slept through all their noise.

"I'll call back later then to talk to them," he said.

"Oh!" I remembered all of a sudden. "Your parents phoned yesterday. They said they want to come for a visit to see the new baby."

There was a long pause. "Okay, I'll call them. Thanks for letting me know. Goodbye."

"But, wait!" I interjected, "Where can I reach you? Where will you be?"

"Just call me on my pager," he said. "I'm still at a motel."

~~~

Hearing the click on the other end, I pushed the phone's off button. The residue of the frosted cereal I'd chewed earlier turned into a tasteless film inside my mouth and I no longer had an appetite for anything more.

"Okay," I talked aloud while pacing up and down the hallway where I could glance at the girls coloring with play soap in the tub. "God, I thank You for seeing this. I thank You for intervening in this. I thank You for Your strength. I thank You for clear-thinking and for Your help. I thank You that You promise to give wisdom to all who ask."

It was an amazing accomplishment that God enabled me to finish getting the girls dressed, fed, and dropped off for their first day of Vacation Bible School on time.

With Kirk's declared resolve to leave me, I drove back home right away in order to make some important phone calls to protect myself financially. I'd heard that in California a married couple shares any debt incurred, regardless of who incurred it. I did not want Kirk to run up a huge balance in my name.

I began with the credit cards, attempting to cancel these joint accounts so that I would not be liable for whatever Kirk decided to do with them.

One company refused to cancel them, but agreed to take my name off the account from that date going forward. For another company, I had to report the card stolen in order for it to be deactivated.

I breathed a sigh of relief when I'd hung up the phone at last. Yet another hard step completed.

~~~

True to her word, Ginny arrived just after the kids went down for their naps after lunchtime. She hugged me and continued to hold me at arm's length and to stare at me with amazement as we stood in the hallway foyer.

"Gene says," Ginny said about her husband, "that he just can't believe it either."

"Ginny," I tried to explain. "God has been so good to me. He has been helping me and giving me peace and steadiness, and clear thinking. This wellspring of praise seems to shoot up from inside of me and I just flow with it, praising Him constantly."

I looked in her face to see if she could possibly understand this, because it didn't make any logical sense.

We walked over to sit down in the family room and began to pray right away, me on the blue couch, her in the rocker-glider. It was not at all hard for both of us to find words to pour out to God in this time of absolute crisis. We sought God and implored Him to intervene on behalf of myself, the children, and, especially, Kirk.

Then Ginny and I stood to our feet and began to move from room to room within the house to pray some more.

We began our tour out in the garage. Kirk had spent so much of his time working out there recently, and this is where his taste in music had surprisingly changed from the old gospel bluegrass songs to the disturbing, unfamiliar sounds of hard rock n' roll that, he'd said, 'his friend,' had lent to him.

"Janice," Ginny said, as we stood in the center of unfinished projects, boxes of nails, hammers, saws, screwdrivers, and different-sized pieces of wood. "I have such a strong sense that Kirk has been viewing pornography out here in the garage," she described, operating in the Holy Spirit's prophetic gift which was not uncommon for her.

"What?" I could not believe that. "No, I've never seen – in our whole marriage – Kirk look at pornography. I've never found any in the house either. Kirk would not do that. He would have told me if he had a problem," I insisted, still standing with Ginny in the middle of the mess.

After all, I would have told him if I had a problem that I couldn't overcome and needed help with.

"Well," Ginny said, not moving. "Maybe I'm wrong, but that is what I have a strong sense about out here when I pray about what the root of this situation could be."

I was fully naive of the danger that pornography presented, or of the possibility that I could be affected by it, especially through someone I loved.

***

"Pornography addiction is the silent epidemic of our nation, a plague spreading at unprecedented proportions. Sex is the number one topic searched on the Internet, and seventy-two million Internet users visit pornographic web sites per year. With the figures growing daily, pornography now poses the single greatest threat to the American family.

Despite statistics, our church body is often lulled into believing we are safe, that our husbands, fathers, sons, pastors, church leaders are somehow coated with 'spiritual Teflon' against the effects of pornography. Numerous surveys show otherwise – rates of pornography addiction are as high within the Christian community as in the secular world.

Viewing pornography can actually become a powerful, mood-altering addiction, causing endorphins many times stronger than morphine to be released into the body. The addict literally gets "high" on his own brain chemicals.

We also found that the images become burned into the addict's brain, just as one would burn pictures onto a CD, a CD that can begin playing at any moment. The younger a person is when he sees pornography, and the longer he is exposed to it, the more imbedded it becomes.

Notes from the article "Pornography: The End of Innocence" By Teresa Cook 10/2006 her web site at www.PornProofYourChild.com. Focus on the Family at: http://www.cbn.com/family/parenting/Cook_pornography.aspx.

***

We tiptoed back inside the house and into Kirk's cluttered office, and then into the bedroom.

"Ohhh," Ginny said.

"What?" I wanted to know, now standing in front of Kirk's empty closet.

"It's just so cold in here – I have such a sense of coldness," Ginny repeated.

We returned to stand in the family room while continuing to pray. After a few more minutes, we both sat back down in our seats across the room from one another, silent.

David woke up with a cry and I went to retrieve him from his nap. I laid him on his blanket on the floor and began to pat his little tummy.

We continued to sit in the room together, feeling somber, and talked more.

"Ginny," I said, sitting on the floor with the baby. "It's the strangest thing, but all I can see in my mind right now is that credit card that I found in Kirk's wallet that I didn't recognize. I do all the finances in our family, so I just assumed it must be an account for his new job at work. But I can't get the picture of that card out of my mind. It's a *giant* card in my mind."

"That is so strange, Janice! That's all I can see in my mind, too! Ever since you told me about it while we were praying in the office it's been stuck there. This must mean something! God must be telling us something! This must be a word of knowledge!" She leaned forward in the rocker-glider with excitement that now beamed from her face.

I was not quite as encouraged. It did not seem like much of anything, and if it were, how could we know? I lay my head down on the floor beside the baby.

But Ginny continued, "My uncle's a private investigator! He's got connections – give me the name and information for that credit card and I'll contact him to see what he can find out."

~~~

"Wisdom will save you
from the ways of wicked men,
from men whose words are perverse,
who leave the straight paths to walk in dark ways,
who delight in doing wrong
and rejoice in the perversions of evil,
whose paths are crooked
and who are devious in their ways."
Proverbs 2:12-15

~~~

12

As a Shepherd, He Leads

Tuesday, July 13, 1999

I woke up early and declared the praises of God before any other thoughts could sidetrack me.

"Oh God, I submit my life and this whole situation to You. I know that You are leading and guiding all of my steps. You are the King of Kings and everybody must bow to You and to Your Name. Nothing ever gets by Your sight. You know all things. You know exactly what Kirk's up to and You are at work in his life and in mine."

I didn't think. I just spoke God's promises out loud. I didn't listen to any thoughts, doubts, or fears. I just heard my voice declaring and agreeing with what the Word of God said. What I heard myself say aloud, I believed.

Now sitting up in bed before any of the children awoke, I reached for the phone and punched in Miriam's number.

"Hello," she answered immediately from across the country, where it was already three hours later. "I'm glad you called, Janice. I found out something really important: You need a lawyer.

"If Kirk serves you papers for divorce like he says he plans to, then you will not be able to leave California with the children until custody issues are settled."

"What?" I responded, feeling again the heavy blow of yet another ugly and unexpected turn of events. "Are you sure?" I asked, sinking back down into the pillows.

"Well, that's what my daughter says. Do you have a lawyer that you can talk to?" Miriam wanted to know.

"A lawyer?! Why would I know a lawyer?" I said, now wondering what to do next. "And anyways, I don't want a divorce."

"It doesn't mean that you want a divorce," she said. "You are willing to stop the process at any time. But you have to protect yourself. He's obviously been thinking about this seriously if he already has a lawyer and papers drawn up. That's what he said, right?"

I nodded, though she couldn't see it.

"Maybe it will give things a chance to settle down if you leave for awhile, and are able to stall the process," Miriam reflected.

Kirk had been bugging me about going home for my annual trip to visit my family, probably because he was making plans to be with her, I thought. "Well, I don't know of any lawyer," I sighed, not at all happy about the suggestion.

"Well, let's pray," Miriam brought us back into focus.

We closed the conversation, and I put on my slippers and bathrobe and walked down the hallway into the office to check my e-mail and to wait for David to wake up to nurse.

The room smelled musty and the computer clicked when it came on.

Then it struck me. In the last month, our whole family had been to a Chuck E. Cheese party with another family we'd met from Nicole's music class. Kirk had spent his time talking one-on-one to the father of the birthday girl, whom later, Kirk had said, 'was a new lawyer' and 'who seemed to be really good.'

Trembling and praying, I read the digital clock in the office: 7:30 AM. Did I dare to call an acquaintance this early in the morning? But I was desperate.

Locating the phone number, I took a deep breath, punched the buttons, and hoped that he would not be offended if I woke him up.

~~~

"Hello," the lawyer picked up almost right away. He was about to leave his home for work.

Quickly, I explained who I was and why I called.

His response toward me was pure graciousness and kindness. I relaxed.

"Is it true?" I asked, sitting in Kirk's office chair, "Is it true that I will be stuck in California if Kirk serves me papers like he has told me?"

The new lawyer fudged. "This is probably not as serious as you think. It will probably all blow over if you stay and work it out. Don't do anything radical like leaving. It might make the situation worse," he advised.

"But Kirk said he would serve me papers and he does not just say things like that. And I always go back to visit my family in the summer, and he's been pressing me to make the reservations. I really need to know. Will I be stuck here if he serves me papers?" I persisted, wanting an honest answer.

The lawyer took a deep breath and responded, "Yes," he said.

Now I knew what I had to do.

~~~

The East Coast stretched 3000 miles away. Using the telephone book, I phoned the airlines. Discouraged, I discovered that it would cost approximately $1000 per ticket for airplane travel because we needed to leave on short notice.

"Miriam," I phoned back only a few minutes later, now resting again against the pillows on my bed. "I *do* have to leave. The lawyer confirmed it."

"What lawyer? Who? I thought you said you didn't know anyone," she questioned.

"I didn't think that I did," I explained, keeping my voice lowered. "But while I prayed about it in the office, I remembered that Kirk had told me about a new friend of Nicole's whose dad is a lawyer."

"That's amazing! Here you have gotten the information that you needed in just these few minutes," she marveled. "What are you going to do now?"

"I'm going to Mom and Dad's," I said, sitting up on the bed. "I never did book the reservations even though Kirk had been asking me to because I just never did have any peace about it. And now I know why the Holy Spirit restrained me."

"But how are you going to get there?" Miriam wanted to know.

"I'm going to drive back," I answered, resolutely.

"What? That is 3000 miles!" she exclaimed. "You have three very young children!"

"I know. But what else can I do? I checked on the tickets and they cost too much to buy them last minute like this.

"And, if I go back home, maybe he will wake up from what he is doing and decide to reconcile. Maybe he'll take it seriously when he sees his kids gone and then he'll realize he wants to change his mind," I hoped.

"Well," Miriam said, "let's keep praying about it. I am sure that God has a plan for how to get you back here."

"Yes, I believe He does, too." I sensed it strongly. We hung up.

~~~

Everyone seemed tuned into the buzz at our home and chose this morning to call. Between answering the phone, I nursed David, woke up the girls for Vacation Bible School, and fed everyone breakfast.

First it was Candy from our preschool playgroup who had recently moved an hour away to Santa Cruz and was calling 'just to catch up.' Shocked with the news, she hung up and then the phone rang again.

It was Vicki, a close high school friend from back East who had become a Christian about the same time I did, so we'd learned about our faith together. She could not believe this was happening.

After this call, it was Frankie on the phone 'just to check in' and I explained that I would be driving back East.

"I'll be over to help you pack after I drop my girls off at Vacation Bible School," she announced.

There was so much to do and so much to think about. I sped through the house readying the girls to leave the house for their second day of Vacation Bible School. While I did so, my mind spun with the preparations needed for leaving so soon.

When Debbie, the pastor's wife, phoned to check in on us, I asked her if she could pick the girls up and take them to her house for another play-date in the afternoon. She readily agreed.

The pieces were all falling into their places without my even having to try – *the exact people I needed were calling me.*

~~~

The phone rang again as soon as I walked in the front door after having dropped off the girls. I left David sleeping in his carseat by the blue couch in the family room where I could keep an eye on him.

"Janice," it was Candy again, "remember how I got bumped on my last trip and the airline gave me two free tickets for being delayed?"

"Yes?" I answered, putting away the breakfast dishes in the kitchen.

"Well, Calvin and I have prayed about it and we want you to take them and use them to go back East," she instructed me.

"Candy! That is so kind of you! Really! But, I need *three* tickets. It would still cost me $1000 for the other ticket," I stopped loading the dishwasher as I stood overwhelmed by her and Calvin's generosity.

"But it would be so much better for you to fly than to drive that distance with three little ones," she insisted.

"Well, I'll keep praying about it. Thank you, Candy. Thank you for being so generous," I said with great sincerity and I felt humbled by their care.

~~~

"Janice, listen," Vicki, my high school friend phoned for the second time that morning when I sat back down in the office chair. "My husband, Vince, has a free airplane ticket from his credit card rewards. He can fly as far as Colorado to meet you there and then he can drive you the rest of the way home. He'd drive you around the clock until you got here, without stopping."

"What?!" I exclaimed. "Wow, that is so kind of Vince," I thought aloud. "Yes, that would be helpful. It would really help me to drive with the three kids if I didn't have to do it all alone." I contemplated the idea and discussed it with her for awhile longer. "Okay," I finally agreed.

The phone rang again. "Janice, this is Frankie. I'll be over soon," she announced her time of arrival.

"Hey, guess what?" I exclaimed, "An old high school friend's husband is going to meet me in Colorado and help me to drive back East," I said, informing her of the latest while turning back and forth in the office swivel chair.

"Really?" she replied. "Hold on a second." I heard whispering. "Janice," she returned to the phone, "Farley, my husband, can drive you to Colorado. I'll follow in our car and then we'll return back home together after getting you there."

"Really?" I exclaimed, standing up now, "Are you sure?"

"You can't drive by yourself with those three babies. We'll help you," she answered.

~~~

Frankie arrived after she'd also arranged for her kids to have a playdate elsewhere after their Vacation Bible School. We had to work at the house, but we also had to avoid the server from delivering papers for divorce.

The shades at the front of the house were drawn, and we only approached the windows occasionally to peek outside. Working together in shadowy silence, we refrained from using any electric lights. Instead, we drew our light source from only the windows at the back of the house.

Tiptoeing, we talked in whispers when we spoke. Frankie cleaned the kitchen. I gathered the many belongings needed to take on a 3000-mile driving trip across the country with three small children.

The goal was to get packed and to leave the house before Kirk could serve me papers. The goal was to stall Kirk's plans to divorce me. Emotions aside, I had much work to do.

The doorbell rang. Startled, both Frankie and I dropped to the ground in the family room. We drew close together, locked eyes, and then I crept on toward a window in the baby's bedroom to peek outside through the blinds.

Was it the dreaded server with the feared divorce papers? Would I now be forced to stay in California indefinitely like my friend and the lawyer had warned me could happen?

I waited until the person moved to one side and I could see that it was Farley. Relieved and breathing normally again, I ran to open the door to let him inside.

"Farley!" Frankie exclaimed, now standing, and then greeting him with a big kiss.

"What are you two doing in here?" he asked, nodding at the piles accumulating in the family room. We explained.

"Well, is there anything I can do to help?" he volunteered. "How is the condition of your car?"

Crossing my arms while standing there in the family room, I realized that there were some maintenance needs. And the car did need an oil change.

"I'd be happy to take it in for you," Farley said. "Can I have the keys?"

I got them, thanked him, showed him to the back door, and pointed to how to get out of the yard.

Back to our tasks, Frankie found some sippy cups especially good for a long car ride. She also packed the snacks.

I pondered over a few toys for distracting the children besides gathering diapers, blankies, and clothes. We would be driving around the clock.

Frankie's husband would drive the kids and me to Colorado. Then Vicki's husband, Vince, would fly in to meet us there and drive us the rest of the way to the East Coast. There would be no long rest stops – just a long, long, *long* drive without respite, all the way to Mom and Dad's.

But there was a problem that I was becoming aware of. Recognizing that I felt troubled and uneasy inside, I excused myself to make a phone call.

~~~

"Miriam," I said from the privacy of our back master bedroom when she answered on the first ring, "It's me. I just don't know what it is – but I don't have a peace about this 'driving across the country thing,' even though it seems like a provision.

"And I remember another time that I had this same feeling of no peace inside – it was when we bought our first house and we did not know that we'd be moving so soon because Kirk got a better job offer – and we lost $10,000! That was my $10,000 mistake! I don't want to do it again! Miriam, I have that same troubling sensation inside of me."

"Let's pray," she advised, and began to do so quickly. After awhile, we paused. "Janice," Miriam spoke with calmness, "I don't think the problem is in leaving California – I think it is the way you're going. Maybe you should reconsider the plane tickets that your friend offered you."

"But, they were only for two people – a third ticket would cost $1000 at the last minute like this – I checked the prices." I said, dismayed, sitting down on my bed.

"Well, why don't you put it on hold while we keep praying about it. Can you phone Vince and ask him not to make the flight arrangements yet?" Miriam asked.

"Yes, but I better do it quick. G'bye." I pushed the off button on the receiver.

~~~

"Vince?" I spoke up right away when he answered on the other end, "Vince, I'm not sure about this – it doesn't feel right – can you wait a little before you book your reservation?"

"Are you sure, Janice? I'm on the line right now with the agent," Vince replied.

"Yes, just give me a couple hours – I feel troubled inside about the whole thing – I want to wait a bit," I explained, pacing in the bedroom.

"No problem, call me back when you're ready." Vince hung up.

"Wow," I thought, "I caught him just in time."

~~~

"Whether you turn to the right or to the left,
your ears will hear a voice behind you saying,
'This is the way; walk in it.'"
Isaiah 30:21

~~~

Now the phone rang again. I answered while still pacing on the hardwood and praying in the master bedroom.

"JANICE!" Candy exclaimed on the other end, "Janice! You'll never believe this! I phoned about those two plane tickets that they gave me when we were bumped last spring and GUESS WHAT?!"

"What?" I asked, bewildered at her excitement, and now standing still.

"They are actually FOUR one-way tickets!!! They will cover all of you! And since baby David is free because he'll be on your lap, you'll have one ticket left to return to California in case you need to attend a court appointment or something!"

"Wow!" I now understood her enthusiasm. "Wow! Boy, am I glad I listened to that disturbing feeling and asked Vince to put his plane reservation on hold just in time. Wow, Candy!"

My feet stopped their pacing and began to dance around the room. "I won't have to drive all the way across the country after all! Wow! Oh, Candy! Are you sure that you want to give up your plane tickets? Weren't you planning a trip to see your mom?"

"Calvin and I prayed about it, Janice. We felt like God laid it on our hearts to give them to you. They're all yours!" She reassured me with a generosity that could only come from God.

"Thank you, Candy. It means so much. Thank you for caring for me and for praying."

"Frankie!" I flew into the family room after hanging up with Candy. "You're never going to believe this! Listen!" I explained how we would not be driving after all, but flying.

"Wow!" she exclaimed, hugging me, "That's incredible!"

"It's God, Frankie! Can you believe it?" Excited, I did another little dance and gave thanks to Him aloud. And that is when we heard it: someone was banging at the front door.

~~~

In the same instant, we both dropped to the ground and cupped our hands over our mouths. I began to move first, crawling to the baby's bedroom to peek outside.

In front of the door on our porch stood a young, unkempt man, probably early 20's, wearing a baseball cap. *Is that what a server looks like?* I wondered while raising my eyebrows at Frankie who had followed me, crawling into the room. We both tried not to move.

Then David began to coo, waking up happy from his nap. The knocking came once more, louder. But finally the mystery man went away.

He returned an hour later and the scene repeated itself.

~~~

Frankie and I inched around the shadowy house preparing for a plane trip instead of a cross-country car trip.

It was Tuesday, and I phoned Southwest Airlines from the office to make reservations for early Thursday morning, only two days later. Frankie said we could stay with them and hide my car in her garage.

Farley arrived back from taking the car in, entering this time through the side backyard entrance. The car, he reported, was 'primed and ready to go across the country.' He insisted on paying for the couple hundred dollars worth of work.

We told Farley all the news about the change of plans and then about the mystery man banging at the front door. We all agreed the man looked suspicious – just like what the promised server must look like, and we shivered.

Farley headed out to go back home. Frankie followed him in order to pick up the kids for dinner – both hers and mine from their afternoon playdates.

Later, I'd meet them all at their home for dinner and bedtimes. I'd have a couple hours more to finish up the packing because Emilie would come by to entertain the baby for me on her way home from working at the church.

Before I settled down to nurse David, Frankie ran back inside the house with a surprise. She jumped up and down with excitement. In her arms, she carried a bouquet of flowers with a card. "Look!" she exclaimed, "Someone sent you flowers! That is who that man was! The flower delivery man!"

"Oh!" I breathed, feeling silly. "FLOWERS! How thoughtful! Look, they're from Candy!"

We both laughed and laughed and fell onto the blue couch for support, holding our middles. Some of the tension of the day broke apart and washed away, and I felt a little bit better.

These were the grace moments – the times that God provides to come up for air and to catch a fresh breath before diving down deep again.

13

Preparation for the Worst, Hoping for the Best

Wednesday, July 14, 1999

W aking up at Frankie's home felt strange and unfamiliar. The bright light of the sun shone through unshaded windows, filling the bedroom and reflecting off the white comforter under which I lay. It was so different from our bedroom at home with curtains covering the sliding glass doors keeping the light out.

Noting the time on the clock and hearing Frankie make breakfast, I rose to nurse David and to get the girls dressed. Frankie would drop all the kids off at Vacation Bible School, and I would meet her at the church at noon when it ended.

Many errands awaited me this morning: more packing back at the house, a few things to buy for the trip, and crucial – keys to our home to be made and delivered to friends and neighbors who would post watch at 707 Strawberry Lane.

Kirk must be at work now, I thought. But where was he staying at night? That was the question. I'd not heard from him in two days.

Instead of speculating any further, I turned my attention to praising God, the One who helps. I drew out memorized Bible verses to focus my mind on and lingered in His Word even as I prepared for the day.

~~~

"You will keep him in perfect peace,
Whose mind is stayed on You,
Because he trusts in You."
Isaiah 26:3 (NKJV)

~~~

Arriving back early to the church to pick up the kids, I entered by the front. Some children sang in groups from their classrooms on the left while others talked inside their rooms as they finished up craft projects.

I walked further into the lobby and noticed two middle-aged women sitting to my right on a couch, each holding a Bible. The one with shoulder-length, silver hair and wearing peach, the older of the two, I recognized as a member of the Precepts Bible study that I had attended. Both looked up and nodded at me as I walked toward them from the entrance.

"Good morning," the unfamiliar, younger one with long blonde hair and a blue blouse spoke first.

"Hello," I returned, meeting her eyes.

"How are you doing today?" the older one asked, appearing to sincerely want to know as she leaned forward on her seat to listen to what I might say.

"Well," I stumbled on the words, and then the tears sprang forth, unsummoned. "Well, really good, considering. But, my husband just left me on Saturday and I have to leave California before he serves me papers in order to try to avoid a divorce and, and... there are so many things I must do!" I rambled, all the time wondering if they actually really wanted to know.

"Sit down right here," the unfamiliar woman in blue spoke with warmness. "Do you know," she said with caring kindness while looking straight into my tear-filled eyes, "that we come here every Wednesday morning to sit and to pray – and we ask that God would send us just one person that we could minister to and pray for – and today you're it!"

The one in peach whom I knew held my hand, and the younger one placed hers on my back, and together we prayed with all our hearts.

~~~

Drying my eyes and thanking the two women whom God had used to send His love, I picked up David in his carseat sitting quietly beside me, and ran to catch up with Frankie, who I now realized had already entered the building and had walked down the hallway past where we sat in the lobby.

Turning around and seeing me, she called as she approached, "How did you do this morning with all your errands?"

"Everything went like clockwork," I said, relieved, but tired, standing in the hallway with David's heavy carseat on my arm while a group of small children passed by in a line on the right. "I even got back here early."

"Well, what do you want to do now? Can you relax in our swimming pool this afternoon?" Frankie asked.

I hesitated. There was one thing which I knew that I should do. "Frankie, I think I need to go to the Kaiser medical building. I think I need to see a doctor – to get tested." I looked down, hating that I should have to pursue this. "You know," I said under my breath, "for possible STDs."

"Why don't I take the girls back for lunch and a swim in our pool, and you can meet us at home when you're done? Okay?" Frankie asked, touching my elbow and quickly coming to my rescue once more.

"Okay," I sighed, looking down still. I was dreading what lay ahead for me that afternoon. But I did not know when I would have the opportunity to be tested again soon, when I'd be back, or when I'd have a doctor available. Kissing my girls after they paraded out of their classrooms, I headed out the door once more.

I felt lost temporarily in the misery and disgrace of what was happening to me. I was reminded of that experience of vertigo when the room had spun upside down and out of control and I'd had to close my eyes for it to stop.

But then another old song came to mind that I used to sing from the Bible from Isaiah 61:3 and I chose to sing its words in the car on the way to the medical building. It talked about how God gives us beauty for our ashes.

~~~

It was a short, familiar drive to the Kaiser complex in the center of town. I began with the general practitioner, signing the clipboard, then sitting, and waiting to be seen even though I had no appointment. This meant that I had to explain the basics of the embarrassing situation to more than one of the many staff personnel.

As everywhere else in Hillside, I ran into families that I knew from church, or from Bible study, or from MOPS. The first mom I recognized cheerfully greeted me, cooed at David, and talked for awhile about the reasons why their family was at the doctor's that day and how their summer was going.

At a loss for words, I stood, nodding throughout her explanation and moved on as soon as I could politely do so.

The second family group I knew simply waved at me from a distance while remaining in their chairs. Thankfully, they didn't approach.

"Janice Lynch," somebody called my name, at last.

I stood up and followed the nurse into a room where she motioned for me to take a seat on the examining table.

"Why do you want to see a doctor today?" asked the nurse in a cheerful voice, her pen ready to write in my folder.

"Well," I began to explain yet again, feeling weak and sick all at the same time. "Well, you see, my husband... he, I mean, I discovered on Saturday that he was committing adultery. And, I actually don't really know what he has been up to, or with whom, or with how many, and I figured, I'd better get tested, you know, for STDs." I finished, with a feeling of total disgrace at my husband for having put me in such a degrading position such as this one.

"I see," she scribbled only looking down at her notes now. "The doctor will be with you soon," she left with abruptness, placing the folder in the holder on the outside part of the door, and then carefully closing the door, avoiding any eye contact with me.

I fought back tears while I waited.

Hearing footsteps, then a pause outside my room, I tried my best to compose myself while irritated at the crinkling of the butcher paper underneath me whenever I made any movement on the table. Then I heard the loud rap at the door.

"Come in," I replied, trying to muster up enough strength in my voice to be heard.

"How are you today?" The doctor asked matter-of-factly, only looking down at my folder.

"Oh, fine. I just needed to get some testing done," I answered, peering at the doctor's bent over head as he took a seat on a black rolling swivel chair.

"Uh-hum," he answered, eyes fixed behind his glasses on the same notes the nurse had left him. "Well, you will have to go down to the lab for this, and explain there what you need."

"Okay," I said, "thank you." I jumped down off the table, grabbed David's carseat, and moved from the room back out into the hallway.

~~~

It was not long before I had located the familiar lab wing and approached its entry. I had been here often during the recent nine months of pregnancy as part of the prenatal care. By the front glass door, a cheery volunteer held out her clipboard. "Sign your name and state your required lab work," she clucked and smiled.

I fudged on the 'required lab work column,' trying to get my mind to focus and to come up with a brief way of stating my embarrassing need. 'Testing for STDs,' I finally wrote slowly. Again, a feeling of disgrace washed over me.

The volunteer glanced at what I had written and passed me a number on a slip of paper at the same time. I reached out to take what she handed me and walked away from her without looking.

It was a long wait. The space was crowded with people of all ages. Warm, muggy, summer air prevailed over air-conditioning. Children cried, mothers attempted to console them, and old men read newspapers in the corners. Only a few chairs remained empty in the noisy, sticky room. I found a vacant one in the back between an old man who snored while leaning with his head back and another chair that was piled with a stack of disorganized newspapers.

Finally, the number on the slip of paper I clutched was called.

Making my way to stand before the staff clerk at the front counter and positioned between two other staff clerks with people in front of them as well, I had to explain my awkward request in a less than private situation yet again. I was in earshot of practically everybody and hoped that nobody was listening.

"You'll have to phone the main Kaiser number to get permission for this testing," the staff worker informed me, pointing with his pen. "Use the phone on the pillar right behind you."

The phone, also centrally located, stood on a column in the middle of the room, in the middle of the crowd, where I would again have to raise my voice above the noise. I cringed.

Turning with reluctance, I picked up the receiver of the Kaiser phone. It slipped out of my hand and hung dangling for a moment in the air. The operator could not hear me and I had to shout my words louder.

I tried cupping my hand around my mouth for both privacy and so that the operator could hear me better. Again, I spoke to first one person, and then was passed to another. I explained my problem in as vague of terms as possible but tried hard to get the assistance that I needed so that I could get the testing done right away, before I left California.

With the confirmation for my testing finally granted and sent through the computer, I went back to the lab tech who motioned for me to come over to the corner of the room where blood is drawn. He did so. And now I had a new appointment with a gynecologist. It was late in the afternoon.

~~~

Tired and hungry myself, I finished nursing David as the woman gynecologist knocked on the door and then came into the room. I recognized her as one of the nurse practitioners I'd seen while pregnant with David. She was orderly, detailed, to the point, with short dark hair. She had attended me a couple times during the pre-labor check-ups for David.

"So, what is the problem?" she wanted to know.

Once again, I explained. This time, though, I couldn't help it and the tears began to gush from my eyes and down my face. I sobbed. She handed me tissues. She did an exam. She was irritated and insulted at the gall of some men.

It seemed like she understood too well, I thought as I lay there, feeling like I'd been run over by a truck or kicked by a horse.

"Honey, you should see a counselor," was her advice, and she handed me the entire box of tissues this time instead of just one.

"Well," I said, sitting up now, "I think my crying would qualify as 'normal.' And really, I am doing quite well."

It was interesting, I thought yet again, how everyone either said you were crying too much, or you weren't crying enough.

"He did just leave on Saturday, just four days ago," I reminded her, pulling the paper drape around my shoulders tighter. It was cold in the air-conditioning and the flimsy garment offered no warmth.

She had been kind. It would take a few weeks to get the results in, and even a couple months for some of them. They would all come back, thankfully, negative.

I thanked the doctor, picked up David in his carseat, and left for Frankie's home, glad to be at the end of a long and humiliating afternoon that I would never forget.

Back at Frankie's, I found both girls bathed, dressed in borrowed jammies, and laughing in their play with Frankie's daughters, who were close to their age. I had returned just before dinner. We all sat down together at the table: Farley, Frankie, their two daughters, me, and my own two.

Farley handed me Candy's airline tickets for which he had driven to Santa Cruz that afternoon to retrieve. Frankie pointed toward the entry to the kitchen where she had assembled suitcases and bags of her own for me to choose from for packing.

As the girls chattered and ate their dinners, Frankie handed me a small, wrapped gift in white tissue paper. Inside, I found a little book that she'd picked up for me that day called *Comfort for Troubled Christians* by J. C. Brumfield. It was an analogy of the master refiner at work using fire to produce pure gold and pure silver.

She could not have known that many years before, Miriam had given me that very same book when her husband had recommended it. This book had been a special favorite of mine, an old friend, one that I had absorbed and had been transformed by, but one that I had lost track of years ago.

My eyes glistened with new tears as I experienced once again God's tender, individual care for me in providing such a personal reminder from the past that Frankie could not have known anything about.

Before dinner was over, the phone rang and Frankie said it was for me. I ate my last bite of taco salad and slipped away into my bedroom to take the call.

It was Kayla, my other prayer partner who had been away at a prison outreach. "Janice," she said, "how are you doing?"

"Kayla, I just feel God's peace inside of me so strong. This has been the hardest thing that has ever happened to me but I am being so well taken care of and I can feel His presence. It is really amazing." I explained to her all the details while relaxing on the bed's soft comforter.

"Janice, I'm so glad to hear the strength in your voice. I've been praying for you," Kayla returned. "I wanted to share something with you that should be of some encouragement: While I was away on the retreat I had a dream that Kirk had walked out on you.

"In my dream, I told you emphatically, 'You need to cancel your credit cards, you need to talk to a lawyer,' and, you need to do ALL the things that you have just told me that you have already actually done! It's amazing, Janice! You have done everything that I told you to do in my dream!"

~~~

The phone rang again only a moment after I'd hung up with Kayla. This time it was Ginny.

"First," Ginny stated, "I just want to say to you that I am so sorry, Janice."

"What do you mean?" I asked, puzzled, and adjusting the pillow under my head. After all, she already knew full well that Kirk had left me. "Why are you so sorry?" I questioned, wanting to know what she could mean now.

"Because, Janice," Ginny spoke in earnest, "remember that I told you that I was going to give that information about Kirk's credit card to my uncle to investigate? Remember? The credit card which neither one of us could stop seeing in our mind after we'd finished praying?"

"Yes," I answered, rolling the comforter's frilly edge between my fingers.

"Well," she continued, "you won't believe this, but my uncle already had a scheduled lunch date with a friend of his who is high up in that very company that Kirk used – if you can fathom that! And Janice, I am just so sorry."

"Tell me!" I demanded, sitting up and wanting to know what she knew right away.

"It was a joint card that he opened up – with another woman." Ginny announced.

"What? He opened up an account with her?" I asked, unbelieving again that Kirk could do any such thing.

"Yes he did. It was on June 1st," she replied.

"But that was only eleven days before David was born," I said, stunned. "Kirk said that this thing was a one-night stand," I added.

"No, he was into this thing big-time, Janice. Listen, I have her name, her address, and her phone number, and all the details. Are you ready for them?" Ginny asked.

Startled and amazed at God's involvement once more, I fumbled to find pen and paper in my purse by my bed.

God had just hand-delivered me incredibly important information through a simple word of knowledge, an amazing connection with a private investigator, and the 'coincidence' of a luncheon date already on the calendar. Now I knew some of what Kirk had really been up to and some of what Kirk had hidden from me.

Knowing this information took away any doubt that fleeing California was the right thing to do.

~~~

Before going to bed for the night, I realized that I needed to make one more difficult phone call before leaving for Maryland the next day. I needed to phone Veronica.

Veronica was the other friend from high school who'd become a Christian about the same time as me. I'd known her since I was twelve.

Now I called her on the phone. I would need baby supplies that I could not transport on an airplane.

"Hello?" I heard her groggy voice from far away – it was three hours later out there on the East Coast and she must've already gone to bed.

"Hello? Veronica? Are you awake?" I barely heard her respond. "ListenVeronica, this is Janice and I cannot talk to you now, but listen to me carefully: Kirk left me on Saturday.

"I am flying home tomorrow. I need baby supplies. Can you bring them to my parents' home tomorrow? Can you call Vanessa, also, and tell her?"

"What?" she responded and began to sound more awake.

But I got off the telephone even though she was shocked and wanted to know more details. There would be time to explain all that later.

Right now I had to get the girls to bed and finish packing. We were scheduled to leave early the next morning.

14

The Escape

Thursday, July 15, 1999

B efore sunrise the next morning, Frankie and her husband, Farley, met us in the kitchen. Frankie set eggs, bread, and yogurt on the table. Then she handed me a carry-on bag full of kid-friendly snacks and treats for the long day of travel.

Pulling me aside before we left, she hugged me tight and handed me an envelope. "Splurge on something for yourself and your girls," she said. Inside I found $300.

Farley nodded his agreement from the door, then took our bags and the baby resting in his carseat, and settled us into the SUV for the 45-minute drive to the airport. He drove us like the travel expert that his work had made him, and landed our family in time at the airport.

~~~

The day had opened for us in darkness, before the sun had had its chance to poke its head over the horizon and to peek through the blanket of clouds. By the time its beams of light caught up to us, we had climbed aboard our first flight leaving San Francisco, California behind in tears of dew and pointing like an arrow toward our target of Washington, DC.

During this first leg of our flight, God provided us with an eight-year-old girl. The stewardess seated her beside us and she proved to be a huge help because she never tired of taking little Nicole and Meaghan to the bathroom while I held the baby.

Now having boarded our connecting flight, we at last rested again, knee-to-knee, staring at one another. We crammed ourselves and our stuff into our seats like eggs in a carton, only we had less room. We waited, or at least I did, with anticipation to begin our escape back up into the clouds.

Because I had little ones, we'd been settled ahead of other passengers. At Southwest Airlines, you choose your seats when entering the plane, and I had opted for the front row 'lounge area.'

In these first rows, three seats face three seats, the only place on the airliner where passengers directly view one another. My two daughters headed in to sit in front of me, with a view toward the back of the airplane.

Stale, muggy air hung like a wet, still-dirty shirt on a clothesline. Inhaling the trapped, used vapors was like taking that soggy shirt down and wearing it before it had a chance to retrieve any freshness. It grew stickier and hotter while the plane's engines idled and the craft continued to swallow its cargo of luggage and passengers.

Noticing hot rays of sunshine inching through the oval window, I maneuvered toward it, hugging my sleeping newborn against my chest. Temporarily drugged with breast milk, he did not awaken even when I tugged hard at the plastic shade and it came down with a slam. Taking a deep sigh, he only let his breath escape with a sweet noise and continued to rest, his mouth hanging open.

Nicole had climbed first into her seat by the window. It was her turn. She placed her backpack on the floor underneath her, patted the stuffed lion in her lap, and positioned her blanket in order to lean comfortably against the side of the plane to watch the crew load the luggage.

Meaghan shifted back and forth in her seat, apparently not able to relax and having no window scenes to distract her. She dropped her blanket first once, and then a second time onto the floor, diving headfirst each time to retrieve it and then pull herself up again with difficulty.

At last, with her blankie tucked safely under her arm, she tried her thumb. After a moment, she pulled it out, looked at it with surprise, then displeasure, and then the corners of her mouth turned downward.

"Mommy, I'm huuuuungry," she whined, sounding dissatisfied and growing grumpier.

Trying not to stir baby David, I pointed to the overstuffed bag I had dumped in the chair across from me, on her right. Sticking out of the top were unused jackets, toys, and leftover snacks.

She scrunched up her face in a wrinkle of disdain and I could see that this picked-through bag of old treats was not what she had been expecting.

Flopping against her seat, she glared at me, demanding that I do something more acceptable.

I did not blame her. It had been a long, unexpected day of travel.

"Wanna cracker?" I asked, hoping.

"NO!" she thrust the saltine I had managed to reach for her from my hand and onto the floor.

Still, I could only think of and be grateful for my friend, Candy, who had given up her free airplane tickets so that we could take this sudden trip without expense.

Strangers passed my left shoulder in a column, one face replacing another in an unending line. With my three children surrounding me, it was almost a guarantee that not one of those passengers would request the empty seat to my right.

I was wrong.

"Excuse me," a low, gentle voice intruded into our world of diaper bags and stuffed animals, "may I squeeze in?"

It was a man in a business suit, a clean-cut beard with hints of gray, and a friendly but distinguished demeanor. Turning to look behind us, I noticed vacant seats still available.

I did not know if this man chose to sit with us because he did not feel like walking any further, or because he missed his own children, or maybe even his own grandchildren. I did not know if he just wanted to be one of the first people out of the plane when we landed.

I stiffened as he moved in. I anticipated feeling sorry for him when the baby bawled because of the change of air pressure, or when Meaghan remembered how unhappy she was.

At last the plane began to budge and the air-conditioning kicked in. Seatbelt lights flashed and bells rang. I covered the baby's ears to protect his sleep and our peace. The stewardess of the day went through her motions, and our plane climbed the staircase into the sky.

It was only a short while before I heard another whimper from Meaghan, who now sat directly across from the man, "I'm thiiiiirsty," she complained, turning toward me and holding me in her look.

"So," interrupted the man in a friendly voice, "are you on a special trip today?"

Meaghan frowned, but Nicole piped in, "We're going to see Grandma and Grandpa!"

"Is that right?" the man asked, eyeing me for confirmation.

Normally, I enjoyed the distraction of chit-chat with fellow passengers. But not today. I had nothing to say. Or nothing that could be said within earshot of my children.

They did not know yet. They did not know yet that their daddy was gone. And I did not know how to tell them.

Surely, Kirk would reconsider. Surely, he could not really have meant it. But he had said it, and he had said that he would 'serve me papers.' I had not even known what the term meant.

As I sat, refraining from talking, I wondered if I would ever think about anything else again. My thoughts wrapped and unwrapped, held and sifted through this information again and again and again, awake or asleep. It was all I could think about. It was all I could pray about.

It was difficult to remember the blissful, ordinary life I'd known only last week as a stay-at-home mom with a happy home and a faithful husband. I had seen no clue that this life would change, though, over time, I would look back and see many.

"Are we theeeere yet, Mommy?" Meaghan wanted to know, drawing my attention back to her.

"Hey," said the man before I could respond to her, "would you like me to draw you a picture of your blanket?" In a flash, he withdrew a sketchbook and a pencil from his briefcase.

"No!" she threw off his kind offer in three-year-old assertion.

But the man began to scribble anyway, ignoring her rejection.

Meaghan hid underneath her blanket, refusing to look. But I saw her one eye, and then both of them, watching his paper and the picture that was unfolding. In seconds, a close likeness of her blanket appeared on the page.

"How do you like that?" asked the man, his eyes holding a twinkle.

Meaghan's mouth dropped open, and her eyes widened in admiration and respect. *This man had drawn her blankie.* He tore out the picture and handed it to her. And then he continued to draw picture after picture for a captivated audience of one. Nicole had fallen asleep.

Surprised by this unanticipated break, I sat back and relaxed. David slept on.

I also felt surprised that I could still be alive and moving when something this bad had happened to me. I was surprised that I could still brush my teeth, that I could still get up in the morning, and that I still got hungry at mealtimes.

The mail had come yesterday at Frankie's house and that surprised me. The clock still registered that time was passing, but time had stopped for me. Why hadn't it also for everyone else?

Something else that surprised me was how close God felt. I felt unexplainable peace when there was still so much unknown to me about what would happen next. Like baby David who lay secure in my lap dozing, I felt that I was being held, too, in secure arms that I could not see, by Somebody bigger than myself and completely trustworthy.

I was surprised at how many things I found to be thankful for when it felt like the world, as I knew it, had crumbled into pieces. Yes, I counted my blessings and I even felt joy. I was surprised.

Descending back down the staircase in the air, the man drew one last picture. The image of a glorious angel took shape and appeared on his pad.

He looked sideways at me, "This one's for you," he said, tearing it from his pad and then pressing it into my hand. Just then we landed, and the sun, which had trailed us all day long, reached through another oval window and embraced me in warmth.

~~~

"Are we there yet?" asked Meaghan again when she saw the other passengers and the man begin to stand up and get into the aisle. I nodded, and she also stood up immediately ready to get off the plane.

Tired and feeling suddenly timid, I leaned over to awaken Nicole, who though still asleep, still held her stuffed lion and her blanket. She began to open her eyes and to look around, blinking.

I gathered the carry-on bag, the blankets, and the leftover snack food. Strangers noticed and helped me to exit from the plane where I found David's stroller waiting outside the plane's door.

It was a long walk up the corridor to the terminal as I wheeled a now wide-awake David and the girls who held onto his stroller on either side. My anticipation mounted with each step.

Who would I find waiting for me when I exited the plane? Would my parents make it back in time from their six-hour trip where they'd been visiting Dad's family in Connecticut? Would anybody else be there? What would the expressions be on their faces? Would they be glad to see me?

Breaking into the crowd after entering from the gate entrance, I scanned the clusters of people. Positioned together on the right side stood Mom and Dad. Coming closer to us, they hugged and greeted us, all the while being careful with their words around the children.

Then my 'little' brother, Michael, broad-shouldered and grown now, joined the scene. He approached from behind and lifted each squealing girl up in the air and gave her a hug.

The girls jabbered away with delight to see everyone, still not aware of the serious situation. However, five-year-old Nicole was beginning to look concerned at times, slightly reserved, like she might have a few doubts.

"Are you hungry?" my brother asked, "Because you know that I can take you all to eat at The Cheesecake Factory." It was a perk of his job that the manager's family ate for free and did not have to wait in the usual two-hour line to get a table.

Suddenly I was famished. The salty goldfish and fruit gel snacks and peanuts had ceased to fulfill long ago. "Yes!" I answered, walking beside him while we both carried bags, "I'm starving!"

It was good for us all to be together at the restaurant, but our conversation stayed on the shallow end and centered on the girls. I was happy to rest and have help with the kids.

After dinner, we rode the two miles back to my parents' home, where I'd grown up. Another car pulled up just as we got there. Veronica and Vanessa popped out.

How good to see my growing-up friends! I received their hugs and felt the comfort of their presence and care. They had outdone themselves with locating baby equipment. In the trunk they pulled out a Pack 'n Play, swing, diapers, clothes, and other kid-friendly items.

Vanessa, with her long, sandy, curled hair, friendly smile, and warm embrace, handed me some new games for the girls that she'd picked up at *Toys R Us*. Then Veronica, tall and strong, a look of concern, and wisps of thin brown hair falling into her face from the sides, handed me a book that was to be a rock for me to lean on: Jerry Bridge's *Trusting God Even When Life Hurts*.

As soon as I could, I grabbed a moment to lift the phone in the upstairs hallway to page Kirk. I also called his answering service to leave a message that said I had decided to take that vacation back East that he was always asking me to book.

I invited him to reach us at my parents' home, and added that I hoped that he would reconsider what he was doing.

~~~

I chose the guest bedroom because my old pink one had just one twin-size bed. Located at the opposite end of the hallway from my parents, the girls would sleep next door to me in Michael's old green room, which had two twins.

Though it was three hours earlier than California time, I was ready to go to bed at the East Coast time. I laid little sleeping David in the Pack 'n Play in my bedroom and stretched out on the queen-sized bed, hoping for unconsciousness after the long, long day. But first I raised myself to make sure that the girls had found their nightgowns and toothbrushes.

Nicole stopped me in the hallway. She looked up at me with her wide eyes and asked, "Mommy, where's Daddy? Why didn't he come with us or say goodbye? What's wrong, Mommy?"

"Well, you know that he's on important business," I stalled, and led her into her new room to lay down, turning off the lights.

Nicole didn't seem satisfied with my answer.

"I left a message for him to call us here," I added.

We all lay there in the dark quiet except for the sound of Meaghan sucking her thumb, probably already asleep.

I just didn't know what to tell Nicole. Kirk had certainly made it clear what his intentions were. But I sure hoped and prayed that he would have a change of heart.

But what do you tell your five-year-old daughter? Yes, what do you tell a very perceptive, intelligent, 5 1/2-year-old girl?

One thing that I did know was this: I would not lie to Nicole. I knew that she'd pick up on that, and it would make her feel worse, more anxious, instead of better. I remembered being perceptive as a child and I hated it if I wasn't given an honest answer.

Exhaustion made it hard to think.

I could sense that Nicole waited for me to answer her and that she was not letting go of her question. I felt a hot tear from her cheek slip onto my arm.

"Honey," I addressed her now, stroking her hair. "The important thing is this: God is taking care of us."

"I want to know, Mommy!" Nicole cried.

"Okay," I decided. "How about this? Honestly, I don't know what to say. So what I'm going to do, Nicole, is to think about what to tell you and I promise we'll talk tomorrow. But right now, we're all okay and you need to get some sleep. Okay?" I asked her.

"Okay," she accepted, unhappy.

~~~

Now, lying back on the stiff guest bed, it felt so strangely familiar and yet extraordinarily unfamiliar.

I was here alone, without Kirk, in a place where I had many memories of Kirk having been here with me. And Kirk wasn't coming.

I was in my happy growing-up home, still married with three children, yet, for the first time, abandoned, and empty.

I could sense the tension my parents were both feeling over the trouble, and I could feel them stretch to adjust to having us all suddenly move in.

How long would I be here? Suddenly, instead of being at my own home, in charge, I was a guest in my parents' home, under different house rules. I felt small in this rearrangement. I tried not to feel like that little kid that I'd been over a decade and a half ago.

Before turning off the lamp by my bed, I sat up to peek at David wrapped in his blanket and sleeping soundly in the borrowed Pack 'n Play. Then, clicking my own prayer cassette tape into place in the borrowed tape recorder, I began to pray and to praise God along with my own confident voice on the tape. Soon I fell sound asleep, as I whispered the promises of God.

15

In My Parents' Home

Friday, July 16, 1999

Though baby David, now five weeks, had awoken me twice, at 6:30 AM I still felt refreshed because I'd gone to bed three hours earlier than usual.

As I lay there, I still had no idea of what I should say to Nicole about her daddy, and I knew that she'd not forget my promise to talk to her.

Sitting up, I pushed the serious thoughts aside and manually chose to begin to praise God. It began as hard work in my new environment.

I made a list of what I could praise God for: our safe arrival, the eight-year-old mother's helper, and the angel. I thanked God for being at work in Kirk's heart and for directing all of our footsteps. I thanked Him for giving me wisdom and help and strength and direction for the day.

Talking to God, I knew that He heard me. I knew that He was with me.

I slipped out of bed to get the cordless telephone so that I could phone Miriam before everyone else awoke. As we prayed, Miriam remarked, "You know, I haven't thought of this song in so long, I mean, in years, but do you know *There's a River of Life Flowing Out of Me?*"

"Oh, yes!" I exclaimed. "I've been singing that one since Kirk left me. It kind of describes the way it really is. I mean, it's like I just put my foot forward to choose to praise Him, and then this river of His Spirit flows through me, almost like He is the One actually doing the praising through me!"

"Yes, yes, I think that is how it works," Miriam thought aloud. "You are obedient to praise Him, and then He fulfills His promise of '*I can do everything through him who gives me strength'* in Philippians 4:13."

"Yes," I added. "It's like He takes it from there after I trust Him and just make that first obedient step of faith."

"Just like when Moses took his first step into the Red Sea and then it began to part," Miriam said.

"And it's like then He carries me," I marveled. "God is so good."

~~~

"Be joyful always; pray continually;
give thanks in all circumstances,
for this is God's will for you in Christ Jesus."
II Thessalonians 5:16-18

~~~

"So, what are your plans for today, Janice?" Miriam asked when we were done praying.

"Well," I explained, "first, I have to think of something to tell Nicole because she is asking questions. And second, I have to find a lawyer so I can understand what I must do next, legally."

"Okay, I'll be praying," Miriam said and hung up just as Mom knocked on the door to say it was time for breakfast.

~~~

Phone calls from friends checking in spotted the day. From California, Frankie, Candy, and Hannah called. Candy had filled Hannah in on the crisis and she had also received a key to our house to monitor our home along with Emilie down the street. Prayer partners Ginny and Kayla called, too. And Vicki, from high school.

Mom ended up doing a great deal of childcare as I took the calls from friends and searched for answers to legal questions.

Mainly, I needed an experienced lawyer's advice. One who knew about divorce, and one who knew about divorce when it involved different states.

Specifically, I needed to know what my rights and obligations were during my visit to Maryland. How long could I stay in this place of refuge? Would I be able to live here with the children if Kirk really left?

Suddenly, my once secure future stared at me as only one big huge question mark. I had no idea what direction my life would take.

But I knew that God did.

Veronica gave me three leads for lawyers she had only heard of, but did not know personally. The first one I phoned said that she did not know what I should do but that if I would come into her office, she would take all the time necessary to figure it out. That didn't sound good when lawyers charge by the hour.

Neither of the other two lawyers knew what to do because they were not familiar with California's state law. Frustrated, I kept on praying to God for direction.

~~~

After a couple hours of fruitless phone calls, Ginny checked in from California and we spent time in intercession while I was in my bedroom. I told her what I specifically needed to know and we prayed about it together.

"Janice?" Ginny said after a bit of time had gone by, "Does your mom go to church?" Ginny didn't wait for me to answer but continued, "Because I think the Holy Spirit is showing me that you need to have your mom phone her church and ask to speak to the church's lawyer. I think he'll know the answer."

"Really?" I said, straightening the covers on my bed, "I would never have thought of that." But I supposed that a church as big as my mom's would indeed have a lawyer connection.

When I got off the phone, I shared this with Mom, who phoned her church. They gave us the name and number of their lawyer, and we phoned him.

He did not know the answer, but he did know someone that would. He gave us the name of his friend whom he highly recommended, and who had experience in divorce/child custody matters, including ones crossing state lines. I phoned and left a message asking him to please call.

Relieved at making some progress, I decided to take a break and play with the girls before their naptimes.

~~~

It was only a couple of minutes before Nicole reminded me of my promise to talk to her. "Remember, Mommy?" she said, pulling me aside again. "You promised to tell me about Daddy today?"

"Oh, honey," I said, dropping to my knees beside her in my old pink bedroom where we'd gone to retrieve a board game. I just don't know how to tell you, or what to say about it.

She looked up into my eyes, not letting go of her question.

"Okay, right now your daddy is at work in California like he always is," I began, sitting down beside her.

She waited and stood still. It was obvious that she was aware that there was more.

I floundered, and I struggled with my words, not wanting to tell her what was true, and yet not knowing how to avoid it, either. *How could I answer her truthfully and yet, at the same time, protect her?*

"And," I stumbled, grasping for words on the spot, "he has broken his marriage promise."

"Will I ever see my daddy again?" she asked, her eyes big.

"Oh, yes honey! In fact, I am sure that he will be calling you real soon. I left a message for him last night when we got here, remember?" I gestured at the phone on the wall in the hallway.

Nicole nodded, still locking her eyes with mine.

"Now," I continued sitting cross-legged in front of her, "we're staying right here with Grandma and Grandpa for a little while so that they can help Mommy with you kids. Baby David is so little, you know, and remember how they came out to help us in California, too? It's really different having three kids to take care of now instead of just two, you know?"

"Okay," said Nicole, blinking.

"You know, Nicole, your daddy loves you very much. We are all just praying right now for our family. And you know, God is hearing and answering our prayers and He is taking care of us," I finished, and I hugged her, having no clue as to what I really should have said or not.

I felt angry at Kirk for putting me in such an awkward position, and for putting his children in such a pain-filled place.

~~~

Saturday, July 17, 1999

It wasn't until two days later that Kirk did call. He'd not phoned since Monday back in California.

Dad answered the phone but Kirk would not talk to him. He only repeated, "May I talk to Nicole or Meaghan?"

Instead, I picked up the receiver upstairs in the hallway first. Kirk would not talk to me either and just said, "I'd like to speak with the girls, Janice."

Meaghan was standing nearby so she took the receiver first. I could tell that Kirk asked her about her plane ride and the fun things that she was doing with Grandma and Grandpa.

Next, when Nicole got on the phone, she answered his questions about the trip in more detail and shared with him about the man who drew pictures and gave one to keep of an angel.

Then, she came into my old, pink bedroom, now partly a mini-office where I sat at Dad's computer, and handed me the telephone. "Mommy," she said, "Daddy wants to talk to you."

~~~

"Hello?" I took the phone from her.

"How dare you tell Nicole about what is going on! How could you say something like that?" Kirk demanded.

I crossed the room to close the door before responding. "Well, honestly, Kirk, I just didn't know what to say. Do you understand what kind of a position you have put me in? She's been asking questions and growing upset. What would you have said?" I wanted to know, sitting on the floor now, and leaning my back against my old twin bed.

"You should have told her something like 'Mommy and Daddy both think that what is happening is for the best.'" Kirk stated.

"What do you mean 'we both think that what is happening is for the best'? I certainly don't think that. It's not like we fought or didn't like each other. It's not like you have tried to work out any problems with me or discussed anything with me.

I continued, now frustrated, "I want you to tell me *why* you left me! I want to discuss it. How can you just up and leave our marriage with no explanation?" I flung my legs straight out in front of me.

Kirk did not respond.

"Well, just for the record, Kirk. I do not agree with what you are doing, and I certainly don't think it's for the best for our children.

"And I want you to know that I love you and I am committed to you for better or for worse, if you will work with me on this. I don't believe in getting divorced, and I think that we should reconcile," I stated, hearing my words bounce back, sounding empty.

Kirk said nothing.

"You know," I added, since Kirk did not speak, "our family can never be the same. But, it could be even better once we work things out. Don't you think we should talk more about this?" I asked now, more gently.

151

"Come back to California and then I'll talk to you," Kirk said, unmoved. Sounding edgy and irritated, he asked, "When are you bringing the kids back to California?"

"You know that I usually stay here 2-3 weeks. Don't you recall how you've been asking me when I was going to come back here for my annual family visit? Well, I decided that *now* was a good time. Don't you think that I need the support of my family right now?" I wanted to know.

"You can bring your parents back with you and they can support you here," Kirk shot at me.

I thought to myself, like my parents can just fly back to California tomorrow.

"I'm going to phone the girls every day so that I can talk to them," Kirk announced.

"Well, good. They will appreciate that. That is the right thing to do," I said. "But don't you think we should talk, too?" I asked. "Don't you think we should discuss what you are doing and you should explain?"

"We can talk about it maybe on Sunday or Monday," Kirk said, and hung up the phone. But this also, I would find out, was just another one of his empty promises.

~~~

Hearing commotion on the floor below me, I peered outside from Michael's old bedroom to see my uncle's taxicab in the driveway. Both Uncle Don and Grammie Lee must be here, I thought. I checked on the napping baby and I could hear Nicole and Meaghan running to greet their great-grandmother and their great big great uncle.

I could not count the dozens of times that my sweet relatives: my grandma, uncle, and back while he was still alive, my grandpa, had come out to our home each week on a Monday night for dinner. Sitting around the table as a child, I'd heard and reheard many old family stories.

I rushed downstairs to join them all, bringing along new baby David. We all sat together on couches and chairs in the dark-paneled family room with its speckled-brown and orange carpet, admiring the baby. Uncle Don started a game of cards with the girls.

"Well," Grammie Lee said when the girls had taken a break to go upstairs and retrieve something to show her, "I just don't know what could have gotten into Kirk. It wasn't all that long ago that he visited our home when he'd been in town on a business trip. Remember that, Donny?" she addressed my red-bearded uncle on the couch, who nodded at her from a game of solitaire.

"All I can think of is that it's a demon," she said from the brown-padded swivel-chair in the middle of the room.

My little old grandmother was a daily Bible reader and a churchgoer but I had not heard her make a statement like that before.

"I'm going to write him a letter," she continued. "Why, I feel like I've lost my own grandson. What could have gotten into him?" she repeated, looking at the floor and shaking her head. "It's a sad, sad thing," she added.

Before my grandmother and uncle left that evening, Uncle Don had arranged to take us out to see the old Star Wars movie that was playing at his favorite downtown theatre. *Just like old times*, I thought, and it felt comforting.

~~~

Though it was difficult to work on both the legal matters and to care for the needs of my children, I was blessed with help from family and friends each day.

Every evening it became routine for Dad and me to meet in his office after the kids had gone to bed. He asked about all that had transpired throughout the day, and if there was anything that he could do to help. And Mom was so great with her grandbabies.

~~~

Sunday, July 18, 1999

The next day was Sunday. So, of course, I prepared the children and dressed myself to go to church with my parents.

"You're brave," Dad said, looking up at me from his stool where he used a shoehorn to get his dress shoes on in the den.

I remembered again Elisabeth Elliot's motto of 'just do the next thing.'

~~~

The church service was over and we were standing outside in the crowded hall waiting for Mom. She visited with different people she knew as they walked by where we stood. They talked and laughed and motioned and cooed over baby David like everything was normal.

I was ready to get home. David was growing heavier in my arms by the second. I was hungry.

This place brought back so many memories. This was where I'd grown up, and this was where Kirk and I had been married.

Suddenly my head felt hot and I needed fresh air. Fed up with shallow chit-chat and meaningless cheerfulness, I walked toward the front door in haste with baby David still in my arms. I could not stand it one moment longer. I went to wait outside for my parents and the girls.

Ugh, that was hard, I thought. It felt awful to be in a place that held so many happy, precious memories, but instead to be so aware of my loss.

~~~

Praising God continually and loudly was more challenging in my parents' home because I was not by myself. Since the kids were so small, I could get away with noisy demonstration of praying and praising and dancing without being questioned by them at home. But I could not really do as much of that in front of my parents and all the company dropping by. However, there was the privacy of my bedroom, and I was so grateful to be in Maryland.

Still, sometimes I stayed longer in my bedroom after nursing David just so that I could quietly 'dance' around the room and just spend time in worship. Refreshment and fulfillment would flood in after I had been doing so for a few minutes and I could feel the strength of the Holy Spirit flowing through me. Faith grew stronger and it caused me to stand buckled to God's truths.

It also helped a great deal that I had three people phoning each day to pray with me: Miriam, Ginny, and Vicki. Emotional comfort along with a sense of being effective in prayer was the result. I felt that I was not alone on this road because my arms were being held up by the support of my friends and family.

~~~

"Though one may be overpowered,
two can defend themselves.
A cord of three strands is not quickly broken."
Ecclesiastes 4:12

~~~

16

Divine Direction

Monday, July 19, 1999

U p and about for the day, Mom and I played with the girls before
lunchtime while David finished his morning nap. The phone rang. It
was the lawyer whom I'd left a message for on Friday. I excused myself to
my old, pink bedroom-turned-office upstairs.

He talked as though he was a very busy man but phoned back because
it was his friend that had referred me. He listened quickly to my brief story
– one that he seemed to have heard far too many times before.

"Go back to California," the lawyer stated. "You must decide the case
out there because that is where you both lived in the previous six months.

"Yes," he continued. "It's alright to have a short visit with your family
for their support on the basis that your husband has just traumatized you
and you've just had a baby. But you need to return to California and show
that you are willing to work things out for the children. Otherwise, it will
be viewed as if you have run with the children. Then no court will look at
you favorably, or listen to what you have to say – especially a request to
relocate across the country."

Well, I thought, hanging up and standing from my chair. I guess that
makes it clear: I would have to return to California sooner rather than later.

"Well God, I thank You that You are in charge of all this, and that You
are ordering all of my steps and showing me exactly what to do."

The thought of facing all that awaited me back in California filled me
with dread. I became aware of my beating heart. But at least I knew now
what I legally had to do.

~~~

The next step was to locate a lawyer in California that might represent me, if needed. I phoned Nicole's new friend's father. When I talked to him this time, he explained that he could not help me because he was too new at practicing law. However, he recommended a friend and co-worker of his, Chloe, and gave me her number.

I phoned Chloe's office and left a message. All this lawyer business was like finding my way in an unknown city. And I was astounded at their quoted prices per hour!

~~~

"Hi Vicki!" I said, glad to hear my friend's voice and ready to pray with her while in my bedroom.

"Janice," Vicki said, "listen, I was just talking to my brother about your situation and I really think you need to phone him."

"Really? Why?" I asked, sitting down on the bed.

"Well, due to his job in taxes, he knows some things about legal matters. Here, I'll give you his number." Vicki relayed.

~~~

I returned to the office bedroom and began to close the door. Before I could do so, the girls ran to me from the stairs.

"Mommy!" Meaghan demanded and glued her eyes on me with great expectance. "Nicole won't play Candyland with me. Remember you said we could play today? Let's play now, Mommy!"

"But Mommy!" cried Nicole, "I don't like Candyland!"

I felt torn. I wanted to spend time with my little girls – especially when their baby brother was asleep – but so much weighed on me that had to be done concerning our future.

Yet again I asked them to go back downstairs to play after I tried to explain how important it was that I make these phone calls. They did not understand. Grandma called to them about a bird's nest outside on the porch and they turned to go.

Quickly, I punched the number for Vicki's brother who picked up right away.

"I'm sorry to hear about what has happened to you," he said.

"Yes, but Vicki says that I should talk to you about Kirk's promise to serve me divorce papers," I began, and sat down in the chair at the desk.

"Yes, well, I just thought you should know this: It is really important who serves the papers first."

"What?" I said, feeling that I had just received another blow in the stomach.

"Well," he explained, "it's because whoever serves the papers first makes a statement about what they want. Then, the second party has to respond to it and try to prove that what the first person says is incorrect. It's harder to do that than to make the original statement.

"Statistically, the judge sides most often with the first person who submits their statement. It's like playing 'King of the Hill.' It's a lot easier to be the first one up than to pull the other guy off."

I felt shocked at the idea. How could this be? It didn't sound at all fair. I put my head on the desk and held the phone to my ear.

"You might want to consider or find out more about it anyway. I mean, you might want to seriously think more about serving Kirk papers first in order to protect yourself and the kids," Vicki's brother finished.

I hung up the phone, flabbergasted at the legal system.

~~~

The phone rang again as I sat there in the chair, and it was the lawyer, Chloe. I ran this new information by her.

"Yes," she agreed. "That's right. It is much harder to dispute the primary statement from the petitioner because that becomes the official court case. Statistics show that anyway."

"But that doesn't seem right! Shouldn't the judge just look at two completely different statements from both people and then decide how to rule?" I asked her, my mind boggling again over this crazy legal system.

"Well," she explained, "the way it works is that the primary statement filed is what is considered the official court case to be ruled upon. Anything said after that will have to be said in reference to that primary statement.

"Otherwise, it would be dubbed a whole different case and have to go through the system from the beginning as a separate matter. So you could not have two different primary statements about the same issue. The first one is the one that counts and where it begins."

"That's crazy!" I said again, deflated, placing my elbow on the desk and supporting my head in my hand. "But I don't *even want* a divorce.

If I were to file papers first, does that mean that I would have to get a divorce?" I asked.

"Of course not. You can stop the process at any time," Chloe answered. "But it would be in your best interest if you did file first as far as putting the needs of you and the children on the table for the judge to see.

"For instance, if you feel strongly about wanting to move to Maryland with the kids, or, say, about their educational choices, then you need to make your position known. If Kirk does so first, it will be harder to convince the judge about what you want because you will first have to prove that what Kirk wants is incorrect.

"And," Chloe continued, "it's true that many women have been compelled to live in California in order to stay near their children when something like this happens."

"But what if I do nothing?" I asked. "Would Kirk still be able to divorce me then?"

"California was the first no-fault state," Chloe explained. "That means that there does not have to be any proven reason for a divorce. It means that any married person may terminate the marriage even if the other person disagrees.

"Once one party files papers with the court and the other party is served those papers, it can take as little as six months from that date for it to become official. However, the process can be stopped at any time by the filing party," Chloe answered.

"Okay," I said, suddenly exhausted and sinking to the carpeted floor to lay on it and rest my aching back, "I'll think about it and call you soon."

I would need to think and pray about this because it was, in my mind, a huge step to consider: me serving Kirk papers when I did not even want to get divorced in the first place.

~~~

"If any of you lacks wisdom, he should ask God,
who gives generously to all without finding fault,
and it will be given to him."
James 1:5

~~~

Hannah phoned in the evening to report that she and Emilie had met at the house to do some cleaning. They both had the keys that I'd made to let themselves in.

"Janice," she said, "it doesn't look like anybody is living there. It looks as though Kirk has abandoned the house and is living elsewhere. The mail is untouched and the trash has not been taken out. But the futon in the office is now missing."

~~~

I began to call her 'Detective Hannah' because she sent e-mail reports every day about her regular trips to our house. It was truly a godsend to have a pair of eyes in California.

"The mail is piling up," Detective Hannah highlighted a couple days later, and I became concerned about the bills not being paid.

~~~

Wednesday, July 21, 1999
"Hello Janice. I'd like to talk to the girls," Kirk insisted as soon as I picked up the phone in the upstairs hallway that evening after dinner. I called to the girls who were downstairs, and then stood nearby to listen.

On the one hand, I always felt glad when Kirk phoned our daughters to talk with them. But on the other hand, I also felt a pronounced ache in my heart that came with each new interaction with him. Not to mention the dread of the scary way he now talked to me.

As Nicole and Meaghan took turns on the phone with Kirk, I understood that he was promising to send them a tape of himself singing songs on his guitar. After just a few minutes, he asked to speak to me and I motioned for the girls to return downstairs to their play.

"Hello Janice?" Kirk began, agitated. "I want to know when you're going to bring the girls back!"

"Well, I'm alright with bringing them back there," I said, thinking of the lawyer's advice for me to do so. "But you know that we always go to the beach in August," I said, stalling from making a commitment to have to return immediately. *I didn't know emotionally if I could handle returning right away.* "And, I also don't have a way back," I finished, still standing in the hallway.

"Well," Kirk said, "I can fly out there and bring the girls back with me," he offered, irrationally.

"How would you take care of them while you're at work if I wasn't there?" I asked him to examine his logic. Lately I felt like I had to take the role of a parent in the absurd ideas that my spouse presented to me.

I thought about how he had cut himself off from all our mutual friends. These included the girls' friend's parents who could help with the needs of our children when they were back in California. He also neglected to consider me in all of this, and worse, I sensed a clear and obvious disdain coming from him toward me.

"Well, I'd figure that out later," he said, sounding vague.

"Where are you living?" I asked, shifting my weight to my right leg, "Where can I reach you?"

"You can contact me on my pager," he refused to give me any information. Kirk ended the conversation after promising to look through the bills and pay them.

Why would Kirk share nothing with me about where he was and what he was doing? Why had he not only abandoned me, but also our friends, and our home? Why would he not talk to me about why he left?

I knew one thing: I could not trust him at all. I stood in the hallway a few more moments after speaking with him, trying not to feel shaky and remembering aloud the Lord's promises to me.

~~~

When I tracked the phone number from which Kirk called, and the location in which he was buying gas on his credit card, I found that it was used in the city where the woman lived with whom he'd opened the credit card account – Kirk was obviously still involved with her. He'd not shared anything more about this outside relationship with me.

With Kirk's refusal to consider any other direction than the one he was taking, I was beginning to understand the wisdom in serving him papers first in order to protect the kids and myself. It was becoming clearer and clearer what I had to do.

I trusted that God was leading me through this new territory because I was praying constantly, asking Him to help me, guide me, show me what to do, and give me wisdom.

17

The Retreat

Veronica, who'd brought me the baby equipment, phoned to check on how we were doing. I retreated to my bedroom and explained all – including how it was that I was still hiding out behind closed doors and wary of 'the server.'

"Why don't you and the kids come over here and hide out with my husband and me and baby Violet for a few days? That way you could relax and not worry so much about a server locating you and handing you those papers?" she asked.

"Well," I thought aloud, lying on my bed, "maybe it would give my mom and dad a break for awhile. We've been here almost a week, so that might be good. How 'bout in two days, on Friday?" I asked.

"Sounds good!" she said. "I'll get your room ready and the girls can be downstairs in sleeping bags."

I was grateful, again, to be well taken care of and have this next provision.

~~~

Thursday, July 22, 1999

Miriam and I tended to have our prayer times first thing in the morning before either of our households were up.

"Miriam," I said, still considering my options, "what should I do about filing papers? Chloe, my California lawyer, confirmed what Vicki's brother told me about it being important who files first in a case, because then that is what becomes the case.

"And Kirk isn't showing any signs of changing his position. He's obviously still involved with this other woman from what I can tell from where he calls from and buys gas.

"But it really bothers me because I don't want a divorce," I said again. "I don't think it's right. Marriage is about something bigger than us. It's about the picture of Christ and the church. It should not just be thrown away," I said, summing up my dilemma.

"You are not saying that you want a divorce, Janice. You've been trying to talk to Kirk, haven't you?" Miriam asked.

"Yes, and he will have none of it. He completely sidesteps me and he's already told me that he has the papers.

"And the lawyer says that California is a no-fault state so that any married person can dissolve their marriage, even against their spouse's wishes. She says it can take as little as six months for the divorce to become legal once papers are served," I explained.

"Well, Janice, I am just amazed at how you are coming across the important information that you need to know at just the right time. I believe that you *do* need to protect yourself and the kids. After all, it's not just about you, but it's about them, too.

"You are willing to stop this process at any time that Kirk asks for it. But in the meantime, you have to use wisdom and protect yourself and the children," Miriam said.

~~~

The whole idea upset me, but it did seem clear that it was indeed the next step. I would say in my statement for the court that if Kirk continued to insist on divorcing me, then I wanted to move back home to Maryland with the children and continue their homeschool education program which had been so successful the prior year.

Perhaps, I thought, this would cause Kirk to want to reconsider the divorce if he saw the possibility of our kids living elsewhere.

I clung to God with the words I spoke. Praising Him and praying aloud when I first awoke and when I went to bed, and when I had alone time in my bedroom. It was God that I focused on in my mind.

It was a choice, and it was work. God's presence continued to envelop me in a very real, almost tangible way.

~~~

Friday, July 23, 1999

Before leaving for Veronica's house, I phoned Kirk's answering service to alert him that we were going to be away at a friend's house, but that we would be back early the next week. I left a number in case he wanted to call.

I also phoned the lawyer and confirmed with her my decision to fill out the paperwork to serve Kirk papers. I conveyed my statement about moving to Maryland with the kids to be near family if he insisted on leaving us.

~~~

When I arrived at Veronica's townhome, I parked the borrowed car far down the street in case it was being looked for by a server.

Entering the foyer weighed down by bags of clothes and toiletries for spending the night, the girls and I took our shoes off while David continued to sleep in his carseat for his morning nap.

Veronica sat in a chair in the little kitchen on the right feeding Violet some oatmeal in her highchair. "Make yourself at home," Veronica said to me as she came over to greet me with a hug.

She turned to kneel in front of Nicole and Meaghan, and asked if they would like to see the downstairs where they would be sleeping. "There are toys for children, and a TV to watch videos. We have bubbles and puzzles and a little play kitchen that Violet is not old enough for yet but that you can enjoy," I heard Veronica say as they all went downstairs together.

I sat down in a kitchen chair to keep watch over little Violet while she finger-painted with her oatmeal.

Veronica returned and cleaned up Violet while we talked for awhile about everyday things. Then Veronica showed me to my room, the guest room, and one that would eventually be one of her children's bedrooms.

She left me upstairs to just be spoiled by being in the bedroom with baby David alone. I nursed him while I lay in the queen-sized bed, rocked him in the chair located to the side of the bed, patted his tummy when he lay on his back in the Pack 'n Play, and sat by him, watching him sleep. Veronica did not come to fetch me out of the room, my sanctuary, and I heard the girls giggling and laughing and playing with her on the floors below.

For the next several days, my main responsibility was to tend baby David and spend time soaking in the Lord and His Word. I prayed and praised in my room and I spent my time reading the Bible and the book that Veronica had given me earlier about trusting God. It helped to guide my thinking along godly paths.

It was a wonderful retreat time of pure rest. I was so grateful to Veronica for providing it. And there was the added benefit of laughter when Veronica and I ate meals together.

One night, after feeling a growing sense of tension due to the possibility of being stalked by a server, Veronica and I slipped out of the house after dark and took the kids to McDonald's. We let the kids enjoy Playland while we talked.

"Well Veronica," I said, picking up another hot french fry, "Kirk said today that he will buy tickets for the kids *and* me to return to California. He wants to book them for Wednesday, August 11th and I agreed, even though I know that means we won't be able to go to the beach with my family."

"Are you okay with that?" Veronica asked, a spoonful of hot fudge sundae in mid-air.

"I know I have to go back," I said, taking a sip of Dr. Pepper. "The thing that bothers me now is that he insists on picking us up at the airport. I think that's a bad idea for sure. The last person I want to see is him after an all-day flight with three small children. And the kids will think everything is back to normal until he turns around and leaves again moments later."

It was an unnerving feeling – that of one's beloved husband turned adversary and not knowing what he would do next.

~~~

As I stayed in my room at Veronica's, I considered the real possibilities of what my future might hold. What would it be like if I were to be one of those women who were required to remain in California against her will in order to take part in raising her own children?

I had no relatives even remotely nearby on that side of the country. How would I afford to visit back East when four plane tickets would cost so much?

Would I be able to continue homeschooling? Or would I be forced to go back to work and put my cherished children in daycare? That idea was so contrary to the family life I'd envisioned for them, and so far from the original plan which I held of being a stay-at-home mom.

Where would I live? Would I be compelled to move to a little place on the outskirts of town? What about the finances and the high cost of living in California? How long would I have supportive friends around me if this continued?

On the other hand, I wondered what it would be like if I actually moved back to Maryland to be near family and high school friends again. So much had changed back here.

What would it be like for my children to be near their grandparents and their great-grandma and their great uncle, and my brother, Michael, while they were growing up? I had such precious memories of extended family nearby when I was a child.

I wondered and wondered about what the future held.

~~~

"Does he who implanted the ear not hear?
Does he who formed the eye not see?"
Psalm 94:9

~~~

Tuesday, July 27, 1999

It was on the last day of staying with Veronica that she had an idea. "Do you want me to see what else I can find out about this other woman?" Veronica asked me from the kitchen where she fed Violet hot cereal and before I went out on some errands.

"Sure, if you can," I said, my hand on the doorknob ready to leave and my mind questioning if anything could really be discovered.

Apparently Veronica got to work on the Internet while I was gone, and when I returned, she had some information.

Walking through the door I heard her call me upstairs to where she worked at the computer in her bedroom. "Well, guess what?" she asked, resting her elbow on the desk.

"What?" I inquired, leaning on the doorframe and listening to the girls play downstairs.

"Well I found out this 'other woman's' previous husband's name: Douglas. She's divorced now and it hasn't been that long. I even phoned him and talked to him! Here's his number." Veronica announced and pointed to a notebook.

"You're kidding? What did he say?" Now I was curious.

"Well, I just asked for his wife and he said that she no longer lives there," Veronica reported. "I also found out about the home that she and her husband bought and all the prices involved."

"Really?" I stood stunned that Veronica had uncovered so much.

"And, I managed to talk to someone who knew of them and sold another family home for them as well because I had a connection through a local office here. She had nice things to say about the grandparents," Veronica informed me.

"Well," I said, "another detective on the case!" It gave us a lot to talk about at dinner that night with Veronica's husband.

Information helped to give ambiguity a name.

18

Road Trip

Sunday, August 1, 1999

D ad and Mom rented a car big enough for both of them and the four of us to travel to Connecticut to see my dad's parents and sister. They wanted to meet baby David while we were still on the East Coast.

Kirk continued to phone the girls even while we were out of town.

At this point, Kirk had reserved our tickets for Wednesday, August 11th, but continued to insist on being the one to pick us up when we arrived back. I was not ready to come face-to-face with Kirk at the end of our long flight. The next time he called, I tried to broach this subject with him again.

"Kirk," I began while sitting on the living room couch in my aunt's New England house, "I just don't think it's best for you to be the one to pick us up from the airport when we arrive back in California."

"Well," he said, "I have every right to do it, and I want to see the kids."

"We can schedule a time for you to see them after we are back, like the next day. But how do you think they will feel if you pick us up and then just drop us off at the house and leave again?" I tried to convince him.

"Janice," Kirk said with roughness, "you just need to *get over* me leaving you."

He just doesn't get it, I thought. Like I can 'get over' him leaving our marriage after just a few weeks. Like he wouldn't be getting his kids' hopes up only to hurt them more.

"Janice, *I am* going to be there and that's final." Kirk told me.

"Okay, well do you want to talk to the girls?" I asked, dropping the argument because it was going nowhere.

~~~

In the meantime, I was running into a glitch with serving Kirk papers first.

Chloe, my California lawyer had prepared the papers, and now I'd hired a server to hand them to Kirk as I was instructed had to be done by my lawyer. However, his company's campuses were large and spread out, and I could not figure out Kirk's exact location. The server had already tried twice to find him and each time he charged a fee.

I did not feel like I could rest from the threat of Kirk serving me first until he was actually served himself.

~~~

Choosing to put all the legal matters aside, I turned my attention to the warm, summer day. My cousin Nancy joined us at her mom's for a visit and brought her kids to play with mine. There was a picnic and a trip to a pool. At night, the adults talked and sipped lemonade on the porch.

My grandmother and grandfather, both ninety years of age, lived nearby in a neat and tidy one-bedroom apartment. The next day my parents drove us to their home where we were greeted with candy and custard.

Grandpa, bald and kind, held each little one in his recliner chair and told them he loved them. Grandma, with never-ending energy, got up and down to cluck and coo and check to see that we were all comfortable and fed.

Before we left, we sat outside on the familiar green iron garden chairs. Grandpa sat beside me quietly, slightly bent over, speaking to me with gentle assurance, "You're okay, Janice. You know, you're okay. Yes, you're going to be okay."

It was a true gift to be with him, and one of the last times I'd see him.

~~~

Thursday, August 5, 1999

It had been a terrific time together with family in Connecticut. It was surprising that in the midst of the underlying, unending, ongoing sting and painful heartache, I could still enjoy moments like these. Even more, I did not take them for granted and I counted each and every one a blessing. Back at my parents' home in Maryland, I was up early again for my quiet time.

I sat silently before the Lord after spending time praising and worshipping Him. Suddenly, the name of one of Kirk's new co-workers who shared an office with him flashed like a picture into my mind. *That's it!* I thought. *Now, I'll be able to locate where Kirk is.*

When 'Detective Hannah' checked in with me next, I gave her the name of Kirk's co-worker who worked at the same location. Formulating her plan, she phoned the operator and got the directions to his co-worker's exact location, which in turn, would uncover Kirk.

It worked. Kirk was served papers within a couple of hours.

~~~

It wasn't long before Chloe phoned to report what had happened when she filed the papers. "Janice," she said, "there's some bad news and some good news."

I braced myself, "What is it?" I asked, sitting down on the office chair and taking a deep breath.

"Well, the bad news is that Kirk had already filed papers for divorce way back at the beginning of when he left you, just as he'd told you he planned to do. Funny thing is, though, his lawyer never had him serve you the papers in person and this is highly unusual.

"Just so you know, he would have had to been thinking about this and making arrangements to have had a lawyer and papers in place and ready to go. He'd obviously been planning on serving you long before you were aware of anything," Chloe explained.

Thanksgiving washed over me to learn that I'd been spared that horrible moment of seeing those unexpected papers. How devastating it would have been to have been caught totally unaware, not even knowing that my husband was contemplating divorce! God was so good to expose Kirk's adultery first. I sunk back further into the chair feeling both weak and thankful all over.

"The good news," Chloe continued, "is that Kirk's lawyer also neglected to have him make any other primary statement other than that he intends to divorce you over 'irreconcilable differences.' In California, you cannot stop him from doing that so it is not like the judge has to make a decision or a ruling on it.

"This means that the judge will instead be looking at your primary statements about wanting to move back to Maryland to be near family and wanting to continue in the homeschool education of your children. It's

169

really good that Kirk did not state his opinions on any of this when he filed papers to divorce," Chloe concluded.

"What will happen now, Chloe?" I asked, standing up as I felt my heart racing. I knew that I was oblivious to the rules and the steps in the legal system.

The girls knocked at the door and I opened it briefly to show them I was on the phone again. They turned back down the hall with unhappy faces because I was not available once more.

"The court will set a date to hear the case," Chloe continued. "At the same time, they will also set a date that will occur before the court date for both you and Kirk to meet with a mediator to discuss issues regarding the children such as a visitation schedule and where the children should live, etc.

"The mediator's opinion will weigh in heavily with the judge because the mediator will be the one who spends more time with both of you. So the next step, *and it is a critical one*, will be to prepare your case for the mediator."

"Okay, Chloe," I said. I was to learn later that though Chloe was not as experienced in appearing before the court, she was extremely good at her role in getting me ready for the mediation date. This would prove to be of utmost importance.

~~~

I could not be thankful enough for regular, faithful friends to share with and to pray with. I was blessed to have three. This meant that if for some reason one could not be there, usually at least the others could.

Ginny phoned in the evening to pray. What touched my heart tonight was that she had scheduled a prayer meeting later that evening with my friend, Paula. It touched me because Ginny and Paula did not know each another.

~~~

Friday, August 6, 1999

It had been a long time since I'd been to a birthday party for one of my relatives. For 15 years I'd been away at college, or taking my first job as a youth director at a church in Ohio, and then I'd married and moved from one East Coast city to another as my husband advanced in his career.

Today Grammie Lee was 79 years old and it was a special time for our family.

In fact, during my month in Maryland, even though under the most tragic of circumstances, God gifted me with many special moments. My uncle took us to the movies and he also brought us to the Capitol Children's Museum. Michael treated us again at the Cheesecake Factory. Vanessa took me out for ice cream. Several high school friends brought their children over for a playdate at Mom and Dad's, and the list of blessings grew longer each day.

How could I experience joy in the midst of feeling such terrible pain and devastation? But that is what happened.

~~~

At night there was time to think and this could be challenging. It was on this night when everyone had gone to sleep and I still lay awake in the light of the dimmed lamp by my bed that I sat up and talked to the Lord.

"O Lord," I cried. "Kirk has not even paid all the bills yet. What is he doing with his time that he is so neglectful of everyday responsibilities?

"O Lord," I cried some more, "what about the finances? Everything looks so insecure from where I am sitting. What is going to happen?" I continued, "And Lord, instead of my loving husband, Kirk now opposes me in the choices I make, and criticizes me. It is so hard, Lord. It is so hard."

Suddenly, as I was feeling almost paralyzed by the ache in my heart, the Lord flashed a picture into my mind: *I saw myself sitting in the bottom of a pit.*

Almost as soon as I saw this picture of myself in the pit, I had a thought to ask God for a new song to sing, and then the typewritten word *'Psalm 40'* immediately flashed into my mind.

I looked up the Psalm, not knowing what to expect. When I read these amazing words, I began to rejoice again because I saw that God had clearly spoken to me once more.

~~~

"I waited patiently for the Lord,
He inclined to me and heard my cry.
He drew me up from the desolate pit,
out of the miry bog,

And set my feet upon a rock, making my steps secure.
He put a new song in my mouth,
a song of praise to our God.
Many will see and fear,
and put their trust in the Lord."
Psalm 40: 1-3

~~~

Saturday, August 7, 1999

I still sat thinking and praying after laying down the baby for his nap. The idea of returning to California in only four days and having to face Kirk at the end of the long journey continued to cause me great discomfort and distress.

Well, I reasoned, while sitting on the edge of the bed, it couldn't hurt if I made a phone call. I phoned Kirk's company and was connected to the travel agency that Kirk had used to book the tickets.

"Hello?" I inquired after giving them my basic information. "I was wondering, how much would it cost if I changed the time or the date on these tickets?" I tried to keep my voice quiet and cupped my mouth over the phone in order to not wake David where he slept in the Pack 'n Play.

"Let me look it up for you ma'am," responded the woman at the end of the line. "Well, let me see here," she continued, "hmmm, this is strange," she said.

"What is?" I wanted to know, my curiosity roused. I stood up and went to look out a window overseeing the driveway where my dad had just pulled in.

"Well," she answered, "it's just that on the day that your husband pur-chased these tickets, it appears that the least expensive tickets available at that time were refundable tickets – that is sure unusual."

"What does that mean?!" I asked, with growing excitement, my stomach feeling it first.

"What that means ma'am, is that you can change these tickets anytime up until even the last minute, and it won't cost you a penny!" the agent informed.

"You're kidding!" I said, seeing God wink at me.

"No, ma'am," the woman assured me. "I am absolutely serious."

"Well, would I be able to book a flight for one week later? On Wednesday, August 18th?" I asked looking at the calendar on the bed to make sure that the date would fit well into our schedule.

She checked and came back to say, "Yes, ma'am, I've booked you and your family on a flight for Wednesday, August 18th."

"Thank you!" I said to the agent forgetting to be quiet about it and hearing David move.

There was only one thing difficult about the date of August 18th: *It was our wedding anniversary.*

~~~

I had to tell somebody what God had done about the refundable tickets. God had such a sense of humor and He made me laugh. He always has the last word on a matter and surprise endings are his specialty.

First I ran downstairs to find Mom and Dad and share the new date that we'd be leaving. Already, the stress dissolved from my heart like melting snow. "Can you believe it?" I said full of amazement, "The day that Kirk booked our flight, *the cheapest tickets were the refundable ones*! Whoever heard of such a thing?" I said dancing in the kitchen, my heart full of worship to God.

The girls were playing outside in the yard with a neighbor so I ran upstairs to make some more phone calls. When I phoned Miriam, we had powerful intercession. Pictures of Kirk in his spiritual predicament flashed into our minds and so we prayed with God's wisdom. We gave thanks for all that God had done.

After our intense prayers, it seemed time to remember that my problems were the Lord's and it was time to go and to have fun with the girls. *Inspector Gadget* was playing at the movies, a nice treat.

When we returned home, I found a check in the mail to helps us from Ginny's church for $200.

~~~

Thursday, August 12, 1999

Kirk sat tight. Even though I'd phoned to leave a message for him about our change of plans and my emotional need to stay a bit longer, it turned out that he'd already been contacted by his work's travel agency as a general courtesy reminder of the ticket change.

When Kirk did phone later for his daily contact with the girls, I braced myself. But this time he was ready to talk with me first. 'His friend,' he said, 'had helped him to see that it was a better idea for him not to be the one to pick us up.' We scheduled time for him to see the girls the day after we returned.

During the conversation, I asked him about us returning to Maryland to live close to family if he was determined to divorce. 'Sure,' he was 'willing to work that out,' he said.

Perhaps he was, perhaps he wasn't. It was only the beginning of his changing his mind on this from one day to the next.

I pled again with Kirk to pay the mortgage which he had not done yet. I told him how our neighbors were now complaining of our backyard being a fire hazard due to the high grass and tall weeds which had now grown up and which he had neglected to cut down after his sudden departure from our home.

Kirk then informed me that he planned to deposit money in the bank which would be representative of monthly spousal/child support on order for me to pay the bills.

Ouch, that hurt.

19

The Return

Wednesday, August 18, 1999

Thinking is foggy when it's early in the morning. Our flight left at 6:30 AM so the children and I piled into the car under the cover of darkness in the wee morning hours, shortly after the alarm clock had beeped. Dad and Mom both drove us.

As I stared out of the window at the familiar landmarks, a sweet gratefulness flowed through me for the time that I'd spent there, being refreshed, and being guided step-by-step by God as we'd prayed for wisdom.

I *did* remember that it was my wedding anniversary. Nine years ago it had been such a different scene here. Who would've guessed that this is what I'd be doing on such a day as this?

It was so sad to contrast these two events, then and now. I tried not to think of it.

And now, what would happen to me and to the children? Those questions raced across my mind again.

But I reminded myself of this: *I didn't know what the future held. But I knew Who held the future.*

~~~

Looking out the window of the plane as we approached the San Francisco airport in California, the houses and the trees and the cars on the roadway began to grow larger. Oh, to stay quietly hidden in the sky behind the clouds for only a few hours longer… to not have to answer questions or to give explanations or to return to all the work that awaited me.

Baby David snuggled in my lap, a little hot potato, and amazingly still asleep during our descent, even with the changing air pressure. Even the girls both sat quietly, not asking questions or moving about. The all-day plane ride from my parents' home back East was coming to an end all too quickly. It was so comforting to just sit here on the plane with time temporarily suspended, momentarily in a whole different world.

What would happen now? I wondered again, for the hundredth time since I'd boarded the plane. Would I be living in California to raise my children, or be granted permission to return back to my growing-up home, family, and friends? God had a plan, and I knew that I was in His Hands. I sensed His Presence, and I kept thanking Him under my breath.

It was so strange to be picked up by somebody other than Kirk at the airport. I wondered if Paula would be there right when we arrived. The last time I'd seen Paula, we'd celebrated her birthday at Mimi's Café.

But to face Kirk, alone, for the first time at the airport since he'd left me seemed too uncomfortable. I could not bear the pain of him walking past me with open arms to meet the children.

Of course they would be so anxious to see him, understandably. And I would have been left behind, left out, excluded from the family as they all reunited, as if he were their hero once more.

Then he'd drop us off at the house, and I would be left to explain why he'd left, again, and why he was not staying, to two tired little preschool girls who had traveled all day long.

I feared how I would react if I saw his face, because, after all, *this was our anniversary.*

~~~

Weakly, suddenly very tired and exhausted, I moved up the gate leading from the plane to the terminal. Others scooted by our group of four, which also included umbrella stroller, diaper bag, backpacks, bottles, and a large carry-on bag.

Blinking our eyes, we entered the bright, crowded, noisy room full of people meeting and greeting others. Tall Paula was by our side instantly, embracing me, greeting the children, taking what she could carry from us, and directing us first to the luggage belt and then right outside to her parked car. "I've done this a million times," she said. "I feel like I could do this in my sleep – my relatives fly into this airport, so I've got it down solid."

Paula flipped open the trunk of her SUV and loaded our luggage. "Are you hungry?" she asked.

I nodded, suddenly aware that yes, I was very hungry.

"I thought I might take you and the kids to *Sweet Tomatoes*?" she offered. This was a favorite outing for our preschool co-op where the kids practically ate for free and the moms enjoyed delicious salads and breads.

"Oh, that would be great," I said, and I slowly began to open up and tell her the stories about how God had been with me during the last few weeks. The girls began to chatter about *Inspector Gadget*, and about what Grandma had given them for their backpacks on the plane ride back.

Bit-by-bit as we drove and talked and looked out the window, I began to acclimate to the sights and sounds of Hillside and feel some comfort in its familiarity.

Still, so many questions and unknowns stared me in the face.

~~~

As Paula pulled us up to 707 Strawberry Lane, I noticed my car, the red Ford Taurus, parked in the driveway. Farley, Frankie's husband, must have returned it from its hiding spot inside his garage earlier that day.

Popping out of the passenger seat of Paula's car, I paused in front of our new, red door. Though it had only been a few weeks, it seemed like a lifetime had passed since I'd slipped away to hide from being served the papers and to flee California.

What would I find inside this house now?

I knew that Kirk had not been living here. Would it be musty? Would there be cobwebs? Would there be other things missing that Hannah or Emilie had not yet noticed in their rounds?

Soon I was joined by short Nicole, a jumping Meaghan, and Paula carrying David in his carseat. I fumbled with my keys. They fell to the ground with a jangle, and finally I found the right one and opened the door. The girls pushed by my legs and burst through first to run to their bedroom to greet toys like old friends.

The front door, still unframed, and the hole in the foyer ceiling from where Kirk's foot had slipped when he'd been working above, remained as before.

But to my surprise, a freshness met my senses. Vacuum marks left the carpet looking clean and neat. I looked left through the family room into the eat-in kitchen and on the table stood a large bouquet of arranged flowers with three cheerful helium balloons attached, and a pile of collected mail beneath it.

"*Wow,*" I breathed. "Who did this?"

"Oh, Hannah and Emilie and I had some fun," Paula smiled.

"Really? This is so nice. It looks like it's from out of a magazine." I wandered through the kitchen noticing the cleaned counters, and some new groceries arranged with care on top. When I opened the refrigerator, there was milk and fruit and eggs, all ready for us. *Welcome Home,* read a sign inside the fridge.

I felt a burden lift as joy flooded me when I realized we'd returned to a clean home already stocked with food. Thanksgiving welled up within my heart and dispelled some of its numbness as I saw the bright gifts of love from my friends.

"Let's bring the suitcases in and I'll stay and talk for a while," Paula offered.

~~~

"Well!" Paula exclaimed as she sat cross-legged on our old blue couch in the family room. She eyed me on the floor where I stretched out beside David who kicked his feet in the air. We were all so glad to be out of cramped places. Playful sounds and giggles came from the girls' room down the hall.

"What are you thinking?" I asked Paula, who looked as if she were bursting with something significant.

"Well," Paula continued, "I just can't believe that I'm saying this, because I would normally just be so angry at a man who would do something like this to his wife and his children. No, I cannot believe that I'm saying this," she repeated before she went on.

"It's just that this love for Kirk is flowing from my heart and it does not make any sense. I just have such a great compassion for him! This is so surprising," she said. "But I know that I would be just the perfect person for God to use to speak to Kirk."

I looked up at her from where I rested by the baby, listening. Paula did not know it then, but she was speaking prophetically.

~~~

The kids were all in bed. Now it was Ginny who had come over to keep me company. In fact, she informed me, she would be staying the first three nights in the guest bedroom because her husband was traveling out of town. I was grateful for how God had arranged for me not be alone when I first got back.

We sat at the round country table in the newly decorated, Mary-Engelbreit-style, eat-in kitchen. Bright primary colors and ornaments of teacups and flowers adorned the upper ledge of the room and the new blue-and-white checkered wallpaper beamed from below the chair rail.

"Why don't I make us one of our favorite treats?" Ginny suggested cheerfully. "I brought over some artichokes and I made my famous parmesan-lemon dip!"

I wasn't that hungry since eating at *Sweet Tomatoes*, but I did love the artichokes and dip that Ginny had gotten me hooked on.

"Whoops," she said, "I guess I left out one of the five ingredients in the dip," she explained. I realized it too, and it reminded me that there was also a missing ingredient in our home: Kirk.

~~~

"So, what's next?" asked Ginny, dipping another leaf into the cheesy mayo mixture.

"We have a court date scheduled for October 1st," I stated. "I'm going to fast desserts until then," I added.

"Janice, I am going to join you. No desserts until October 1st," Ginny agreed.

I was so touched that she would join me in making this sacrifice. It wasn't long before others, who found out about my fasting, would also join us. I was not alone.

~~~

A knock sounded on the front door even though it was now almost 9:00 PM. Looking outside, I saw Kayla. "Kayla!" I exclaimed, rushing to unlock the door. My hearted lifted at seeing her.

"Oh," she said, setting down her purse when she entered our home and wrapping me in a hug, "I thought we'd have one of our three-cord prayer meetings tonight since Ginny was over."

And we did. We put away our food, and we prayed together until midnight. I had a better understanding, now, of why God had led me to ask Him for *two* prayer partners when I had first moved to California.

Amazing providence.

20

Adjustment

Thursday, August 19, 1999

The beeping alarm clock woke me up the next day and I lay in bed looking up at the ceiling framed by the forest-green valances on the canopy rails.

I was back in California. Ginny slept down the hall in the guestroom, and David lay asleep in his bassinet beside me. The praise and worship music sifted into my thoughts and I joined my voice with the words.

How good it had been to pray with Ginny and Kayla until late last night. How good it had been for Paula to pick me up from the airport. And how good it had been to come home to a cleaned home with fresh groceries.

Today Kirk would come over and pick up the girls at 5:00 PM for dinner. It would be the first time I'd seen him face-to-face since he'd left me.

~~~

"Hello?" I answered the phone. It was Hannah.

"Janice! Welcome back!" Hannah greeted me. "Listen, would it be alright if Hailey and I came over to hang out with you and the girls after naptime?" she asked. "Hailey really wants to see her friends and I want to visit with you."

"Okay," I said, figuring that I could run to do a couple of errands in the morning before naptime. It would be nice to see them.

It was comforting to have Hannah's companionship. Ginny had gone back to her office at home to work during the day but would be back later in the evening. The three girls enjoyed playing and running and making noise.

"So, Kirk is coming at what time, Janice?" Hannah asked, planning our schedule.

"He's supposed to be here at 5:00 PM," I said.

"Do you think it would be alright if I phoned Henry and had him come over here for dinner?" she asked. "I'll make us all a dinner from the groceries we stocked your fridge with!"

Gladdened by her idea and happy not to be alone when Kirk arrived, I agreed. The clock ticked away the seconds, and the time approached when I'd have to face him.

Henry read the newspaper at the kitchen table and Hannah cooked our dinner. I held baby David on the couch after having nursed him and it was then that Kirk burst through our front door, unlocking it himself with his old key. He had not knocked first.

"Girls!" Kirk called out and little feet came running from the bedroom down the hall. Both girls flew into the open arms of their daddy.

"Daddy!" they squealed, happy to see him.

"Nickie! Meg!" he called to them. "Look how big you both are now!" He held his hands up to where they came to his waist. "And who do we have here?" he asked, pointing to the stuffed animals they held.

Then Kirk walked over to me. And, disregarding my existence altogether, he pulled back the blanket near David's head and whispered, "Look at little Davie." He pointed at the baby and looked back at the girls still in the foyer.

Davie? Nickie? Meg? Why was he changing all their names?

Henry, Hannah's husband, jumped up from the kitchen table and greeted Kirk.

"Hey," Kirk answered but did not look at him and did not linger. Instead, Kirk grasped the girls' hands and walked outside with them to his waiting truck.

Henry followed, but apparently he did not exist either. At least, Kirk did not seem to see or hear him.

Returning inside the house after he'd driven away, Henry reported that he'd gotten nowhere with Kirk.

Later, as the clock reached the scheduled time of 8:00 PM, I heard a knocking at the door and opened it to find only Nicole and Meaghan standing outside.

I looked up just in time to see Kirk speeding away in his white truck.

~~~

Friday, August 20, 1999

The next morning the phone rang early before the alarm clock.

"Hello? Janice? This is Kirk."

"Hi." I said, my heart beginning to race.

"You know, I know that I wasn't supposed to see the girls again until Sunday afternoon, but I'd like to have them with me this evening, also. And I plan to have them spend the night with me."

"What?" I asked, feeling alarmed at the sudden change of plans and sitting up. "But what about Courtney's birthday party tomorrow morning in Santa Cruz? They've been talking all about it with Hailey and they are expecting to go. Everyone from their old preschool playgroup will be there."

"I'll have them back in time for the party," Kirk assured me.

"At 10 AM? Are you sure?" I asked, feeling uncertain about this whole new idea but also unsure about what I could do to stop it.

"Yes, I'll pick them up at 5:00 PM tonight after work." I heard a click. Kirk had hung up.

I sat in bed with the phone still in my hand, feeling like I'd just been run over. The whole thing made me feel uncomfortable, and like I'd had no say in the matter. But I was just so tired, still adjusting from the jet lag, still adjusting to everything.

"Who was that?" Ginny called from down at the end of the hallway.

"That was Kirk," I confided. "He says he's going to come to take the girls at 5:00 PM, and then keep them overnight."

"Are you going to let him?" Ginny asked, her voice rising as she moved a few steps closer toward my bedroom.

"Well, I don't know if I have a choice. He surprised me by changing the plans. I guess so." I said, placing the phone back in its holder.

"I don't know, Janice." Ginny left the discussion to get showered and dressed to leave for her office. I was grateful that she'd been staying with me at night, but this was the last time because her husband would now be back home from his trip.

Pushing aside the disturbing wake-up call, I began to choose to thank God that He was in control. I thanked Him that He knew everything and that He saw everything. I thanked Him that He cared and that I was not alone. I thanked Him that my children were in His Hands.

After a while of hearing my voice declare what was true in His Word, I felt God's peace fall over me with the confidence of His strong presence.

~~~

When Kirk arrived at 5:00 PM, I met him at the door before he could open it and burst through it again. It disturbed me to not really know when he might be entering. The girls joined him in the foyer and he herded them outside.

I followed them to the truck with the girls' backpacks and the things they might need for their overnight. "Do you want their pajamas or tooth-paste?" I asked. "Because here they are." I said, holding them toward him.

"Nope." Kirk said, not looking up while he adjusted their seats, "I have everything they'll need."

Perplexed, I did not move but asked, "Where will they be? What is your contact information?"

"Just phone my pager," Kirk again refused to give me any details, or eye contact.

The girls waved from the window as he drove them away.

Alarm rose in me and I cried out to the Lord. As I prayed, I did not have direction to take any action but I felt a definite confidence and a peace from the Lord that I could rest. I went to bed very early, worn out com-pletely, knowing that I had the nighttime feedings ahead of me.

~~~

Saturday, August 21, 1999

I knew that I had to wake up early the next morning to get David ready and to pack for the day. Santa Cruz was at least an hour away and we had to leave immediately when Kirk returned the girls at 10 AM.

But I was still so tired, just dragging. I really did not know how I would manage to have energy for this long day trip. Should we all just stay home? But I also couldn't see that I'd get much rest by staying home either, because 5 and 3-year-olds require lots of interaction.

After packing the diaper bag and the snacks, I got into the shower at 8:30 AM. When the phone rang, I didn't hear it.

I nursed David in the rocker-glider in the family room so that he would be ready for the long car ride. I was just so tired.

Dozing while I nursed him, I became aware that it seemed like they should have been home by now. I forced my eyelids to open and look at the clock on the wall: 10:20 AM.

Where were they? Kirk knew we were on a tight schedule. He promised to have them back. Rousing myself from the rocker and depositing the sleeping David in his bassinet, I discovered a message blinking on the answering machine.

Kirk's voice interrupted the silent house, "Janice, the girls miss me so much that I have decided to keep them another night. I'll have them back at 5:00 PM on Sunday."

My mind sprang with alarm. *Where were they?* Kirk had refused to give me an address or a phone number. Should I call the police? I pushed aside visions of them crossing the border into Mexico. I couldn't really imagine Kirk taking them. But I couldn't really imagine Kirk committing adultery, either.

I prayed in my spirit. I declared aloud what God's Word says is true and the promises He gives us. I felt God's peace wash over me and in me and I discerned that it was alright.

Now, thoroughly exhausted and still recovering from jet lag, I literally fell back into bed, clothes and all. I slept the rest of the day.

~~~

When I began to feel better and really wake up, I looked at the digital clock to see that it was 9:00 PM. Wow, I thought, I'd really needed that rest.

"God, I thank you that Kirk is a tool in Your hand used to bless me. I thank You that everything You allow him to do only serves to bless me. In Jesus' Name. Amen."

~~~

I felt good enough to find something to eat in the kitchen and that is when the phone rang. "Janice! You'll never guess what!" Paula exclaimed to me on the other end of the line. "You know how I was at Courtney's birthday party today in Santa Cruz?"

"Yes." I said, still holding the refrigerator door open and looking inside.

"Well, normally I don't go shopping at night, but I decided to stop by the grocery store on the way home," she explained, her words zipping out.

"Yes?!" I said, realizing that this was leading somewhere important and pushing the fridge door closed.

"Well, when I walked inside the store, I looked toward the produce section because that is where I was headed, and you'll never guess *who* I saw!" she exclaimed.

"Who?!" I said, standing up straight and tall and alert and reaching for a notepad and pen on the counter in case I needed it.

"Nicole and Meaghan both seated in a shopping cart," she said. "And there was Kirk – with the other woman!"

"You mean, Kirk is already having that woman involved with my girls? Right when they just arrived back home?" I asked, thunderstruck by this information.

"Yes, apparently so," Paula confirmed.

"Well, what happened next?" I insisted. "Tell me word-for-word."

"My knees felt wobbly and I forgot what I was even doing there. I would've gone home except that the girls saw me! They both began calling to me and saying 'Hi Mrs. Paula!'" Paula reported.

"Then what happened?" I asked, excited.

"I was caught and so I had to go over there and talk to the girls," Paula said. "So, I told them, 'I missed you at Courtney's birthday party.' And they said, 'We had to stay with Daddy instead because we missed him and tomorrow we're going on a boatride!' So I said, 'Oh, I see. Is *somebody* trying to spoil you?' And then I looked straight into Kirk and the other woman's eyes!"

"Janice," Paula confessed, "as soon as I said it, I felt a terrible conviction in my heart and I knew that I'd sinned by speaking that way to Kirk in front of the girls. But Kirk and the woman began to walk down the aisle away from me, pushing the girls in the shopping cart."

"So then what happened? Did you see or talk to them again?" I wanted to know.

"First," said Paula, "I figured that hundreds of prayers have gone up for Kirk and this situation so it was no accident that I ran into them tonight. Then, I remembered how God had poured out love in my heart for Kirk which was so unlike me to feel in this situation.

"Then I looked up, and to my surprise, there was a man standing there whom I know and he is someone who knows how to pray like no one else

I know! And he was standing there late in the evening in a grocery store! So I said, 'this is no accident either!' And I went straight over to ask him to pray for me that God would give me an opportunity to talk to Kirk," explained Paula.

"Then what happened?!" I asked, clutching the phone.

"So now I moved up and down the aisles going the route I normally do," said Paula. "But I forgot to add anything to my cart and I thought my knees would give out and my heart pounded so hard that I felt it coming out of my chest!

"After a few aisles, I saw Kirk with the shopping cart, the girls, and the woman again. So I approached him and I said, 'Kirk, can I talk to you privately, please? I need to ask your forgiveness for something.'"

"You did?!" I asked, holding my breath.

"Yes, and Kirk came over to the side with me, and first I asked him to forgive me for saying that snide remark in front of the girls.

"Then I said, 'Kirk, I know that you cannot pray right now. But please, think about what you are doing. Please, think of all the consequences. I know you can't see it right now, but you will have many regrets if you continue down this path.'"

"What did he do?" I asked.

"He just thanked me politely and left," said Paula.

"Wow!" I said. "God really used you just like you said you thought He might! Remember that?"

"Yes! It's amazing!" Paula said. "How that all came together."

"Just think, Paula," I said, "this is just one divine appointment that we know about. Just think of how many other circumstances and people that God has also set up for Kirk because of all the people praying," I said, excited. "And, guess what else?"

"What?" asked Paula.

"Now I can rest easier tonight because I know that Kirk has not crossed the border into Mexico. Isn't God good? To show me generally where my girls are?" I asked her, unable to stop moving my feet as I stood in the kitchen and danced up and down. "God is good!"

"Yes, God is good!" Paula agreed.

~~~

What I didn't know at the time was that because Kirk unexpectedly changed our agreed-upon schedule, a more rigid visitation with the children would soon be put in place with the help of legal counsel.

One of the consequences Kirk had not thought through was this: the loss of liberty with his children.

~~~

"Do not be deceived:
God cannot be mocked.
A man reaps what he sows."
Galatians 5: 7

~~~

"Sin takes you further
than you want to go.
Sin makes you stay longer
than you ever wanted to stay.
Sin makes you pay more
than you ever wanted to pay."
Anonymous

~~~

21

How Odd it Feels

Sunday, August 22, 1999

I t was Sunday morning again, and I knew it was best to maintain normal activities. So I went to church.

It felt strange to be there without the girls because Kirk had kept them overnight. I walked on the outdoor sidewalks between the buildings. Pastor Logan, the senior pastor, stood by the sidewalk along the way. I'd heard that sadly he'd just lost his father.

"You're brave," Pastor Logan said, when he saw me walking by with the baby.

I paused and looked at him, "You're brave, too," I added quietly.

We both nodded without saying more. Both statements were painfully true so we just moved on in separate directions.

~~~

Hannah and Henry and their daughter, Hailey, came over again after Sunday naptime. Hannah again made dinner in my kitchen, this time bringing more food from her own house. Again, I felt grateful and relieved to not have to wait alone for Kirk's return, or worry about what to do for dinner.

Around 5:00 PM, knocking sounded at the door. Holding my breath and opening it, I found my two tired girls, who were in need of their previous Saturday night baths, standing there looking up at me. Looking past them, my eyes caught sight of Kirk whizzing away in his vehicle.

After supper, Hannah and Henry watched the baby while I put the girls to bed.

"Leanne spent the night," Nicole confirmed the name I suspected, and shockwaves at Kirk's audacity took my breath away.

"Daddy gave us a kitten!" Meaghan piped in sitting up in her bed.

Nicole reported from under her blanket, "Daddy had to leave us so that he could take care of his stray kitten. He says we can bring it back here if you'll let us."

"Will you let us bring home the kitten to keep it, Mommy?" Meaghan chimed in.

The report was distressing, but I was just so glad to have them safely back home.

~~~

"For a man's ways are in full view of the LORD,
and he examines all his paths."
Proverbs 5:21

~~~

Monday, August 23, 1999

I awoke to the worship music playing in the background so my thoughts flew first to Him in praise and in worship, and then followed in supplication.

"Lord, I can't believe that Kirk has had this woman over while the girls were there! And for their first overnight!" The lack of morals he had displayed for our children appalled me. His actions so contrasted from the Kirk I'd thought I'd known. Jolts of shock stabbed at my consciousness once again.

Watching the clock, I waited for the lawyer's office to open. Then I phoned Chloe.

I explained to her how Kirk had changed the agreed-upon schedule by taking them on Friday, and then refusing to bring them back as promised on Saturday. Next, I explained about the other woman spending the night while the girls were there!

"Well, it sounds like there needs to be a visitation schedule in place so that he knows when it's appropriate to come by," she counseled. "That is generally the way it's done. When you meet with the mediator, he'll help you go over that. But in the meantime, you might want to already have something in place," said Chloe.

"What about him having this other women spend the night while the girls are there?" I asked, frustrated and horrified that Kirk would do that. "How can he do this? And in front of our kids? He is a married man!"

"Well, it's too bad that he's doing that," Chloe said. "I can request that he not do it when I write a letter to his lawyer, but there is not much you can do about it, I'm sorry to say.

Chloe continued, "However, another reason that you might want to steer away from overnight visitations besides that," she counseled, "is because the court calculates child support based on the amount of hours with each parent.

"So, if he has them overnight," she continued, "then he'll have them for more hours, and then he'll be required to pay less child support. This could have a huge effect upon you and the children."

I felt another stomach blow as I digested the new information which tasted like sawdust.

Chloe sent a letter to Kirk's attorney recommending a possible visitation schedule and requesting that the other woman not be involved in the visits. She also asked that money be deposited for the bills, and then she added the routine requests of no drug or alcohol allowed present during visitations, and no critical comments made about the other parent in the presence of the children.

I was quickly getting an unwanted education about the legal system and divorce law.

~~~

Every day was busy because it held all the regular activities of caring for the children. The house still needed cleaned and the bills still required attention. Many hours, in addition, were being consumed in learning the court system and in praying through the crisis.

Sometimes, the girls and I took walks to the park with David in his stroller. My senses seemed heightened and I noticed the little things which I'd overlooked before.

For instance, the row of rosebushes growing inside the white picket fence of our neighbor's yard – I found them striking and felt privileged to see their beauty. I couldn't believe I hadn't really seen them before. And, I so appreciated the sun warming us from the sky.

I did not take anything for granted anymore. Every small blessing was a gift that I noticed, and I thanked God for each one.

Today, Nicole had another swim lesson and thankfully, another meal was being dropped off from the Hillside Mother's Club.

Emilie phoned to ask if she could come over to visit with the girls and to help out by reading stories at bedtime. It was great to have an extra set of hands in the evening so that I could give each child individual attention and talk time.

And daily, there were the prayer times with both Miriam and Ginny.

~~~

"Finally, be strong in the Lord
and in his mighty power.
Put on the full armor of God
so that you can take your stand
against the devil's schemes.
For our struggle is not against flesh and blood,
but against the rulers, against the authorities,
against the powers of this dark world
and against the spiritual forces of evil
in the heavenly realms."
Ephesians 6: 10-12

~~~

Tuesday, August 24, 1999

Kirk phoned early in the day. His tone sounded frustrated and threatening. He played on my fears that he might take away the children and not return them when he had them for scheduled visits.

He changed his mind from what he'd promised before and said that now he would not let the children move back to Maryland. "And," he added, "California courts rule in the favor of the father."

It was tiring and draining to have to face Kirk on a continual basis. Kirk, once my protector, was now the one from whom I felt I needed protection.

But I knew that in actuality, Kirk contended not against me, but the Lord who was completely in charge of my life.

~~~

"Who is this uncircumcised Philistine
that he should defy the armies of the Living God?"
I Samuel 17:26b

~~~

"You come against me
with sword and spear and javelin,
but I come against you
in the name of the LORD Almighty,"
I Samuel 17:45

~~~

22

Walking it Out

"Janice?" Kayla questioned when I picked up the phone.

"Hi, Kayla!" I responded, very glad to hear the sound of her voice.

"Hey, how about having my daughter, Kit, babysit your girls tonight and you and I go to an Aglow prayer meeting? You can bring the baby with you," Kayla offered.

"Oh, that sounds great!" I said, already looking forward to an evening out and heading to the closet to thumb through the clean clothes.

~~~

Kayla dropped by with Kit after dinner and we left her teenage daughter with my girls to play.

"Can you drive?" Kayla asked.

"Sure," I agreed, walking with her toward my car with David in his carseat.

Kayla tried to remember the directions of where we were meeting. As we drove out of Hillside, we talked about what had happened with Kirk most recently.

Soon we drew nearer to our destination. But the closer we got and the more that we talked, the more that I could not withhold the tears. At last, we arrived and I pulled the car to a stop.

Kayla popped out and called, "Let's go inside, Janice. They're waiting for us."

We knocked at the front door and my tears continued. There was nothing I could do to stop them.

Several strangers met us at the door. The one that knew Kayla took her into the kitchen where they assembled refreshments. The others, about three or four ladies, guided me into the living room.

These women gathered around me, one touching my shoulder and another handing me tissues, and they began to pray in the Spirit. I knew none of them, but it didn't matter because we all knew the Lord.

"You know," one lady in a pretty red scarf spoke up, "I believe the Lord is saying that He is ultimately causing what is best for you and your children in all that is happening to you right now, and to be assured that He has a good plan for your family."

I wondered if this could mean that Kirk might come back.

The prayers continued on with me sitting in the center seat.

When Kayla and the hostess returned to the living room for our meeting, I felt a peaceful refreshment and I knew that God was touching me with His healing care.

~~~

"And pray in the Spirit on all occasions
with all kinds of prayers and requests.
With this in mind, be alert
and always keep on praying for all the saints."
Ephesians 6:18

~~~

Wednesday, August 25, 1999

Preparing to meet the mediator in the midst of caring for the children was a huge burden, but many friends helped out. Still, there was much nursing, changing of diapers, laundry, grocery shopping, and tucking little ones into bed with special talk time.

My lawyer assured me that the time spent in preparation was even more important than my court date because of how seriously the judge would lean on the mediator's opinion.

Chloe directed that I prepare my requests clearly with documented support to include the following:

1. <u>Request to Move Back to Maryland</u>
   <u>with the Children.</u>
   - • I have no family in California.
   - *- Include letter from parents who request we move home and can support us emotionally as well as through homeschooling.*
   - *- Include recommendation letter from family counselor at Kaiser stating the importance of family support during a crisis such as this one.*

   - • We have lived here only 3 years and husband has moved us around frequently taking better job offers.
   - *- Include list of 7 addresses we have held in the last 9 years.*
   - • Maryland has been a place of stability I have always returned to on vacation to see family and growing-up friends.
   - • I have a plan in place for children to maintain significant contact with their father if permitted to live in Maryland.
   - *- Include well thought-out workable plan.*
   - • Include report from realtor about the housing market and specifically our home in California which would need to be sold.

2. <u>Request to Continue</u>
   <u>Homeschooling Children.</u>
   - • Husband and I agreed and have been successfully home-schooling since last January.
   - *- Include recommendation letter from Paula who has seen me perform as a teacher and is also a veteran homeschooler.*
   - *- Include Nicole's progress in reading at a 2nd grade level at age five.*
   - *- Include list of homeschool field trips we have taken.*

   - • In previous discussions, husband has requested to take part in the homeschool process and we have discussed how he might do it in these ways:
   - *- Include list of specific ways.*
   - • I have researched the umbrella school we would use in Maryland

- Include packet of information from Family Schools Program in Maryland.

~~~

*"Shadrach, Meshach and Abednego
replied to the king,
'O Nebuchadnezzar, we do not need
to defend ourselves before you in this matter.
If we are thrown into the blazing furnace,
the God we serve is able to save us from it,
and he will rescue us from your hand, O king.
But even if he does not,
we want you to know, O king,
that we will not serve your gods
or worship the image of gold you have set up.'"*
Daniel 3:16-18

~~~

"Well, it sure needs work before it could be listed," Robyn, the realtor, said as she peered through the house.

Robyn was the woman who had helped us acquire this fixer-upper home two years before. We had enjoyed her quip and laughed at her stories and she'd been accurate as to her predictions of the housing market.

I'd phoned her to get an estimate and some advice in order to provide the mediator with all the possible information needed so I could get permission to move back to Maryland.

"Okay," she continued, "the front needs some landscaping. I would just give an allowance of $3000 for the backyard because it needs so much work.

"All that Kirk was in the middle of – like the front door and the sliding glass one in the living room – needs to be finished and framed. I think the yellow cabinets in the bathroom should be painted white. In the office and the bedroom, either the hardwood floors need to be repaired or covered with carpet."

Robyn continued on and on adding items to the to-do list with every step she took. I studiously took notes of all that she said.

A huge amount of work had already been accomplished in this fixer-upper home that we had been able to purchase just because of the poor condition it had been in. But the list of work that needed to be completed was greater than I had expected.

After Robyn left, I phoned Kirk to suggest we decide on a visitation schedule. He didn't answer, so I left a message. Then I had a short time to clean and work before Frankie returned the girls, whom she'd picked up to take on a homeschool field trip to the bakery.

~~~

Thursday, August 26, 1999

Before walking out the door to attend an informational orientation at the courthouse, Kirk phoned.

"Hi, Janice," Kirk said. "I'm going to come over tonight and have a visit with the kids."

He didn't ask me, he just told me. I felt bullied. He hung up after he handed me his newest edict without waiting to hear if I had anything to say.

Emilie then phoned and I explained to her the call I'd just received from Kirk. "Oh," she said, "how 'bout my husband, Ed, coming over and just being there, too, so that you are not alone, Janice?"

"Yes," I agreed. I felt much more comfortable with that.

I phoned Kirk and left a message that Ed would also be there in the evening.

Kirk phoned back and announced he would not be coming over.

~~~

"Hello?" I answered the phone again in the afternoon while the kids were playing. It was Chloe. Shushing the kids with a finger over my lips and slipping into the garage, I did not want to postpone her as I was aware that every minute of her time counted in coins.

"Janice," Chloe said, "I received a fax from Kirk's lawyer in response to my letter earlier this week and I thought you should know about it."

"You did?" I asked, dread rising.

"Yes, the letter from Ms. Rochelle states that they believe you will not allow Kirk to see the children unless you are present and so they threaten to request that the sole physical custody of the children go to Mr. Lynch.

"Also, the letter states: *We hereby provide notification to you that Mr. Lynch does not consent to the homeschooling of any of the children. Nicole is now of public school age and should be enrolled immediately in kinder-garten, to begin with her classmates on opening day in September."*

I felt fear rise from this intimidation and the emptiness of speaking through attorneys, whose benefit was financial.

~~~

"Even though I walk through the valley
of the shadow of death,
I will fear no evil, for you are with me;
your rod and your staff, they comfort me."
Psalm 23:4

~~~

23

Fear in the Night

Thursday, August 26, 1999

A t night, after the kids were in bed, I'd climb into the green-canopy wrought-iron bed anticipating a few hours of sleep before the baby awakened to be nursed.

In the background, soft familiar words of the praise and worship music played on repeat. By my bed, a cup of water sat on a table to help with hydration. By it, the baby monitor rested with its small red light, and behind it, the telephone lay in its holder.

Usually I fell asleep feeling secure and peaceful. Like a baby, I sensed that I lay on my heavenly Father's chest during the night season, safe in His embrace, carried by Him as if I were a newborn like David. I slept deeply, and I returned to sleep quickly after nursing baby David in the middle of each night.

But one night it happened in a different way.

This night, right before bedtime, I had been talking with a friend about Kirk and the whole situation involving his leaving me. "How could it be that he was acting so strange? How could it be that he said the things he did that did not make logical sense?"

We began to speculate: "Was he on drugs? Were there other people involved in some sort of a crime ring? Did he get whomever it was pregnant and then feel cornered into his decision to leave and keep another promise made out of total desperation?" Our thoughts and our imaginations stretched as my friend and I talked.

Instead of focusing on God in prayer and praise before bedtime, I continued to dwell on all of the possibilities my friend and I had discussed.

Then I heard it: a noise. *What was that?* I wondered. Kirk still had the keys to our house and he could enter it any time he wanted. My body tightened and I listened closer. I heard another noise. What should I do?

I knew that usually houses settle and there are noises to be heard at night. But what if somebody were there?

My heart began to pound. My hands began to shake. My breathing slowed and I took careful, shallow breaths, trying not to make a sound.

Our bedroom was in the back of the house so I felt cut off from other entryways and views. Could somebody be in our fenced backyard?

I kept listening. I kept hearing more suspicious sounds. I kept wondering what Kirk was really up to, and what was really going on, and who else was involved, and what they were doing, and what they wanted.

In my mind, I made a decision. I reached for the phone, trying not to move more than I must and trying not to make a sound. Well, I reasoned, Hillside is a small town and the police don't have much to do. I dialed 911 by feeling the buttons in the dark.

An operator answered.

"I think there's someone in my house," I whispered.

"Okay, hang on," she said. "What is your house number and street name?"

I gave it to her as quietly as I could.

"Do you have any dogs?"

"No," I responded in a low voice.

"Okay, two officers are already nearby and they'll search around the outside of the house first. Just stay where you are and stay on the phone, okay?" she commanded in a calm, directing tone.

"Okay," I answered, thankful for her support. "Hey, I see flashlights outside."

"That's them. Just hang on, they'll come inside next," she talked me through.

Soon, I heard a loud rapping on the front door. Pulling on my rosy bathrobe and slippers, I scurried as fast as I could to open the door.

Two large men dressed in uniform stepped inside. I felt flushed, stupid, and thankful at the same time.

"Ma'am, do you mind if we check inside?" they asked. Carrying their flashlights, they went into the kids' bathroom, and then looked in their bedrooms, closets, the living room, dining room, and then the garage.

I continued standing there feeling awkward, but at the same time, glad to have their assistance.

They were kind. They understood. They offered to come back again if I phoned.

I fell into bed, and this time I focused on God and His care for me and mumbled Bible verses aloud. Soon I was asleep.

~~~

"'Because he loves me,' says the LORD,
'I will rescue him;
I will protect him,
for he acknowledges my name.'"
Psalm 91:14

~~~

Friday, August 27, 1999

The phone rang the next morning before I was ready to wake up.

"Janice?" I was beginning to get used to the coldness of Kirk calling me by my given name now.

Tired from the sudden adrenaline rushes, I sat up in bed and attempted to sound alert and focused.

I had to be on guard at all times. I had to wear a façade and never share any weakness or failure. For that was what he was looking for to capitalize on, to point a finger, to accuse, to attempt to tear down.

The lawyer had warned me that my actions now would determine how the judge would rule. Praise music reached me and soothed me as I stood to attention, trying to be awake.

"My parents are coming into town for a visit and I wanted to have the kids over while they are here," Kirk informed.

"Sure," I agreed. That idea appealed to me. I suspected the other woman would not be in this picture, and I wanted the children to see their grandparents. I ran my fingers through my tangled hair.

"So how about I have them Saturday, September 4th, overnight to Sunday?" Kirk requested.

"Sure, and then can we talk about what has happened and *why*, while your parents watch the kids, okay? You've promised to do so, remember?" I was still looking for a chink in his armor – something in that shield that he had up toward me that might crack open and allow me in again.

Kirk paused, then answered, "Okay." He didn't want to fix anything between us.

"Did you write down your thoughts in a letter as you offered?" I persisted, switching the phone to my other ear.

"Not yet. But we can talk while my parents are here watching the kids," Kirk said.

"Kirk," I began, changing the subject. "I received a very disturbing fax from your attorney to mine yesterday."

"What?" Kirk asked.

"It stated that you were against homeschooling and that Nicole should be enrolled immediately in public school," I blurted, now swinging my feet over the edge of the bed.

"I didn't say that," Kirk denied. "I just want to make sure that I can take part in the homeschooling process is all."

Feeling some relief, I said, "Really? Well, that is what my lawyer read to me that your lawyer faxed."

Hanging up after talking with Kirk, I fell backwards onto my bed to ponder the words he'd said. Kirk seemed calmer and less agitated this time. I was glad about his parents' soon arrival.

I didn't know what to think about the discrepancy between Kirk and his lawyer regarding the homeschooling.

I began to sing a praise song I knew from the Psalms.

~~~

"Some trust in chariots and some in horses,
but we trust in the name of the LORD our God."
Psalm 20:7

~~~

Thursday, September 2, 1999

"Hi," Ida said, when I answered the phone while still kneeling on the floor and pulling a dress over Meaghan for the day. I knew this conscientious woman from our church and also from the church's women's Bible study which I'd hosted in my home.

"Listen Janice," she continued before I could say anything. "I heard about what happened and I'm sorry. What I want you to know is this: I'm available today. Many days I'm not, but today I am. So I wanted to know if I could do anything for you."

"Well," I answered her, walking to the office and glancing at my calendar. "Do you know, we actually have nothing on the schedule for today.

I can't think of anything I need right now," I replied. "But I'm so grateful that you would ask."

"Okay, then. I'll just spend time interceding for you today then, okay?" she responded.

"That would be great," I said, hanging up the phone and marveling at how kind it was of her to think of me. I didn't know at the time that this woman's gift of availability would be a godsend.

~~~

Opening the mail, I noticed one of the letters was from my lawyer, Chloe. Inside she noted that she had spoken to Kirk's lawyer on the telephone and that she was now offering me her advice in light of this conversation.

My heart began to sink deeper as I read the letter.

He does not want you to move, my lawyer's letter stated. I thought about how Kirk had fluctuated back and forth over whether he would agree to my moving back to Maryland.

You may need to be prepared to pay $1500-3000 to a custody evaluator, if I wanted to 'prove' that my small children should live with me.

His lawyer states that 'Mr. Lynch should be able to see the children whenever he is not working or traveling.' Why is he so concerned about this now? He has spent so much of his time away from us.

Next the words suggested, *Perhaps you could plan to start babysitting other children, so as to give you earnings of minimum wage, approximately $950/month.* Now they want me to begin a new career? With a two-month-old baby and two small children, and right after my husband has left? When I haven't worked outside the home in so many years? Yes they did. I read on.

She (Kirk's lawyer) *will probably expect you to start working once your son is 3 months old. Perhaps you could plan to start babysitting other children. This way you could still breast-feed your son.* What? Can Kirk and his lawyer get away with these demands?

At the end, Chloe's letter read, *Your husband does not want the children homeschooled anymore, and therefore, your oldest should be immediately enrolled in kindergarten. I think the motivation is to get you to work asap so that support will reduce after awhile.*

The feeling of devastation crept up from my toes, covering my heart, dizzying my mind. I tried to blink back tears because the children were down the hall. They would need me soon.

How could this happen? I sat dazed on the blue couch, not moving a muscle. How could Kirk's lawyer be so against me and so crafty and so uncaring? How could Kirk endorse what she did and attempt to use her as a tool to lash out against me?

I wondered, do lawyers even think about what they are doing and how it will affect someone's life? Or, do they just plow on seeking the prestige of winning another case, regardless of the consequences to people?

I felt very, very defenseless. I felt like everything had been ripped from me. First my innocence in marriage, and now my motherhood was at stake.

Now was the time to remember that God was my Defender.

Meaghan called out for me from her bedroom, and so I stood up.

~~~

A few minutes later the phone rang again. Marcy, the leader of a local homeschool support group, phoned to check on us. Her group had recently sent a $200 check.

It turned out that Marcy's timing could not have been better. She knew California law in regards to homeschooling.

"Janice," she confided with softness in her voice, "our state law holds that children do not have to begin formal education until the age of six."

I breathed a sigh of relief for receiving that piece of information just when I needed it. Nicole still had another year before she could be forced into the public school system based on her age.

"Thank You, God! Thank You for showing me that Kirk's lawyer does not really know everything she is talking about." Her threats were aimed at bowling me over with intimidation, and she was attempting to hit a strike even before the court date arrived.

I made a note as to what I would add to my mediator's report: In California, children are not required to attend school until the age of six.

Include documentation.

24

Another Attack

Thursday, August 26, 1999

Meaghan awoke from her afternoon nap with a tummyache. Within the hour she was sick.

"Are you feeling better?" I asked, carrying in towels and lifting her back into bed to rest with a bucket by her side.

When she nodded from under her blanket, I went on to nurse a hungry David. Before I'd finished, I heard crying from her bedroom.

Nicole came into the family room to announce the news, "Mommy, Meaghan says she feels bad again." I could hear it.

After Meaghan had vomited for the third time in only an hour, I remembered Ida's offer to help. Maybe that is why God had led her to phone me today? Maybe she could pick up some Gatorade and drop it by the house?

I didn't think I could get all three kids into the car, and into Safeway and out, without Meaghan possibly being sick again. But we did need some groceries now.

"I'll pick up some things and be right over," Ida promised.

"Oh, but, you probably don't want to be around this flu bug," I reminded her.

"It's okay, Janice. I've got a medical background. I'll come and help you today," Ida replied.

And help me she did. Ida came over at 5:00 PM and stayed until midnight. All evening long, two-three times an hour, Meaghan got sick to her stomach. I would have been 'scared silly' if Ida hadn't been a trained nurse and known what to do.

The other amazing fact that I had not been aware of was that Ida had experienced a similar type of betrayal. She ministered to me from her experience which she had come through whole and healed, and as one who could really understand.

While we conversed, we fell into a routine: 'It's time, pass the bowl'; 'She's done, dump the bowl'; 'Now she needs her fluids, pass the Gatorade.' And, less than a half-hour later, 'Pass the bowl again.'

We sat by Meaghan's side as she lay in the family room on the blue couch. We wiped her brow and smoothed her hair and helped her to sit up when needed.

I marveled again at God's perfect provision for me and the children in providing Ida for this day.

~~~

"'And why do you worry about clothes?
See how the lilies of the field grow.
They do not labor or spin.
Yet I tell you that not even Solomon in all his splendor
was dressed like one of these.
If that is how God clothes the grass of the field,
which is here today and tomorrow
is thrown into the fire,
will he not much more clothe you, O you of little faith?
So do not worry, saying, "What shall we eat?"
or "What shall we drink?" or "What shall we wear?"
For the pagans run after all these things,
and your heavenly Father knows that you need them.
But seek first his kingdom and his righteousness,
and all these things will be given to you as well.'"
Matthew 6:28-33

~~~

Friday, September 3, 1999
Meaghan slept through the night and had only been sick a couple of times in the morning. Hopefully this flu was ending and none of the rest of us would get sick.

Hannah dropped by another bag of groceries when she heard about our dilemma. She dropped it and ran, because she was newly pregnant and couldn't take a risk.

Before I even called, He answered. Before I even knew I had a need, He provided.

~~~

Dread filled me when I spied another letter from the lawyer on the garage floor where it fell from the mail slot. When would receiving the mail stop feeling like a nightmare-in-the-making? Was this another ridiculously high lawyer's bill? Or some more discouraging advice?

"God," I talked to Him first, "You know all things and You are not surprised by anything. Help me to be more aware of You than I am of whatever new piece of information I might find in this letter. Thank You, God, for how You've shown incredible care for me already."

Inside, I found Kirk's *Responsive Declaration* to the statements which my lawyer had filed with the court.

Kirk Lynch declares as follows:

1. The Respondent and I have lived in California for three years. During that time we have become well connected to our community. I intend to make California my permanent home.

2. I have been very actively involved in my children's upbringing. I live in an apartment close to our family residence. I have arranged for my work hours to be flexible in order to spend as much time as possible with the children.

3. Now that the Respondent and I have ended our marriage, the Respondent will need to return to work. I believe that our children will be best cared for under a joint legal and physical custody arrangement, spending equal time with both parents. While we are working, they would be cared for by a daycare provider. I oppose the Respondent's request that she be allowed to move away with our children. Our oldest child, now age five-and-a-half should begin kindergarten in public school.

4. I agree to pay guideline child support. I oppose the request for spousal support and request that Respondent be ordered immediately to seek work. Respondent's request for attorney's fees and costs should be reserved until our marital assets have been divided.

The lawyer had drawn up the statement.
And Kirk had signed it.

~~~

Saturday, September 4, 1999

I awakened early to the praise music as usual, but though the words soothed me, I just didn't feel right.

The Promise Keepers men's group planned to come this morning to fix some of what Kirk had left undone. I had to get up and get dressed.

It had not been so long ago, I thought, that Kirk *had been* a Promise Keeper.

It was then that the bitter taste came into my mouth. Running to the bathroom, I made it just in time. "Ohhh," I stayed there on the floor, weak, and trying to recover, hugging the toilet. And that's when David's cries to nurse penetrated the bathroom.

Next it was Nicole who got sick.

Picking up the ringing phone, I heard Kirk's voice. He wanted to remind me of his parents' arrival and how he'd be there at 5:00 PM for the girls.

I explained that we all had the stomach flu.

Reluctantly, he said he would phone later to check, but he still wanted to take them.

Before I knew it, Ida was back, along with Kayla, to give nursing care to the girls and me.

The seven men doing repairs walked in and out of doors and throughout the house. I answered their questions without moving from my spot on the old, blue couch.

They covered outlets, cut the long grass in the rear, fixed the broken gate leading to the backyard, and, most of all – changed out the deadbolts so that I didn't need to fear if or when Kirk might try to re-enter the home with his key.

I felt fragile laying there, but thanksgiving flowed for all the people who took care of everything we needed.

By 5:00 PM everyone had gone home and Kirk had picked up the girls as scheduled. He wanted them with him when his parents arrived.

Searching for more clues as to what Kirk was doing, I checked the credit card. Kirk had been buying gas in the location near the address of the 'other woman' earlier that day.

~~~

Sunday, September 5, 1999

I poked through the refrigerator looking for ideas for dinner because the girls were supposed to be home any moment. But the phone rang instead.

"Janice," Kirk said, "Meaghan has been throwing up again so I am going to keep her here. I'll bring the girls back tomorrow at 3:00 PM along with my parents, and then they can meet David."

Again Kirk had kept the girls and changed the schedule at the last minute. Kirk still withheld information about where he took the children.

"God," I prayed again, "I thank You that Kirk is a tool in Your hands used to bless me."

I continued my much needed rest and recovery from the flu, and thankfully the baby did not get it.

Unfortunately, Kirk's parents did come down with a bad case of it later in the week.

~~~

Monday, September 6, 1999

I waited and watched out the window for Kirk, the girls, and his parents to arrive at 3:00 PM.

I tried to look my best which felt hard to do after recently giving birth. I wondered what were they thinking of me. Would they be in agreement with their son that this 'East Coast girl' deserved to be tossed aside like an old garment?

Dressing David in a cute little blue-and-green jersey with a matching cap, I played with him on my lap while I waited.

Finally, just a few minutes after the scheduled time, an SUV that I did not recognize pulled into the driveway. The girls and their grandparents piled out and approached the front door, talking as they came.

Dick and Darlene, though gray, were still active and greeted me as they had in the past, hugging me and smiling as if nothing had happened.

They took David from my arms and sat down on the old, blue couch to admire him, check out all his features, and elicit little smiles from his sweet lips. Kirk stood over the baby also, obviously proud of him. The girls scurried off to get favorite toys from their bedroom to show their grandparents.

Soon Darlene offered to take the girls outside so that they could ride their trikes. Dick followed, leaving Kirk and me alone in the family room for the first time since he'd left.

Facing each other while sitting in chairs across the room, he looked at me, but his lips were shut tight. His jaw was tensed and he appeared determined to remain silent.

"Is that your SUV outside?" I began since he said nothing.

"A friend lent it to me," Kirk replied.

A female friend? I wondered.

Now Kirk stared at the floor, still not offering anything for the conversation. I could see that he did not want to be there.

"Why is it that you left me?" I asked him with distress.

"I don't want you to move the kids to Maryland." Kirk ignored my question altogether.

"What?" I said, feeling the tears come. "But you said that I could."

"I want to co-parent the kids, Janice. I want to have equal time with them. You can find some work. I don't intend to pay spousal support for longer than six months." Kirk finished his rehearsed statements.

There was nothing left to do but to let him go. Discouragement, but not surprise, attempted to sweep over me because I could not do anything to effect Kirk's mind.

I could not seem to touch Kirk, or to reach him, or to find him even in there. He was like an empty shell whose heart and soul had moved out. But when had that happened?

To me, it seemed all of a sudden.

His heart was so cold toward me. If I had felt any inkling of response from him, I could have told him how angry I was at him for what he was doing to me, and to our own beloved children. But how could one express anger at someone who was not even there, who was gone, who did not even care?

Kirk left to go outside. I went to the bathroom.

"But," I declared aloud to my mirror image, "God's ears are not too dull to hear, and His arm is not too short to save," (Isaiah 59:1).

Tears streamed down my face.

~~~

"You will forgive him, won't you?" pleaded Kirk's fair-skinned mother, Darlene, privately, where we stood in the foyer. Kirk and his father talked on the driveway, watching the girls play during their short visit.

"I do and I will," I said, realizing that my own mental health depended on it.

"I just know that Kirk will change his mind and regret what he is doing," she said, connecting with my eyes through her glasses.

I looked at her but did not respond, because I just wasn't quite so sure. My heart welled up in more sadness as I realized the likelihood that I would not only lose my husband, but also his family.

Darlene must have recognized my doubt. She touched my elbow and added further, "I think, *I know*, that sometimes he feels that he is losing his mind these days."

Her words confirmed to me that our prayers were effective. Much spiritual warfare was undoubtedly taking place.

I knew that God was reaching out to Kirk, giving him every opportunity to repent and to turn from his destructive course.

This new glimpse from his mother gave me fresh hope.

25

Prejudice

Thursday, September 9, 1999

I t was toward the end of the work day and the large Kaiser campus in Hillside was quiet. I found my way to the pharmacy to pick up a prescription for Nicole just before the office closed.

The day was pretty and sunny and I walked in the outside corridor made of see-through glass and leading over the green lawn between the buildings. At the last moment, I decided to take the outside shortcut back to the parking lot.

I pushed through the heavy door still declaring praises to God under my breath to keep my thoughts focused. I found myself face-to-face with Nurse Taylor. In her 50's, shoulder-length gray hair, thin, and one who did her job with quiet excellence, she was the nurse practitioner who had seen me the most during my pregnancy.

"Nurse Taylor!" I exclaimed, disregarding small talk, "You wouldn't believe what happened to me. I had the baby, and my husband walked out on me. He left me for another woman!"

Within an instant, Nurse Taylor threw her arms around me. "I am so sorry, I am so sorry," she said, then released me, and shook her head while speaking with her Irish accent, "it happened to me too."

She looked into my eyes with sadness and understanding. We both just stood there then, quiet.

"I'm writing a book about it," she added. "The title is *What Women Do to Women*."

I knew that it was no accident that I had opened the door to come face-to-face with Nurse Taylor who could understand and encourage me just by being there, just by knowing. I came to realize that there was an unspoken club out there of which I had become a member – the *Left-By-Your-Husband Club*.

It was an exclusive membership of which only, hopefully, a few could belong – and there existed an unexplained camaraderie, and a strong tie between even strangers.

~~~

Sunday, September 12, 1999

It was Sunday, so I sat in a church pew again, alone, but with the comfort of my little baby to hold in my arms.

He needed my care and he was so sweet and so warm and so appreciative of all that I did for him. He rewarded me with smiles and cooperation, and the joy of having him with me. I stared down into his little sleeping face during the sermon.

Afterwards, I felt another warm body sit next to me and I looked up to see a new, caring face.

"Janice," the unfamiliar woman whispered, looking at me directly and speaking softly. "Here is the number for one of the key judges in the city.

"Call him at home," she continued, "because he will help you to understand what you will be facing in court. He will also tell you if there is anything more that you can do to help your case. Also, he knows all the people in the system and will tell you specifics about whom you'll meet."

"A judge?" I asked, not quite believing my ears. "A judge… would talk… *to me?*" I looked at this stranger, and I wondered how could this middle-aged woman in silver high heels possibly know about my situation. Who could have told her?

It turned out that she was a friend-of-a-friend, someone's neighbor.

"Yes, and he cares about what happens to families. Phone him, okay? I've told him about you, and he is expecting your call," she said, then slipped away.

"Yes, I will," I called after her, holding the little slip of paper. New excitement infused me as God amazingly provided yet again! God truly owned 'the cattle on one thousand hills' and could use each one of them for His purposes as He chose.

~~~

My attempt to phone the judge that evening yielded no results as he was not in when I called. So instead I worked more on my list of questions to ask him.

Meanwhile, I had concerns about my lawyer. She had helped me to prepare with excellence for the mediation, it seemed, but she also acted intimidated by Kirk's lawyer. She appeared to bow to her threats. This would not do. I needed someone to stand up for me. But I had already enlisted her and I felt stuck.

Did anyone see, or care, that Kirk was the one who had committed adultery and left me? Didn't that count against him? How could he and his lawyer tell me I had no say about my husband's choice to divorce me and now little say about my children's future?

Such is the case of no-fault divorce law – the only concern of the courts is to divide up assets (and children) logically, impartially, and equitably.

Where was God in this equation?

I remembered His Word and that He was ultimately in charge. I submitted my life and its outcomes to Him.

~~~

"The thief comes only to steal and kill and destroy;
I have come that they may have life,
and have it to the full."
John 10:10

~~~

Monday, September 13, 1999

One of the hardest parts of the experience was that of other people's opinions and prejudices – especially, sometimes, when they came from a close friend. I lost at least one.

Some people seemed driven by their own preconceived notions of what a divorce is about with little regard for my specific circumstances.

While sitting at the desk in the office, I received a call. "I just don't understand, Janice, why you are letting Kirk leave you?"

"*Letting* him leave me?" I repeated, wondering if I had heard her correctly.

"Yes, I mean, you are helping him to leave you," she explained.

"Well," I said, feeling the air knocked out of me at her accusation, "what do you think I should be doing about it?" I paused, taking in what she'd said.

Maybe I was missing something. Maybe there was something different that I could do to save our marriage.

I continued, "How can I do things another way? Really, honestly, I do not want him to be leaving me. I pray for him all the time, asking God to change his heart."

Now suddenly I felt weary all over and exhausted by the many challenges arising from so many different places. This time I had to struggle with it coming from a good friend. But I stayed in place on the chair in our office while I held the phone to my ear, and determined to listen.

"Have you tried marriage counseling?" she asked.

"I would love to try it," I said, picking up a pencil. "Truthfully, I just don't think Kirk will do it."

"Well, have you tried?" she pressed.

"No, you're right. I should try. Do you know of any place where we could get counseling?" I asked. "He's refused to talk to anyone from the church. In fact, he has turned down contact with any of our friends." I poked with the pencil on a pad of paper.

"Why don't you try calling your medical insurance to see what they offer? He might be open to something that's not Christian, and maybe it could still help?" she suggested.

"Okay, thank you. I will try." I hung up the phone.

Maybe... maybe... maybe it would work. But, deep inside I asked myself, who was I kidding? I knew Kirk. He didn't change his mind when he made a big decision. But I would try anyway.

Phoning Kaiser, I scheduled a counseling appointment.

Barbara, a grandmother who served in AWANA Club with me had called earlier that day with an offer to babysit. She agreed to work out her schedule in order to come over during the appointment the next evening.

Then I phoned Kirk at work. "Hi Kirk," I said. "It's me, Janice. Listen, our friend suggested marriage counseling. I thought it was a good idea. So, I set up an appointment with Kaiser and I have a babysitter worked out. Do you think you could make it tomorrow at 7:00 PM?" I asked.

"Uh, I don't have anything on my calendar. I... I'll try to make it," he said, hesitating, sounding like he was caught off-guard and did not have words to answer this unexpected request.

~~~

There were other friends, too, who added to the stress – all without meaning to, and all who had very good intentions. I loved them dearly – but their expectations of me from their worlds – far outside the realm of what I was living – sometimes tempted me with confusion or discouragement.

I've heard others say that this is common with almost any major crisis that one goes through. Well-meaning friends, or even strangers, try to find something helpful to say. But instead the words can be like sand thrown in one's eyes. I know because sometimes I've said the wrong thing myself to those I've cared about and tried to help.

One friend told me that I should wear certain clothing to allure Kirk – that doing this might fix the situation. So I tried this one evening when Kirk was due to pick up the kids. Kirk just looked at me and seemed amused.

Somebody else said that she knew a woman whose husband had left her for someone else, so she stationed herself physically on the sidewalk outside of where this other woman lived and where her husband was staying. Day-in and day-out, she positioned herself there until he eventually did return. I wondered what she did with her small children while she set up camp on his sidewalk?

Yet another person said that she'd known about a woman who had sought out the 'other woman' and allowed her to abuse her verbally and otherwise, again and again, to show her God's love. Eventually, the 'other woman' broke down, accepted Jesus, and stopped the affair. Then her husband had returned to her.

~~~

I had to remind myself that I was praying constantly, and that God was leading me each step of the way. I trusted Him.

I did not want to divorce Kirk over his adultery even though I knew that the Bible stated that divorce was permissible under these circumstances. I still believed it was possible for God's love and healing to work through us to restore our marriage.

Another reason I did not want a divorce was because our decisions would have far-reaching effects on our children and all those who knew us.

When the opportunity presented itself, I continued to remind Kirk that I wanted to consider the option of reconciliation even now.

~~~

In the evening, I phoned the judge once more after I'd settled the children in bed. This time he came to the phone and my heart pounded in my chest.

"I've heard what has happened to you, and I'm sorry," said the judge.

"Thank you, and thank you for taking the time to talk to me," I said, trembling and sitting in my rocker-glider, pad and paper ready to take notes. "First," I asked, "does the court really not care about how my husband left me with three kids including a newborn, for another woman?"

"That is not something they would allow you to bring up in your report," he answered, too matter-of-fact for the emotional tearing, the hurt, and the wrongness that I felt over the situation.

I moved to sit on the floor instead. "How can it be that they don't care about the circumstances?" I asked, incredulous, but I already knew that California was a 'no-fault state.' I continued, "Well, what do you think about the lawyer that I have employed, Chloe?"

"She is a good associate, but I'd be more comfortable with the head of her firm just due to more years of experience," he answered.

"What about Kirk's lawyer?" I asked, scribbling down the judge's answers as fast as I could.

"His lawyer is known for being very aggressive and often successful. She is one who has openly 'come out' and values an anti-traditional family belief system," he informed me.

"Well, that certainly lines up with what I have seen of her actions. Would you recommend that I switch lawyers?" I asked, sitting cross-legged now.

"I'd feel more comfortable if you had someone better suited to stand up for you against the lawyer that your husband has chosen. I would recommend a man named Mr. Maxwell." He gave me his phone number.

"But can you switch lawyers midway?" I asked, fearful of making her feel bad.

"It happens all the time," the judge answered.

"I am so glad that you can give me some insight about all this," I said, relieved to have his perspective. Holding the phone tight to my ear so that I would not miss a word, I asked, "What about the judge that has been assigned to hear the case?"

"I'd say he is conscientious, that he listens, and that he is coming from a liberal point-of-view," responded the judge.

"And how about the mediator that has been assigned to our case?" I asked, standing up now and then taking a seat on the couch.

"I'd say he's very good at his job," the judge told me.

"If Kirk agrees that I can move to Maryland with the kids, how much time would the court recommend for visits?" I asked.

"Very minimal. Two to four weeks during the summer. Maybe a week for Christmas and Easter," he said.

"And alimony?" I wanted to know, turning to a blank page in my notebook.

"Alimony is generally paid for half the life of a marriage. Unless the marriage has lasted for over ten years, and then it can be more," the judge said.

"That's too bad," I said, "we are so close to that ten-year mark."

"Protect yourself if you can tax-wise. Choose less alimony which is taxable, and more child support which is not taxable and lasts longer," informed the judge.

"Thank you so much for taking the time to answer my questions," I said, laying my pen down. "It has been really helpful and I am so grateful."

"Glad to have helped, goodbye now." The call concluded after only a few minutes – I was aware that his time was valuable.

The judge had been guarded and careful to give only basic, public information that most people would generally know about in the system. But it was information that I would not have come across in my stay-at-home mother world, and it was information that would prove extremely important in preparing for my case.

Again, I marveled in amazement at God's provision and help for me. I felt His closeness, and I knew that I was not alone. The battle and the outcome were His.

~~~

"The horse is made ready for the day of battle,
but victory rests with the LORD."
Proverbs 21:31

~~~

26

God Leads Again

Tuesday, September 14, 1999

The next morning, I gathered the notebook with the phone number of the lawyer that the judge had recommended, and I closed the door of our office before the girls had awakened.

"Hello?" I said to the secretary who picked up at the firm. "I would like to schedule an appointment with the lawyer of your office as soon as possible."

"Ma'am," the secretary informed me, "Mr. Maxwell is not currently accepting any new clients. His caseload is full."

My heart sank. I had expected this to be easy. "Oh," I said. "Well, can you ask him about taking me?" I pursued. "He was recommended to me by a judge that he knows." I gave her the judge's name and sat, tense in the chair.

"Well, that is very nice, ma'am," she said, obviously not believing what I said was true, "but I doubt that he will be able to take you. However, I'll give him the message."

"Okay, thank you very much." I said, full of suspense again and dreading the wait that would follow when I had such little time left. The court date was approaching in less than a month, on October 1st.

"God, I thank You that You can accomplish Your best plan. If this is the lawyer that I am supposed to have, You can make a way where there seems to be no way. And if he is not supposed to be my lawyer, then I thank You for closing this door, in Jesus' Name."

I continued to thank God aloud as I re-entered the hallway and began to get the girls dressed for the day.

My daily prayer partners agreed with me in prayer over the phone, and I met the demands of the day while praise and worship music filtered up into my ears whenever the activity of the home grew quieter.

~~~

I exited the Kaiser complex once more, this time leaving from the evening counseling appointment. Kirk had been a no-show, never called, and never even answered his pager to tell me why he did not make the appointment.

"Ginny," I phoned my friend while standing in the lobby, "I have some time. Barbara is all set taking care of the girls this evening, and I'm done with my counseling appointment at Kaiser because Kirk never showed."

"No surprise there," she said.

"Yeah, you're right, but I wanted to give it a try anyway. But guess what? Instead, I got to tell the counselor all the things that God has been doing since Kirk left. I talked to her about forgiveness and praising God in all situations, and more!" I looked out the glass doors as I talked, my voice full of excitement.

"Really? How did she take that?" Ginny asked.

"Well, she seemed to enjoy the stories. She said that she didn't think I needed counseling so she didn't set up any more appointments. The best part was that she wrote a letter for the mediator to read beforehand that says, 'In my professional opinion, my client should be allowed to return home to Maryland with her children in order to be near her family.' Isn't that great?" I asked.

"God just used the whole situation for your good, again!" Ginny said. "Hey, Janice, tonight is the weeknight that Gene and my brother, Gabe, and another friend of theirs get together to praise and pray and prophesy. It's their men's prayer meeting. Do you want to meet me here and then we can drop by and ask them to pray for you?"

"Yes! That would be great!" I said.

~~~

Ginny's husband, brother, and their friend were expecting us. So when we knocked at her brother's door, it opened right away. Ginny and I sat down with them in the living room on the couches and chairs provided and they dived right into praying for me.

Ginny's brother, Gabe, who didn't know as much about my situation as her husband did, took the lead in prayer. After awhile, he opened his eyes and stared at me and said, "Janice, you are doing everything right, aren't you?"

"Well, I don't know," I said, looking up at him, not knowing if I could be sure of a thing like that.

"You're just doing everything right," he repeated, unwavering, not moving his eyes from mine. "You are walking this thing out and you are in the right place," Gabe paused. "In fact, when I pray for you, your future looks so bright that I am actually feeling jealous!"

~~~

Wednesday, September 15, 1999

Frankie had started to pick up my girls regularly for weekly home-school field trips and I was grateful. Today was only two days away from the appointment with the mediator. I had to go to the courthouse to drop off more paperwork that I had collected for the case.

In the courthouse was a room of about twelve available computers which I'd learned about from the required orientation. On these computers was a software program called *The DissoMaster*.

If variables such as the number of children, wages earned and by which parent, other assets or tax concerns, daycare expenses, and the number of hours each parent spent with the children were plugged into the computer, then it would spit out a yearly, monthly, or bi-weekly figure for spousal support and/or child support. This figure was called 'Guideline Support' and would be used to support the judge's ruling.

Kirk's figures for monthly deposits into my bank account were on target with the basic software recommendations.

I spent many hours playing with the numbers at the courthouse while I rocked David in his carseat with my foot, and while the girls were being cared for by friends and neighbors. I looked again and again at all the different scenarios and outcomes dependent on the different variables.

Before leaving, with the click of a button I could print out the files to take home for further study.

~~~

An important time of my day was spent 'soaking in the Word.' This meant that I prayed for God to give me understanding and then I'd read a passage from the Bible. Next, I'd just sit there giving time to enjoy the words and time to let God speak to me from it.

Often the Holy Spirit seemed to highlight certain verses that I'd read that day that seemed meant just for me and my situation. Mulling them over was like eating food. It left me strengthened and refreshed.

For a while now, I'd been in the passage of Moses inquiring of the Pharaoh to 'let my people go!' If I couldn't have my marriage, then I prayed for the kids and me to return to Maryland to be near family.

~~~

> *"This is the confidence we have in approaching God:*
> *that if we ask anything according to his will,*
> *he hears us.*
> *And if we know that he hears us—*
> *whatever we ask—*
> *we know that we have what we asked of him."*
> I John 5:14, 15

~~~

Thursday, September 16, 1999

Rosalyn and Rhoda both lived over on another side of town, amongst large, beautiful, newer homes. They were friends of mine from church and from my first days at MOPS.

I'd met them shortly after we'd relocated to Hillside, and their husbands had extended offers to Kirk to join their small Promise Keepers men's meeting which took place early before work. Kirk had been part of Promise Keepers before, but Kirk had not found the time to join them.

"Why don't you bring the kids over for a playdate?" Rosalyn offered. "We'll have lunch and Rhoda and her kids can join us."

Relaxing on a couch with my two friends while our little children played, I told them all about what God was doing in my life. It was a restful morning, a nice break from the world of legal paperwork which I'd been forced to dive into, and it encouraged me as much as them to recount all the ways that God had been actively at work and answering prayers.

Refreshed, I began to gather the children and return to my car. As I left, they slipped me $100 in grocery gift cards and another $50 gift card to buy some new clothes for the kids at Gymboree.

I felt blessed over and over again. My time rehearsing God's goodness with them prepared me for the next day which was the mediation appointment at 9:30 AM.

~~~

With all the children home, tired, and down for their naps, I picked up the phone in the office to call the lawyer recommended to me by the judge.

My heart felt heavy as I remembered the secretary's discouraging words from before, but I reminded myself that God was in charge and that it was good whatever His answer would be. God alone knew what was best. True, I desperately wanted to have this new lawyer take my case now.

"Hello?" I said, when the secretary picked up the call. "This is Janice Lynch again. I was phoning to see if Mr. Maxwell could see me and take my case?" I moved some papers in front of me to the side of the desk.

"Well, ma'am," she answered, sounding friendlier and softer this time, "he's going to take your case."

"What?" I asked, shocked, putting the cap on my pen. "He is? I thought he was too full?"

"Well, he is full, ma'am," the secretary explained, "but the judge personally asked him to take your case this morning when he saw him in court.

"And this is the ironic thing, Mrs. Lynch. The client who held the spot that you needed for the court date on October 1st cancelled just five minutes before the judge asked Mr. Maxwell to represent you. So he had the opening available," the secretary explained.

"Wow!" I said, feeling so excited that I stood up and began to move. "That's great!"

"Yes, ma'am," she said. "So, let's schedule you an appointment to meet Mr. Maxwell."

~~~

"And my God will meet all your needs
according to his glorious riches in Christ Jesus."
Philippians 4:19

~~~

27

Kirk's Agitation

Kirk, who had been upset about the visitation with the kids, had agreed to meet me at Borders in the evening to discuss it. The senior pastor's wife and daughter had phoned to ask if they could babysit the girls, so it seemed right to meet with Kirk during the time he had requested.

I waited for Kirk at a table in the bookstore, pretending to take interest in a magazine. The truth was, it was hard to think about anything other than the circumstances I faced and the up-and-down teeter-totter that I felt like I was riding.

Kirk arrived shortly, and roughly pulled out his chair to sit down. He did not greet me or smile.

But my heart still sang praises because I'd met with friends in the morning, and then because the new lawyer had taken my case. Now I observed Kirk with steady eyes, not knowing what to expect from him.

Looking evenly back at me, Kirk stated his agenda: "I think we should divide the time with the kids equally."

I stared back, not responding.

"In fact," Kirk continued staring me down, "what do you think about switching them every other year?"

"What?" I said, not believing my ears again, and shuffling in my chair.

"You could have all three of them the first year," Kirk went on as he leaned over the table toward me, "and then I could take them the year after that. You could even have them with you in Maryland that way."

I could not believe what he'd just said. I refused to agree with it, noting that he was the one who had left, noting that he was still welcome to return and work things out, and noting that I planned to raise the kids with the Christian values that we had both determined from the beginning.

And I also noted that I intended to be part of their lives more than just every other year!

Kirk's face grew red and his chair screeched as he stood up. He stomped out of Borders, unwilling to share, discuss, negotiate, or have any real conversation.

I sighed. *That sure didn't get us any further.* I had hoped that we could have come to some agreement before the mediation appointment the next morning.

~~~

The pastor's wife and daughter had now gone, and the kids slept undisturbed by background household noises. I stayed in the family room in the rocker-glider, anticipating the next day and the important appointment with the mediator.

Having already prayed with my two prayer partners and wanting to relax for a while, I flipped on the Christian programming. It was comforting to hear the testimonies of God at work in others' lives.

On the screen was a phone number displayed if one wanted to call for prayer. I'd never broken out of my comfort zone or humbled myself before to call such a number. But I was desperate, and I phoned the number.

The Christian on the other end came alongside me to carry the load. Encouraged, I found that phoning a prayer ministry late at night when there was no one else available to talk with was yet another provision for me as I walked through the upcoming challenges.

28

God Convicts Me

Friday, September 17, 1999

The much-prepared-for mediation date had finally arrived. Many trips to the courthouse had now been run in order to use the infamous *DissoMaster* located in the room of computers, and in order to drop off the collected paperwork which Chloe had recommended.

Allison, the leader of MOPS, had phoned me and asked to babysit. Again, I stood amazed at how God kept providing others who came *to me* to fill each and every need.

On the short, two-mile drive to the courthouse, I declared the praises of God aloud in the car. I declared what God's Word said was true and reminded myself that God was ordering my steps. I verbally submitted the entire situation to the Lord and thanked Him ahead of time for intervening.

Before 9:30 AM, I managed to get David and myself inside the courthouse and ask for directions to the correct hall where I would wait for the mediator's door to open.

Sitting on one of the many folding chairs lining the hallway, I took a deep breath and closed my eyes for a moment. When I opened them and turned to see who was sitting to my right, I noticed someone I'd known from MOPS, though I couldn't remember her name.

The young, dark-haired woman was crying as she sat with another woman only a few chairs away. It turned out that she was in a similar grievous situation – yet another member of the unadvertised club of women left by their husbands.

"We'll be praying for you," the woman and her sister both nodded and encouraged me as the door to the mediator opened. I was invited inside the office by a short man with trimmed brown hair and a mustache.

~~~

I sat alone on the plaid couch in the office across from the mediator, with David awake in his carseat, moving his arms, bumping my feet. Soon there was a sharp knock at the door, and Kirk entered to sit down in his chair, evenly spaced from myself and the mediator. He was a few minutes late.

"Your baby is so handsome," the mediator said, looking back and forth at both of us.

I nodded. His comment made me so sad, and I blinked back a tear.

"Let's talk about the children's visitation schedule," Brandon, the mediator, said. "What are your concerns?" he turned to me.

"I truly want Kirk to have an important relationship with his children. I believe that is so necessary and crucial," I answered.

"But my concern is the way that he surprises me with calling me up at the last minute to say he wants to see the kids. Especially the way he phones me while he already has them and informs me that he is extending their time with him, changing what we had agreed-upon. It makes me feel very uncomfortable when I do not know what to expect next from him."

The mediator turned to face Kirk and to invite him to talk.

"I believe it is important for the children that we are both involved in their lives. I think their time should be divided equally," Kirk spoke up, and crossed one leg over the other.

"Okay," the mediator said, sitting forward, "do you have a schedule in place right now?"

"We've talked about the standard every-other-weekend," Kirk answered. "But I'd like to have them during the week as well. And I want to see the baby, too."

"To be honest with you," I looked directly into the mediator's face, "I have been doing research on *The DissoMaster*. I have discovered that if he has them overnight, he is entitled to pay me less child support, and that could make or break me on my ability to care for our children. I have always been a stay-at-home mom."

"I see," Brandon nodded, clearly appearing to recognize the legitimacy of the words I'd spoken.

Kirk leaned forward now, "I'm not interested in changing the amount of money I deposit in her bank account. I just want to see my children more."

"Well," Brandon offered, while folding his arms across his chest, "how about we say this: The father can have all-day visitation with the girls every Saturday, let's say 9:00 AM-5:00 PM. Also, the father can take all three children on Tuesday and Thursday evenings for a set time of three hours. Would that fit in with the baby's nursing schedule?" Brandon asked me.

"Yes, definitely," I agreed, nodding my head. "I could work around that schedule."

"Okay," Kirk said, visibly not as enthused.

"And you can be the one to pick the children up and drop them off, right?" he looked at Kirk, who nodded reluctantly.

Brandon dismissed us after setting another date for a follow-up mediation.

~~~

Full of sudden relief because things seemed to have gone the best that could have been expected, I followed Kirk into the elevator holding the baby in his carseat. Neither of us said anything on the way down. I looked at Kirk, but he only looked at the door in front of him, standing rigid, unwilling to communicate.

I followed behind Kirk into the parking lot where he turned to the right to walk toward 'his friend's SUV.'

"You shouldn't have left us," I taunted, standing by the car next to his. "It was a crazy thing to do to not be in the lives of your children as you should. Is this how you wanted things to turn out?" I asked, mad.

"How could you go off with that 'floozy' anyway?" I asked, remembering a term that someone had used to describe the 'other woman' that Kirk had involved himself with. "That sure was a stupid thing to do!" I cried out more.

Kirk's face grew steely and he said nothing. He opened the door, climbed inside, backed out, and zoomed away.

I watched him zip off down the street, angry at him for all the misery he caused and the stupidity of it all.

Maybe I sensed that what I had done was wrong, but in that moment of weakness I only focused on the fury that I felt.

~~~

"For though we live in the world,
we do not wage war as the world does.
The weapons we fight with
are not the weapons of the world.
On the contrary, they have divine power
to demolish strongholds."
II Corinthians 10: 3-4

~~~

As I drove home to an empty house, I did not feel so good. I grew more and more anxious and worried. The solid peace I'd been enveloped in seemed to have almost instantly disappeared with my angry, hateful words.

Back home, I nursed David and placed him in his borrowed crib. Somebody had brought this one over and set it up for me since Kirk had neglected to assemble my own baby crib waiting in the garage.

Collapsing on my bed because I'd hoped for a nap, the what-ifs flew at me from all sides, assaulting my mind until I felt buried under an avalanche of worry and fear.

It was then that I called Beverly. Beverly, who had been the president of Women's Aglow where I'd met her in North Carolina, who had become my co-worker at the afterschool care program, and who had served as my mentor and close friend.

"Hello?" Beverly answered her phone from across the country.

"Beverly?" I asked, but when I heard her voice, I began to sob before I could talk. "The mediation went so well," I tried to explain between blowing my nose, crying, and catching my breath. "But I feel so bad now – so worried and so afraid."

Then I told her about what happened afterwards – about how I'd followed Kirk out to his car and mocked him for his stupid stupidity. I still felt the anger rise inside of me when I told her about it.

"Janice!" Beverly exclaimed, sounding shocked.

"What?" I asked, sitting up and blowing my nose again.

"No wonder you have lost your peace. *You sinned.* God was taking care of you all the way, but then you stepped in and sinned against Kirk by saying those words to him. God is the only One who will bring Kirk to justice. You need to repent," Beverly stated clearly.

"I need to repent?" I asked, flabbergasted and throwing the tissues on the floor. "Have you happened to notice all that he has done to me?" I declared, thinking that Beverly was thinking a lot like the California judicial system – the no-fault divorce law.

"Honey, you have the Lord. You know better than to talk to Kirk like that. You need to ask his forgiveness," she said as gently, but firmly, as she could.

We sat in silence. I was still mad. Beverly waited. I sniffed and blew my nose again. But slowly understanding and revelation began to filter into me. It made sense to me. I felt a growing awareness of the Holy Spirit's conviction in my heart over what I'd said to Kirk.

"Oh Beverly, you're right," I said, now knowing and leaning back on the pillows. "I have sinned. I do need to ask Kirk for forgiveness and I cannot wait to do it!"

"You go, girl!" Beverly encouraged. And with that repentance and decision in my heart, God's beautiful, holy, wonderful peace returned and blanketed me once again.

I hung up the phone with Beverly awhile later, laughing, feeling relieved and so much better. I felt so much better that I didn't care what God's peace cost me – I would obey Him and do it His way!

I could not wait to see Kirk when he picked up the girls for a visit that evening. He'd asked to have them for dinner because he'd already made plans for the next day, and could not take them at the time that the mediator had suggested.

So I would see him shortly.

~~~

Kirk arrived at the house on time and manually opened the garage door to look for something inside. I approached Kirk quietly and explained that the girls would be out in a minute.

"Kirk," I said, "I want to ask for your forgiveness for the remarks that I made to you today," I spoke, standing a few feet in front of him and feeling the Holy Spirit's conviction, leading, and satisfying presence. "Also, I'm sorry for calling 'your friend,' a 'floozy.' That was wrong of me."

Kirk actually looked up from where he bent over a pile of tools in the garage. "Thank you," he said, "that means a lot to me that you said that."

Feeling God's peace soaring through me, and encouraged by the response I'd received from Kirk, I pushed ahead further. "Kirk," I said, "I'm sorry for anything I did that caused you to want to leave me."

Kirk nodded at me, but did not say anything more.

Oh well, I thought, sighing. I'd hoped that maybe Kirk would open up and talk to me, but again, he'd stopped short. I went inside and hurried the girls out to meet him for their dinner date.

After they left, I danced down the hallway feeling peace and joy. I didn't care what I had to ask forgiveness for, God's presence and peace were worth it! I sang, "I'm so glad that Jesus set me free!"

29

More Steps in the Journey

Sunday, September 19, 1999

To go to an event or a family outing by myself, where I'd been used to the comfort and security of going with Kirk, proved to be challenging again and again.

Today was 'Fairgrounds Sunday' at church which meant we'd meet for the large service outside and then have a huge potluck. I struggled even as the car took me there carrying only David in his carseat in the back. The girls were with Kirk.

Aloud, as I drove, I declared praises to God and spoke His Words of promise so that I could hear them myself. "Thank You for ordering my steps, Lord. Thank You for knowing about how I feel right now – miserable – and for caring for me."

I drove into a dirt parking spot, put the car in park, sighed deeply, and turned around to unbuckle David from his carseat. I really did not feel like being there by myself.

When I turned around from getting everything out of the car and had David, diaper bag, water bottle and stroller all hanging from me, I noticed that while I'd been busy gathering it all, others I knew had arrived. Emilie and Ed had driven up and parked beside me on the right, Hannah and Henry and Hailey were on the other side of me on the left, and soon, my homeschooling friend from church, Angela, also drove in and parked one car down.

Before I knew it, this group of caring friends joined me and carried my stuff, pushed David in his stroller, and seemed genuinely glad to see me.

Suddenly I was very glad that I'd come. I breathed out thanksgiving to God as I thoroughly enjoyed the church service and the afternoon picnic.

~~~

Monday, September 20, 1999

Rocking back and forth on the glider in the family room while still holding baby David, I noticed that it had been a couple of hours since I'd sung the girls to sleep in their bedroom. I still rocked, thinking, awake.

The court date loomed before me, eleven days away.

The idea of me not being with my children made me feel wobbly, like I'd lost my footing, seasick. My stomach hurt. My head swam. My eyes teared. I looked down at my sweet baby's face, sleeping peacefully on my chest. I held him closer. *But it was my job to be their mother.*

I was not leaving them! I did not believe in this idea of divorce! I wanted to be with them. I homeschooled them. I wanted to train them. I wanted to love them, and to be there for them.

Could they just be taken from me? How could this be? Would they love someone else as their mother instead of me? Would they be confused? This idea, especially, was a nightmare.

It hurt. It hurt deeply. I did not know what would happen. The room spun.

"Lord," I prayed aloud, squeezing my eyes shut and freeing captive tears, "Lord, this seems too hard," I trembled.

I began again with resolve, "But Lord, when it is hard, that is when we can give You a sacrifice of praise, I said, tears flowing. This is the only time we can give You this gift – a sacrifice of praise – when things seem and feel so awful.

"So I praise You now because I remember that You are the One in charge of my life. You have the final say in these matters that concern me. You can give favor in the courts and You can cause the judge to make decisions according to Your best plan. You are giving every opportunity to Kirk to repent and to change his ways so that we can be a family again. You are intervening in every matter of my life today.

"But I thank you for whatever You do, God. And I will trust in You, Lord. And I will praise You."

My voice began to sing feebly, wobbly, mirroring how my body felt, "We... bring... the sacrifice of praise... into the house... of the Lord," my voice rasped with congestion and with tears.

As I sang, I felt new strength well up inside of me from somewhere deep down. "We bring the sacrifice of praise, into the house of the Lord. And we offer up to You, our sacrifices of thanksgiving." I set the baby in his carseat and I lifted up my hands. Many tears fell while I sang, "And we offer up to You, our sacrifices of praise."

~~~

"Through Jesus, therefore, let us continually
offer to God
a sacrifice of praise —
the fruit of lips that confess his name."
Hebrews 13:15

~~~

Tuesday, September 21, 1999

It was one afternoon during the children's naptime when I felt like crying. But I was too numb inside and I couldn't.

I thought of my friend, Jennifer, from church. Jennifer and her husband were kind and generous, and lived in a home not too far away in Hillside. Jennifer had taken over hosting the church's women's Bible study for me when I'd had to stop due to the house remodeling projects.

I had not talked to Jennifer since I'd been back from Maryland and I wondered if she knew that Kirk had left me.

"Hello?" Jennifer answered the phone. I could hear her two children, ages eight and ten, talking and laughing in the background.

"Hi, Jennifer?" I asked, walking down the hallway in my bedroom.

"Oh hi, Janice! I haven't talked to you in a while. How have you been? How's the baby?!" she greeted me with gladness.

"Have you heard what's happened?" I asked, sitting on the thick, soft, green comforter on my bed.

"What do you mean? Are you okay?" her voice changed its tone to one of sudden concern.

I told her. Her end of the line grew very quiet. Then I could hear her sobbing.

"Jennifer?" I asked, now concerned for her. "Are you okay?"

"I am just so upset that Kirk would do that to you!" she cried.

"I know, Jennifer," I said, pulling part of the comforter over my legs. "But do you see God at work and how He is helping me? And today I needed to cry, but I couldn't, and I called you. I knew you had the gift of mercy. You have really helped me by crying for me. Thank you," I said, now feeling my own tears well up.

"Oh, Janice. Is there anything I can do for you?" Jennifer asked.

We talked further. Soon we'd come up with a plan: We decided that I would phone Kirk and leave a message that the kids were at Jennifer and James' home and needed to be picked up there.

It was a Friday night and Kirk was scheduled to have them for dinner. James, her husband, would be ready to intervene and try to get a word in with Kirk. James and Kirk had done some biking together, so maybe Kirk would listen to him.

Kirk did pick up the kids from Jennifer and James' home, but he ignored James' attempts at conversation.

As Kirk walked out of the door of their home with our children in hand, Kirk turned to me and said crisply, "Never set me up like that again."

~~~

Kirk had returned the girls. I'd settled them into bed, and I sat on the old blue couch in the family room, thinking.

I felt like I had been ripped apart. I felt torn and bleeding. I felt like the dull ache I now lived with would never stop; the stinging, the pain, the dull throb was ever with me.

Would it be possible to ever feel happy again?

Another person, the person closest to me – who had shared my life, my heart, my thoughts, the one whom I had tried my best to take care of and to please and to support – it was he that said I was unworthy, not special, not important. I was judged not valuable in his eyes.

My heart was broken, crumpled, trampled on, bleeding.

He had not only harmed me, but our children, whom I loved as my own self, and whom we'd agreed to rear in the Christian faith based on those values. Divorce was not one of them. What was he teaching them? How would this affect my beloved children?

And my family, and all those who loved us, all those who looked to us in any way as an example, were wounded.

How did God fit into this picture? I thought.

Slowly, with tears, I rose from where I'd been sitting on the couch hugging a pillow. I walked down the long hallway leading into our bedroom, crying out to God in the misery that I felt with extreme acuteness.

As I did, I saw this typewritten text in my mind's eye: ***Psalm 55***

Recognizing that the Holy Spirit had just spoken to me, I ran to the side of my bed where I kept my Bible. I was not familiar at all with Psalm 55, and I knew that God must be saying something to me. Astonished, I read the whole psalm, and took note especially of these verses:

"If an enemy were insulting me, I could endure it;
if a foe were raising himself against me,
I could hide from him.
But it is you, a man like myself,
my companion, my close friend,
with whom I once enjoyed sweet fellowship
as we walked with the throng at the house of God."
Psalm 55:12-14

~~~

"But I call to God, and the LORD saves me.
Evening, morning and noon
I cry out in distress, and he hears my voice.
He ransoms me unharmed from the battle waged against me,
even though many oppose me.
God, who is enthroned forever,
will hear them and afflict them—
men who never change their ways
and have no fear of God.
My companion attacks his friends;
he violates his covenant.
His speech is smooth as butter, yet war is in his heart;
his words are more soothing than oil,
yet they are drawn swords.
Cast your cares on the LORD and he will sustain you;
he will never let the righteous fall."
Psalm 55:16-22

~~~

I sat on the edge of my bed with stunned amazement. God had supernaturally shown me to look up this psalm, and the words pinpointed my feelings and my circumstances exactly.

God understood me! God saw me! God knew me!

It was late at night, but I jumped up to dance around the room. Breathless, I sat down and read it again. I praised God!

I phoned Ginny to tell her and I couldn't wait to tell others the next day the newest thing that God had done! I sang aloud again, "Look what the Lord has done!"

~~~

Wednesday, September 22, 1999

When I awoke the next morning, the refreshment of how God knew me and my situation streamed through me like fresh spring water. The praise & worship CD greeted me and I sang along, directing my praises to God.

I climbed out of bed early because today we planned to go to the Berkeley Science Museum. Before long, I made my way through the family room to the kitchen to get some water.

But as I passed the garage door, I heard something funny sounding... what could it be?

Grasping the handle, I opened the door to our garage to see a waterfall gushing out of the hot water heater. I stepped backward, my mouth wide open, staring at the scene in front of me.

"Well!" I said speaking aloud over its noise. "Well!" I declared. *"This* problem is no surprise to You either, God!

"You knew this was going to happen and I thank You that you have already provided for it! I thank You that the water is running outside and not inside! I thank You that You let it burst at exactly the right time and that I came out here early. I thank You that You are ordering our steps and that You are in charge!"

I got the idea to call Emilie. She picked up the phone at Hillside Community Church and said that she had just arrived at the office. "Oh!" she said. "Well, here. Let me give you the name and number of George. He goes to our church, and if anybody can help you, he can. He's helped Ed and me out a number of times."

I phoned George.

Within thirty minutes, George had arrived and shut off the water. He knew exactly what to do and I left the garage open for him when we left on our field trip. When we returned home a few hours later, a brand new hot water heater had been installed.

Eating dinner early, we left for our Wednesday night AWANA Club with the peace that our latest problem had been fixed.

While there, Marlene, also a member of our church, slipped me an envelope. Inside was $100 in grocery gift cards.

~~~

" ...the joy of the LORD is your strength."
Nehemiah 8:10

~~~

30

A Sacrifice of Praise

Thursday, September 23, 1999

The phone rang early in the morning and I grabbed the receiver from the table beside my bed. "Hello?"

"Hi Janice," Ginny said.

"Hi Ginny!" I was glad to hear the voice of my prayer partner. Ginny had continued fasting desserts with me as we prayed together every day about the upcoming court case and all that was involved. Eight more days.

"Well," Ginny said. "I kind of have some bad news."

"Oh no, what is it?" I asked, sitting up and wondering if she was alright.

"Well, I kind of have to go out of town this week with Gene to visit his parents, and that means I won't be here to pray with you this week, or the next," she explained.

"Oh, no!" I cried. My heart sank. Both Ginny and Miriam prayed with me every day and I depended on it.

"Yeah," she said. "But you know, God's got this under control, too. And I will be praying for you up at Gene's parents house. I promise."

~~~

Right after I set the receiver back, the phone rang again. Thinking it might be Ginny phoning back with something she forgot to say, I picked it up eagerly.

"Hi Janice," Kirk said brusquely, "I just wanted to let you know that my co-worker will be with me when I get the kids tonight because they're the one driving. And I'm planning on taking David tonight, too. Have him ready."

"What?" I asked, suspicious that it was the 'other woman' whom he was bringing along. "Who is this co-worker?"

"Just somebody from work." Kirk answered.

"Okay," I answered, feeling that I didn't have any control again and still wondering about who it could be coming with him.

~~~

Hannah had plans to watch the girls while I met the new lawyer to set up for the next week's court date. However, the day's plans turned out even bigger than expected when Suzy, the mother of one of Nicole's friends from church, called.

"Janice," she said, "I've set up an appointment with my hairdresser to get your hair done with me. My treat. Believe me, this is an experience that you won't want to miss. Can you come tonight?"

I agreed, thanking God for a new hairstyle in time for the court date.

~~~

Late afternoon...

"Oh, God!" I dropped to my knees, once again in our family room. "Oh God, Kirk is picking up the girls *and now* baby David for the very first time! I have never sent the baby off before, God!

"And now, this co-worker of Kirk's is coming here to laugh at me also! He knows that I am 'the wife that Kirk left.'"

I felt undignified and shamed and did not trust Kirk.

Tears sprang to my eyes. It just wasn't fair. I had to send my precious baby away, and some stranger who probably didn't believe in family values either, would be there with Kirk to watch it all.

Humiliation washed over me. I dreaded Kirk's arrival.

~~~

The knock at the door came, and I answered it. Kirk stood alone.

"Hi," I said, "do you have the special buckle to help hold the carseat in place?" I asked, concerned about the baby's safety.

"No," he said, distracted, looking past me for a glimpse of the children.

"Well, there was a seminar at MOPS on how to attach one correctly. Can I come and show you?" I asked, standing in the doorway.

"Sure," Kirk said, stepping aside so I could exit the house.

I grabbed the carseat I'd left on the porch for when Kirk arrived and walked out to the black SUV parked in the driveway.

Another young man, Kirk's co-worker, jumped out from the driver's seat to join us at the back door of his car. I managed to fit the carseat inside, and began to wrestle with the buckle.

I felt drained, and my eyes were worn from the crying I'd done before they'd arrived.

To my surprise, when I looked up at this dark-haired stranger, his eyes, also, were brimming with tears. He took over and helped me to secure the carseat.

I could just hear the sad story that he told his wife that night.

Kirk, oblivious, enthusiastic, and with loud exclamations, welcomed the girls who stepped out of the house ready to go. Then he reached out his arms for David who was waiting for him in his stroller by the door.

Again, it was a moment that I was able to offer as a precious gift – a sacrifice of praise.

~~~

(Hagar said of the Lord)
"She gave this name to the LORD who spoke to her:
'You are the God who sees me,'
for she said, 'I have now seen the One who sees me.'"
Genesis 16:13

~~~

Suzy, slight and fiery, arrived shortly after I'd had a quick dinner and the kids had left. "Are you ready to go?" she asked, standing in the doorway.

Suzy and her husband, Sam, along with Debbie and Donald and Kirk and I, had enjoyed going to 'The City' together before Kirk had left me. Now things were so different.

Suzy returned me to the present. "You're going to love Victoria's Salon," she said. "And it's lots of fun to get your hair done at night. The salon is on the top floor and there is a good view of Main Street below.

"You know, Jan wanted to be here, too, and she sent me with some money. Let's go!" Suzy said.

I grabbed my purse. It was so strange to not have the baby to grab also for the first time.

We drove the few short blocks and Suzy parallel parked. Up the stairs I followed her through the doors and into a snazzy looking salon where Suzy was greeted as an old friend.

She introduced me and I was taken to sit in a chair with a view of the lights, the restaurants, and the people strolling on the sidewalks below.

"So, what do you want done tonight?" my hairdresser asked.

"Oh, do whatever you want," I said. I really didn't care. I had no opinion and I didn't feel like talking, either. I tried a smile, though.

"How about a little dye? Do you mind if I cut it short?" she asked pulling my dark brown hair back and forth. Currently it was shoulder-length.

"Sure," I said, not moving. "Do whatever you think looks best."

"How about a glass of wine?" a hostess of the salon came by and asked.

"Sure," I said, looking up at her.

The stylish woman handed me a tall glass along with a bowl of popcorn.

"Isn't this fun?" asked Suzy from a few chairs over.

It was. I sat in the shadowy room spotted with few lights. I enjoyed the view overlooking the activity of Main Street, sipped my wine, and ate my popcorn. I appreciated Suzy for taking me there.

But there was a dull, numb ache inside of me and I wondered if it might remain there forever.

The hairdresser dyed and rinsed and conditioned my hair. Then I became aware of heaps of it sliding down to the floor. I didn't care. Soon, the 'new me' emerged. I glimpsed my new look and listened to tips on styling it. She had cut my hair short, highlighting the wisps and curls atop my head.

~~~

Suzy and I drove back to the house since we had a short time to visit before the children returned. We settled into the family room.

"So the court date is coming up soon, right?" asked Suzy, taking a seat on the old, blue couch.

"Yes, but I am really unhappy that one of my prayer partners has to go out of town and won't be here to pray with me up until the date," I said, taking a seat across from her, on the rocker-glider.

"Really?" Suzy asked, moving her purse off her lap and onto the floor.

"Yes, we've been praying every day and even fasting desserts together. In fact, Ginny is someone whom I've been praying with regularly since I moved here to Hillside over three years ago, along with another friend, Kayla," I explained.

"I could pray with you daily, Janice." Suzy offered, suddenly sitting up, leaning forward.

Suzy and I, though we'd enjoyed our church Bible study together, had never talked one-on-one about spiritual matters. "Do you know much about spiritual warfare, Suzy? And how to pray standing on the Word of God and believing His promises?" I asked her. I needed to know if she had confidence based on the Bible that He could hear and that He *did* want to answer prayer.

"Oh, I do believe that," she assured me, and she shared a few stories involving her children and how she'd prayed for them.

Convinced, I thankfully agreed to her offer. We would begin praying over the phone together the next day. She made arrangements with her husband to take over the childcare of her four children as soon as I called in the evenings.

Again, what seemed like a loss in having Ginny go out of town turned into a longer-term gain. Now I had a third prayer partner who would pray with me every day.

So Miriam from back East, Ginny when she returned from her in-laws', and Suzy, all made praying with me each day their priority. They held up my arms.

~~~

"For where two or three come together
in my name, there am I with them."
Matthew 18:20

~~~

31

A Plan and a Future

Saturday, September 25, 1999

K irk had the girls from 9:00 AM-5:00 PM for Saturday. *Free baby-sitting,* I thought, deciding to count my blessings and to see 'the glass half-full.'

"Let's go to the Fall Aglow Retreat for the day," Ginny offered. "Gene said he'd like to pay for you to go with me. My new friend, Lacey, is coming too, and she wants to buy your lunch."

When we arrived at the registration table, we discovered that the chosen theme for the event was, *He Delivered Me From the Miry Pit,* based on Psalm 40.

"Hey, Ginny! That's the same scripture verse that God gave me one night while I was in Maryland," I said, amazed at how He had ministered those words to me already. We moved into the conference room, which was also a church sanctuary with pews.

"Janice, that is so cool. Hey, listen, I see Joan over there, and you have to let her pray for you. She is very prophetic." Ginny led me over to the left side and up to the front of the large room.

Ginny and I waited in the prayer line where Joan was ministering after the morning session along with several other women. "Joan," Ginny said when we took our seats in the pew in front of her, "you have to pray for my friend, Janice."

"Don't say a word," Joan instructed. "I don't want to know anything about her circumstances. I'll just pray and share what I sense the Lord is saying." She began. Ginny took notes.

"There is great favor on you, Janice,
much favor on you.
God has a destiny for you!

Even though there have been rough times, yes,
you knew to go to The Rock!
He is healing every offense!
He is filling in your pit and covering it
with beautiful flowers, and a tree!

You have warrior feet!
You will walk into the enemy's camp
and the enemy will not see you coming
and then the enemy will only see Jesus
when he looks at you!

Fear and doubt are bound from you.
He has taken up your case –
He is your advocate – your attorney –
the case is settled.
It is going to be alright.

He is like an umbrella covering you.
Your seed is also
under His umbrella of protection –
they are going to be alright!
He is providing, providing, PROVIDING!

The Holy Spirit has gone before you
robed in splendor –
He has taken care of every detail,
wow, every detail!
And no, you shall never, never,
never be in want.

You are a vessel that can be used
and God has a plan to use you.
You will walk in signs and wonders.

He is bringing you to a new place in Him.
He is launching you into ministry.
I see you holding a basket of fruit.

You would say in your own eyes, 'Who me?'
And God says, 'Yes, you!'
He is going to use you!
He is working out everything in you
that needs to be purged.
The Lord is putting you in a new place!
It is a new time!"

~~~

Tuesday, September 28, 1999

The office of my new lawyer phoned to say that Kirk's lawyer had now been informed that Mr. Maxwell would now represent me. It was only three days until the court date.

~~~

Wednesday, September 29, 1999

Driving the few blocks into downtown Hillside, I located Beatrice's house on a side street off of Main Street. Beatrice, the co-leader with her husband at the AWANA Club, had asked if she might watch the girls today. This worked out well because I had an appointment with Ginny's friend, Lacey, to find clothes to wear for the court date.

It was amazing how God orchestrated all my needs by using different people from different groups from all over Hillside. Each day someone different called from either church, or one of the homeschool groups, MOPS, Aglow, or AWANA Club and said that God had put on their heart exactly what I needed for that day. Only God could coordinate this so perfectly.

It seemed that my job was to submit each day and each need to the Lord, and to spend my energy and thoughts in praising, worshipping, and praying. He took care of all the rest.

~~~

Ginny's friend, Lacey, managed several Glamour Shot stores in California and back on the East Coast in the Carolinas. They'd met one day when Lacey had gone to Ginny's church to find out about becoming a Christian. The pastor had connected Lacey to Ginny for support and they had become fast friends.

Lacey, single and glamorous herself, with stylish long blonde hair, big eyelashes, and perfect make-up, greeted me at the front door of her home on the outskirts of Hillside's short borders.

"Come inside!" she greeted. "Have I got the clothes for you!" She led me into her newly finished, painted, two-car garage-turned-closet. Both sides sported top and bottom racks boasting dozens of stylish outfits. Each store hanger held a carefully folded suit or dress protected by a clear plastic cover, many tagged and brand-new, never worn.

I stared, my mouth dropping open. It looked and smelled like an upscale store instead of a garage.

"Well, begin trying some on!" she said, amused by the look on my face. "We'll get you looking really good for your court appearance this Friday!" Lacey laughed.

I remembered from my studies at Gettysburg College that research had shown that looking attractive and well-dressed was important when appearing in a court trial.

With Lacey's professional make-up help, her personal wardrobe, and the fact that we wore similar sizes, I left with a top-notch look.

~~~

Thursday, September 30, 1999

It was the day before the court trial.

What would happen tomorrow? How would my life be different after this next day?

The soil of my life appeared dark, trashed, and dirty. All that Kirk and I had built had collapsed. The surface was barren, broken, and unlovely. I could see nothing of what might someday grow there, or of what my future might hold. Large, gray question marks loomed before me as I awaited court dates, judges, and answers.

Here is how I explained it to Mom later in the day: My hopes were like seeds that I was planting in the soil of my life and I was dying to each and every one. Reminding myself of what the Word of God said was just like watering those hopes while they were still out of sight.

Now we would wait and see exactly what would poke through the soil and grow and blossom in my life because of His Hand alone.

~~~

"Well God," I said, as I continued to rock in my glider during the children's afternoon naps. "You always promise us the victory in the end. So I am going to proclaim a praise celebration right now – just as if I were already on the other side of this – and just as if it were the time to celebrate!

"I am going to disregard the fact that I don't know the details of what is going to happen and I don't know my future. I am going to praise You – *with enthusiasm*, even though inside I feel very small and weak. And, I will worship You. And I will thank You no matter what!"

I praised Him with the fervor and the energy and the excitement as if the outcome had already happened, and as if I could already see from His perspective the answers to my prayers.

I could do this because I knew that His plans for me were good – no matter how they turned out.

> *"'For I know the plans I have for you,'*
> *declares the LORD,*
> *'plans to prosper you and not to harm you,*
> *plans to give you hope and a future.'"*
> Jeremiah 29:11

~~~

> *"The steps of a good man are ordered by the LORD,"*
> Psalm 37:23 NKJV

~~~

I prayed that God would direct the judge's heart:

> *"The king's heart is in the hand of the LORD;*
> *he directs it like a watercourse wherever he pleases."*
> Proverbs 21:1

~~~

I prayed that God would confuse the enemy – and that Kirk and his lawyer – and whatever was behind them – would not be able to communicate:

> *"Confuse the wicked, O Lord, confound their speech,"*
> Psalm 55:9a

~~~

My traditional, godly values were being put down. But this is what God said: I should not be surprised about it, but I should leap with joy!

"Blessed are you when men hate you,
when they exclude you and insult you
and reject your name as evil, because of the Son of Man.
'Rejoice in that day and leap for joy,
because great is your reward in heaven.'"
Luke 6:22-23a

So I practiced leaping for joy.

~~~

I thought about the eternal rewards building up for me, and how one day I would be so glad that I had believed God through this trial.

"Blessed is the man who perseveres under trial,
because when he has stood the test,
he will receive the crown of life
that God has promised to those who love him."
James 1:12

~~~

I also remembered how God laughs at his enemies and at dire-looking situations.

"The One enthroned in heaven laughs;
the Lord scoffs at them."
Psalm 2:4

~~~

"But you, O LORD, laugh at them;"
Psalm 59:8a

~~~

So I practiced laughing aloud like God laughs at His enemies, understanding that they are no match for Him.

I remembered that God could see everything and be everywhere. HE IS ABLE TO HELP – HE IS GOOD – HE IS IN CHARGE OF MY LIFE – HE IS LOVING and HE IS STRONG.

The noise of my laughing must've sounded silly. I looked up to see my little girls emerging from the hallway from their naptimes, coming into the family room to join the fun that I was having.

It was a marvelous praise party!

~~~

"Be joyful always; pray continually;
give thanks in all circumstances,
for this is God's will for you in Christ Jesus."
I Thessalonians 5:16-18

~~~

32

The Court Trial

Friday, October 1, 1999

The day I had been on my knees praying for, preparing for, hoping for, and dreading – the day of judgment – had finally arrived. I woke up early to get showered and dressed and to eat breakfast.

Kayla's daughter, Kit, came to the house and settled in to watch the girls.

Everything in Hillside was so close that it was like living on a college campus. I'd only put 3000 miles on my car in three years. I drove slowly to the courthouse, declaring and singing praises to God, making the most of the minutes.

Baby David sat snug in his seat in the back. My lawyer's secretary had phoned late the day before about Kirk's lawyer being irate that I'd brought the baby to mediation. "I don't know what the details are, but the mediator gave you a good report," said the secretary, "and she blames it on you for bringing the baby to the mediation meeting."

So because my lawyer had recommended it, Suzy also planned to meet me at the courthouse in order to care for David and to keep him outside of the courtroom.

~~~

When the elevator came to a stop for me on the second floor of the courthouse, my lawyer was already there waiting for me in the lobby.

He motioned for me to follow him into a private meeting room. "Sit down," he said. He opened up his briefcase on the short table, took out some folders, and handed me the stapled report from the mediator.

"Is it good?" I asked, feeling uncomfortable in the hard chair and only seeing nonsensical words.

"Fairly," he said, not smiling. "Ms. Rochelle is not pleased with it, anyway."

"Is that good news? Does that mean anything?" I asked.

"Nothing's certain 'til it's certain," my lawyer offered, closing his briefcase and snapping the lock.

I skimmed the mediator's report, my eyes widening.

Although Janice is still reeling from Kirk's decision to end the marriage, she is attempting to put her life back in order...

Given the issue of finances, her feelings of isolation, and her need for a support system, she is requesting permission to move...

In short, her actions do not appear retaliatory...

Her stated position is that regardless of her feelings for Kirk at this time, she wants the children to have an important relationship with him....

Toward that end, she is willing to find him free lodging in Maryland when he comes to visit...

She is also willing to come to California for a month in the summer so that the children might have daily contact with their father over an extended period...

Recommendation: Physical custody of the children will be awarded to their mother and she will be authorized to live with them in the state of Maryland under the following terms...

~~~

I entered the room by the side of my tall lawyer. I noticed Kirk already there on the right toward the front, seated beside a woman with short, prickly hair, Ms. Rochelle.

It was a medium-sized room with a black-robed judge at the large mahogany desk in the front. A stenographer typed to the right side of the judge. About ten rows of benches held a couple dozen people waiting to be called up for their hearings.

Only one or two prior cases were called before the judge announced, "Lynch vs. Lynch."

Lynch vs. Lynch, I thought, what horrifying words to hear. I looked at my lawyer for direction.

"Will the parties please rise," said the judge. I stood up beside Mr. Maxell, my lawyer, who had an air of confidence in this environment which I did not feel at all familiar with.

The judge shuffled our papers around at his desk and then looked up to observe us. Looking at his notes, he stated, "The petitioner requests a divorce from his wife based on irreconcilable differences. He also requests that his wife remain in California so that he can be near the children. By the way, you have a beautiful son, Mr. Lynch. I saw him out in the lobby."

"Thank you," Kirk answered. But Kirk's lawyer, Ms. Rochelle, turned a shade of red at the judge's comment.

The judge questioned, "Now, why shouldn't the mother be near her family? After all, emotional support is important if she is to be a good mother."

"I want to know my son," stated Kirk.

"Long-distance relationships have been done before," the judge looked at Kirk over his bifocals. "Could you possibly find employment in the Washington, DC area?"

Kirk's lawyer took a step forward, interrupting to change the subject, "I want to propose a new schedule of visitation, Your Honor, one that would help the father to know his son better."

The judge nodded at her to give her permission to proceed.

Ms. Rochelle read off a list of how she proposed that the children should split their time equally between each parent, including dividing up holidays.

My heart attempted a catapult through my chest at that. My face paled at her business-sounding legalese as she tried to implement major life-altering decisions for me in under a minute.

"And," Ms. Rochelle wrapped up her proposal, "based on the greater amount of time that Mr. Lynch will be spending with his children, I have come up with a new figure in the amount of child support that Mr. Lynch should be obligated to pay."

Kirk looked at his lawyer, surprise registering on his face when he heard the words that she'd just said. He raised his hand, "May I say something, Your Honor?"

"Go ahead, Mr. Lynch," the judge permitted.

"I do not wish to drop the amount of child support," Kirk asserted.

Kirk's lawyer looked like she was about to gag, grew red, even purplish in the face, but remained composed and said no more.

"Alright, Mr. Lynch," the judge agreed. "The child support will remain as it stands." The judge added, "Ms. Lynch should be permitted to return to her home in the state of Maryland with her children to receive the emotional support from her family that she requires."

Kirk's lawyer spoke up again, "Your Honor," Ms. Rochelle appealed, "I feel that there should be a psychological evaluation and an in-home study completed to qualify the status and the correctness of the children spending so much time at home with their mother."

"Do you really think that is necessary?" the judge asked, nonplussed at Ms. Rochelle's tactics.

"All possibilities must be examined in the best interest of the children," Ms. Rochelle held her ground and raised her shoulders, standing an inch taller and looking like she withheld a smirk.

"Alright then," the judge conceded.

Next a date was discussed between both lawyers and clients and the first date available for a follow-up to the case was scheduled into the following year!

The craftiness of Kirk's lawyer shocked me! She had simply planned to get at her goals from a different route, drawing the case out indefinitely and thus multiplying her lawyer fees and my pain.

After what was less than ten minutes, I found myself walking back out into the lobby by the side of my lawyer who quickly abandoned me to make his next appointment.

Rounding the corner, I heard Suzy's voice. "Janice! How did it go?" she rushed over to me from where she'd been standing, holding baby David for me in the lobby.

"I don't know," I said, feeling bewildered, "I think good."

"Well, guess what?!" Suzy rushed on, "Guess what happened while I was walking around the lobby with the baby while you were meeting with your lawyer beforehand?"

"What?" I asked, wondering why she was so excited.

"The judge came up to me and said, 'Is that the Maryland baby?' That is what he said, Janice! Can you believe it? He called David 'the Maryland baby'!" Suzy radiated.

~~~

As I drove the two miles home from the court trial, the reality of what happened began to develop in my understanding like a picture on an old Polaroid camera.

Yes, the judge had stated that he favored letting me go back to be near my family, and that was positive. But Kirk's lawyer obviously had a plan to prolong the wait for that freedom for months, or even years! The costs would mount up with new court dates and with her request for the psychological evaluation and an in-home study by a social worker and who knows what else!

Yes, Kirk had stood up and said that he intended to pay the agreed-upon child support, but his lawyer had planned to switch the schedule for the purpose of lowering the child support. How long would it be before he succumbed to paying less if he had the legal support to do so?

Yes, the judge had referred to David as 'the Maryland baby.'

Yes, the mediator had written a report completely in my favor after meeting with us.

But would the case go on and on and be appealed to the point that all would be lost? Discouragement and devastation crept up inside me, leaving me weak and stripped of all hope.

Somehow I'd thought it would be over after today. Instead it looked like the whole process had just begun.

~~~

The babysitter had left, we'd all eaten lunch, and I'd put the girls down for their naps.

I crawled into my own bed and began to cry.

It looked like even with all the good reports, Kirk's lawyer was so crafty at her job and so against family values that I could be stuck in California for a very long time. I wept.

And now I must prove I am a fit mother! And that my own children should live with me! And where was the money going to come from for all these ludicrous legal diversions?

Once my best friend, legally still my husband, Kirk had become a dreaded enemy.

The kids were so young that they could be confused over who their real mother was. What if they thought that this other woman was their mother! After all, if she was the one with their daddy, it would be natural for them to think that.

And what if I had to be apart from my children on Christmas Day? I was devastated at the thought.

And what if I had to go back to work and wouldn't be able to stay at home with my children to spend my time with them? What if strangers had to raise my children?

My mind flashed to the lady I'd met at the gift shop on Main Street who told me that her ex-husband had not allowed her to move back to her hometown to be near her family. The stepmom in her boys' lives hugged and kissed this lady's own children right in front of her and she said the boys had become confused over which parent to follow.

Would this be my story?

~~~

Fully worn-out, I began to close my eyes as I lay in a heap on the bed. Discouraged, I still said the words aloud, "Praise You, God!" But in my thoughts, my future was rolling out before me like a gray carpet.

Work. Separated from my children. No homeschool? If it hadn't been bad enough losing my husband, then my dignity, now my children?

Before napping, I turned over to pick up the phone. I called Beverly in North Carolina.

~~~

"Well hello, Janice," she answered cheerfully.

I crumpled at the sound of her voice. "Beverly," I sobbed, "It's terrible! Kirk's lawyer is awful – she's going to drag this thing out. What if I get stuck in California? What if I have to go back to work? What if I have to leave my children and stop homeschooling them?"

"Wait a minute," she stopped me. "Haven't you been telling me how you've been praising Him?"

"Yes," I sniffed, cradling the phone.

"Don't you think God is in control now?" she asked.

"Well, yes," I admitted.

"Don't you think it is Him who will decide all those things you just said? They're not settled yet, are they?" Beverly asked.

"No, they're not." I informed her, sniffling some more.

"Honey, I want you to stop right there and repent from forgetting that He is in charge of all that concerns you. I want you to start speaking the truth again.

"Remember all the ways He has already intervened and helped you and showed Himself able?" she said. "Nothing can happen without God knowing it. God has the final say on whether you will go back to work, or if you will homeschool, right?"

"Yes," I agreed, the tears beginning to slow.

"God knows what is best for you and your children and He can provide it – whatever it is – right?" Beverly asked.

"Right," I agreed again, and blew my nose. "But, what if I don't like what it is that He provides?"

"God has a plan for you, Janice – for you and for your children. You have given Him your life, right?" she asked.

"Yes," I acknowledged, confident of this.

"Then you know that you can trust Him. Whatever happens, I want you to be praising Him like you've been doing. If you don't get all that you hoped for, I want you to see God's opportunity for you – and for the kids – in that. Know that He has a plan."

As we dialogued, I began to relax. I began to rest in God's goodness once again.

I surrendered it all to Him.

I determined once more that I would praise Him no matter what.

~~~

"Trust in the LORD with all your heart
and lean not on your own understanding;"
Proverbs 3:5

~~~

33

The Choice to Praise

Saturday, October 2, 1999

As I lay in bed the next morning, not knowing what my future would hold but trusting in God who did, I was reminded of the life of Corrie Ten Boom as told in her book, *The Hiding Place*. She always made the choice to praise God – even when imprisoned for helping the Jewish people in WWII – and even when she got head lice. God proved Himself faithful to her time and again. I determined that I would praise God, too, no matter what.

~~~

I'd felt freedom since the afternoon before when I'd decided to trust in whatever God's best plans were for me and the children. I knew that He was intimately involved in our lives, I knew that He had the power to intervene and to keep us in His will, and I knew that He had good plans for us. I spoke aloud what I believed and was encouraged by the words I heard myself say.

Waking up early, I got the girls dressed and fed and ready to go with Kirk. At 9:00 AM he knocked on the door. He entered the foyer and I sat down on the family room floor to tie Meaghan's dress in the back, feeling spent, and reluctant to engage in conversation.

"The girls are ready," I stated, still looking at the strings on the back of Meaghan's dress, resigned.

"I wanted to talk to you about yesterday," Kirk said.

I looked up at him, bracing myself once again, not knowing what Kirk would say this time.

"I fired my attorney," Kirk stated, standing there.

"You what?" I asked.

"And I want to settle out of court," Kirk said, not moving.

"You want to what?" I asked.

"You can have your lawyer draw up the papers and I'll sign them," Kirk said. "You can go to Maryland as soon as you are able. I will plan to relocate by June 1st to be near the kids."

I looked at Kirk but was afraid to say anything. I had wanted to hear those words so badly, the words which said that I would not be stuck in California against my will, that we could stop this court carousel marathon, that things could settle down into place somehow.

But I was afraid to say anything just in case I had heard wrong or just in case he might change his mind.

So I continued to stare at him, unreacting, not sure what to believe, or to think, or to say.

"Also," Kirk added, "I don't like the way the visitation schedule was left yesterday. I want to have visitation every other weekend instead of every weekend."

I spoke up, standing now, "Well, I'd like the children to still go to church. So can we do Friday at 5:00 PM to Saturday at 5:00 PM for two weekends, and then one full weekend for each of us? That way they'll get three Sundays in at church."

"Okay," Kirk said, "and we'll keep the Tuesday and Thursday evenings from 5:00-8:00 PM with the girls and David."

"Okay, but if you want we could do 5:00-9:00 PM?" I offered, trying to be generous.

"Let's keep it the way it is," Kirk stated and turned. "Come on girls, time to go. I'll have them back at 5:00 PM," Kirk said abruptly and walked out the door.

~~~

I looked out of the corner window as Kirk helped the girls get settled into the car. I watched him back up and turn onto the street and disappear from my view.

I didn't know what to do.

I felt giddy. I felt relief. I didn't know who to call first. I didn't know if I could believe what had just taken place. *Kirk said I could move to Maryland*. Kirk said that I could move to Maryland!

I walked down the hallway and picked up baby David. Holding him out in front of me, I said to the baby, "Your daddy said we could move to Maryland! You *are* 'the Maryland baby,' just like the judge said!" I breathed deeply and did a little skip as I thought about what all this meant.

"Oh God," I prayed, "I thank You! I thank You that You alone '*direct the king's heart as a watercourse*!' I thank You that You '*order my steps*!' I thank You for having Your way in my life and the children's! Thank You!"

Then, I began to make the phone calls.

34

The Next Step Begins

Monday, October 4, 1999

It was Monday morning and I still felt dazed about Kirk's sudden decision to close the case and allow me to move to Maryland with the kids. A great burden had been lifted and I felt surprising relief.

Could I be sure about it, though?

I prayed and I trusted God.

During my quiet time I parked in the account of the Israelites' being released from Egypt in order to go and worship the Lord. These words came alive to me:

> *"And I will make the Egyptians favorably disposed toward this*
> *people, so that when you leave*
> *you will not go empty-handed.*
> *Every woman is to ask her neighbor*
> *and any woman living in her house*
> *for articles of silver and gold and for clothing,*
> *which you will put on your sons and daughters.*
> *And so you will plunder the Egyptians."*
> Exodus 3:21-22

~~~

I knew one thing that I really wanted and that was to be with my children on Christmas Day.

~~~

Much work had to be done: the house needed to be listed, the items inside needed to be sold, research needed to be done in order to write a contract that Kirk and I would sign, and plane tickets needed to be purchased.

Marlene from church and AWANA Club had arranged to take the girls out for the day. It was an opportunity to chip away at my to-do list.

Later in the afternoon when she returned the girls, each one wore a new smile, along with a new dress, new socks, new shoes, and new stories of adventures with friends.

~~~

Thursday, October 7, 1999

Our routine stayed the same: MOPS on Tuesday, AWANA on Wednesday, and homeschool co-op on Friday.

Kirk asked if we could meet to discuss details about the out-of-court settlement. Our dentist's wife, also a friend and leader from MOPS, phoned to ask if she could babysit and she agreed to do so on Thursday night when Kirk returned the kids at 8:00 PM.

Kirk and I would meet outside on the porch while she cared for the kids inside. I would feel much better having her there in case things got uncomfortable with Kirk. I still did not always know what to expect from him.

I felt like the situation was 'iffy' until I had something from Kirk in writing. I wasn't fully ready to believe it was all going to work out. My three prayer partners and I continued to seek God daily for the details.

~~~

Before the meeting was to take place, Miriam and I prayed together over the phone. After awhile we quietly listened for what direction the Lord might have.

"Janice," Miriam said, "I don't think you should say anything. Let Kirk do the talking first. Just see what he has to say and then, you might not have to say anything."

"Do you think?" I asked. I had my list in hand and ready to go. It described the agreement that I had researched for hours and I had in mind.

"Don't speak, Janice. Listen to what he has to say. I believe that this is the key to the whole conversation," Miriam repeated.

"Well, okay," I said, already trying to bite my tongue. It was hard.

~~~

Now I sat across from Kirk with a notebook in my lap and with the porch light on. It was cool and comfortable and pleasant, except for the reason we met.

It almost seemed normal, but it was not.

I looked at Kirk and waited for him to talk, just as I'd promised Miriam that I would do.

Kirk started, "I'd like to keep my truck, the futon which I've been using as a bed, the executive office furniture, and of course, my musical instruments." Kirk paused. "The only other thing that I would like is the video camera."

I jotted down the items he listed in my notebook. "Okay," I replied, "you don't want to keep anything else in the house?"

"No," he said, leaning back in his chair.

"Okay," I said, resting my pen. This was easier than I thought it would be.

We confirmed the visitation schedule which gave each of us one full weekend with the kids and two half-weekends so that the children could be in church most of the time.

Kirk wanted to make sure that he had two evenings a week with the kids for dinner.

The main disagreement centered on the holidays. I just could not, could not, *could not* get used to the idea of not having my children for Christmas.

"Kirk," I pled, sighing, "the children need to have some sort of tradition to count on every year. I do not like the idea of it being different year-to-year."

I continued, "I cannot imagine not having them with me on Christmas. Why don't you take them on Thanksgiving every year so that they know what to expect and will look forward to it?"

"No," Kirk said. "If we were in court, they would divide the holidays evenly."

Just then, our dentist's wife opened the door and peeked out, "Do you mind if I go home?" she asked. "The kids are all asleep and it's getting late."

"Sure," we both agreed and rose from our chairs.

We decided to continue the discussion on the next Tuesday evening when Kirk returned with the kids.

35

Still Praying for Kirk

Friday, October 8, 1999

Suzy's husband, Sam, had called a prayer meeting for Kirk. We met at our home after Kirk had taken the girls for their overnight and David had been nursed and put to bed.

A circle of precious friends gathered in our family room – all with a huge heart for Kirk and for our family. Suzy and Sam sat on the couch to the right of my glider. Paula joined them, and Hannah and Henry took chairs to her right. Ginny sat beside her and Gene rested on the floor. I was so grateful that all these people had chosen to get childcare and to come together and give up a Friday night to pray for something that we all felt was so important.

"Let's open to Proverbs 2," Sam led us and began to read aloud. Solemn and serious, we listened to the words of wisdom, and our group sought God at length in prayer and supplication for Kirk's soul.

~~~

Tuesday, October 12, 1999

"Daddy is going to marry Leanne," my oldest daughter said as I helped her with her nightgown. Kirk had just dropped them off from their Tuesday evening outing.

"Yes," added my three-year-old, standing beside me, "and her boys get to have a slumber party with Daddy every night!"

It was another splash of cold water in my face and a hard blow to my stomach. Yet again, I was shocked at Kirk's actions.

It appeared that since we were settling out of court, Kirk felt the freedom to pursue his new agenda openly. No lawyers or mediators or judges stood there to check him or to direct him to paint a more virtuous picture.

Putting the girls to bed quickly, I hurried because Kirk waited for me out on the porch to continue our discussion. Sam and Suzy were on standby in the family room while Kirk and I talked outside.

"Oh, God!" I prayed as I headed for the front door, "Please help me to be careful and to use wisdom in what I say," I pled.

~~~

"Kirk," I said bluntly. *"How can you do this?* How can you move in with another woman and her children when you are a married man? What kind of an example is that for your kids?"

"I am not married to you in my mind, so it's okay," Kirk stated flatly. "And," he added, "there is nothing you can do about it."

I looked back at him and felt my insides collapse like sand pouring out of an upside-down bottle.

When two people can't resolve something and it goes to court, then everyone must wait for the judge to tell them what to do. If those involved don't follow the judge's orders, then they are 'in contempt of court' and there are consequences. Maybe privileges are taken away, or fines are given with interest, or, perhaps, even jail.

But when one is settling out of court, the pressure to 'keep up appearances' also goes away. Kirk handed me his address and phone number.

It was not the last time that Kirk's actions would make me feel like I'd been knocked down. Before long, he would take my little girls shopping with him for a wedding ring for this other woman.

~~~

Later I found Nicole crying in bed. "Daddy says he has to live with Leanne because she loves him. But I love Daddy, too! Why doesn't he live with me?" she sobbed.

The pain a mother feels penetrates smoothly and deeply like a sharp knife.

I had to keep the truth in full view: God, my children's true Father, saw, cared, and, in His perfect timing, acted.

~~~

> *"The eternal God is your refuge,*
> *and underneath are the everlasting arms."*
> Deuteronomy 33:27

~~~

Wednesday, October 13, 1999

An uplifting break came in the form of AWANA Club on Wednesday night. The girls participated, I was a small group leader, and the baby was allowed to stay with me.

Caring for our family, Beatrice, the co-leader of the club, offered to babysit when needed, and she always offered to help me by simply talking with me.

"Janice," she said after we'd spoken more after the evening meeting inside the gym, "I've been hearing what has been going on for some time now, and I believe that I know what the root of the problem is. I've seen all of these same developments before in my close friend's marriage, and I know."

"What do you mean?" I asked, wondering what she saw.

"The root of this situation is pornography. I'm sure of it," Beatrice explained. "Yours is a classic scenario and when you know what to look for, the signs are all there.

"I have a book which will help you to understand. It's called, *An Affair of the Mind* and it's published by Focus on the Family." Beatrice pulled the book out of her bag and placed it in my hands.

"It's funny that you should say this," I said, "because when Ginny and I were praying at the very beginning, that is what she felt that God was telling her, too. Someone else also received the same idea while they were praying," I said, still turning this information over in my mind. But I had not ever seen Kirk look at pornography.

However, I now realized that I did remember a magazine coming to our house once which he'd denied he'd ordered.

"Well," Beatrice said, "if you read the book, you'll understand more."

"There's something else, too," I added, still standing beside Beatrice near the bleachers in the church gym while others finished the clean-up. "A couple of the women with whom I've been praying with regularly have sensed that there is something more for God to uncover in all this.

"We have been asking that God would expose all that is in the darkness and bring whatever it is into the light. I wonder if the root of pornography is what God has been wanting to reveal?"

"Read the book and see if you discover anything else," Beatrice answered. We began to walk toward the door of the building where the girls waited for me.

~~~

"For there is nothing hidden
that will not be disclosed,
and nothing concealed that will not be known
or brought out into the open."
Luke 8:17

~~~

The book, it turned out, was painful to read. It was glaringly obvious that a similar thread ran through my own marriage story.

Beatrice had known what she was talking about. But God would confirm this revelation even further.

~~~

Thursday, October 14, 1999

I wondered if Kirk and I could come to an agreement on our own outside of the court system.

Suzy and Sam sat inside the house a third time while Kirk and I met outside on the porch. I was beginning to feel hopeless over our discussions.

Kirk, sitting with his legs crossed in his folding chair, began, "I'd like for the girls to spend the night with me on Tuesdays and Thursdays since they are already at my new home for dinner," Kirk stated.

"No, Kirk," I answered him. "I do not believe in joint custody. I think the children should have a stable environment."

Kirk's face reddened. He kept his eyes locked on my own.

I added, "I think living in two places would be unsettling and confusing, Kirk, and look how young they are." Not to mention, if he were ever to take me back to court, then the precedent would be set and we'd probably have to continue it that way. The child support could likely be altered as well.

"Janice," he insisted, shifting in his chair, "the girls need to get to know their new family better, and to spend more time with them."

I tried not to register the horror that felt like a severe slap on my face, but I know I paled. *Their new family?* And a new mother? Would my little children recognize that I was their mother? Would they want to be with this new group instead of with me?

I asked him to reason, "Don't you think that would be very disruptive to their schedules to have to wake up two hours early on two days of the week?"

"I think that it would make it easier for you to find a job and go back to work," Kirk challenged, ignoring our precedent in homeschooling.

Overlooking that digression, I said, "Kirk, I need to talk to you about something. David's diaper was unusual after you brought him back the last time. Were you feeding him formula without telling me?" I asked, knowing that he had just by the way the baby had refused to nurse when he'd been returned.

"Well, I think that David should be able to spend longer periods of time with me – even overnight," Kirk demanded. "I watched David for any allergic reactions and he had none, so I didn't think I needed to tell you."

"You know that I nursed both girls for over a year, Kirk. You know that we'd agreed previously that that was best for them," I reminded him again of his prior life.

"Well, I don't think that I should have to ask your permission to take the kids for extra time, and I think that I should be able to have them whenever I want," Kirk said. "We need to decide on our holiday schedule with them," he added.

"You know," I reminded him, "that I want to have the kids every Christmas. I can't bear the thought of not having them with me on that special day," I said, frustrated, but remaining calm. "And I think you should build up the tradition of Thanksgiving with them instead. That will give them stability. Traditions are important."

"Well," Kirk answered, "I think disruption is good for kids so that they can learn to be adaptive as adults and not value things too much. Besides, they have a new family to celebrate holidays with now, and I want the kids to be there."

"Kirk," I stated with conviction, "I am telling you this: I cannot bear the thought of being separated from my children on Christmas Day. You will have to take me back to court if you want that."

"You know that the courts would rule that the holidays would be divided equally," Kirk said.

"That may be so, but at least I would ask. You are the one who left this family, and I do not want to be without my children on Christmas Day," I said firmly looking into eyes.

"You know, Janice," Kirk said, "you just need to *get over* me leaving you." Kirk got up and stomped off again, leaving me on the porch.

We would have a similar disturbing conversation at our next meeting on the porch while Suzy and Sam again watched the children inside.

~~~

I didn't believe that my beloved husband could actually do this terrible thing. For a long, long time, I could not.

No picture in my mind matched this stranger that I now observed in our foyer actually saying goodbye to his small children, his daughters pulling on his legs.

When I closed my eyes, I could see the real Kirk again – his gentle, calm eyes looking at me – his enthusiastic grin and determination to accomplish jobs at home and at work – his helpfulness, respect, caring, his kindness toward me – both me and the kids.

Where had the real Kirk gone? I wondered. What would the real Kirk think or say or do if he knew that this was happening to me?

This man, so recently my best friend, my confidant, and the father of my three babies. This same man, now suddenly my adversary, my enemy, my worst nightmare. He'd taken me to court to wage war. And he'd suggested that I could not be with my little ones on Christmas Day.

To me, the marriage vows had been like an ark of safety, deciding and sealing our future forever. But Kirk had jumped ship and swam to another shore – an unfamiliar place – one where I was unwelcomed and uninvited.

I had visions of numbly staring across the huge expanse of water which now divided us from where I stayed in my ark, into the new world of Kirk's choosing, where he sat under the beach umbrella with her, instead of me.

They sipped intoxicating drinks from tall, dazzling, fancy glasses, and ate mouth-watering food. It momentarily sizzled.

With teary eyes, I watched him get up and walk after her into the deep, dark forest – further and further away, without looking back even once. Like one under the influence of drink that had long been sealed in a barrel and washed up ashore.

But he had planned it. He had decided without my knowing, without consulting me, out of earshot, in cahoots with someone else – what his future and what my future would be.

'Love,' he said, had 'dried up' for him. 'Now,' he said, 'his heart belonged to another.'

My mind reverted back to all those love notes he had written to me, 'Dear Sweetie.' Every day he had written me from ten hours away, for more than a year during our engagement. They were still in a box. Fictionalized.

God, I knew, had been a silent observer of the secret rendezvous that Kirk had pursued and attended. God had heard the plans that Kirk had made in hidden corners of booths in the dark, noisy rooms of bars, and from the insides of steamy windows of his musty-smelling, cramped, white truck.

And God Himself stood by my side, not breaking His covenant with me. He never would leave me, He never would forsake me as Kirk had done.

I could not trust my husband, I now realized with shock and profound dismay. The weight of this new revelation bent my lips downwards, sent quivers, and drew waters from the wells of my eyes.

But... I could... I would... trust God.

I would have been shipwrecked, but God. I would have been drowned, but God. God... I remembered. God... I believed. God... had... plans... for me.

Good plans... plans for my future... not to harm me... but to give me hope.

If He had not been real, I would have gone under.

36

A Question That Would Pop Up

W henever something of this nature – a betrayal – happens, the question pops up again and again: "Could I have done anything different? Could I have avoided this?"

Of course, no one is perfect and I could have been guessing for years to come if I had kept the house clean enough, or made the food good enough, etc. You can guess what I mean.

One day I talked to the Lord about this because it was a subject that had been brought up more than once by a well-meaning friend. She asked, "What did you do to cause your husband to betray you?" As you can imagine, this was very hard to face.

"Lord," I spoke to God, "what can I say to this? I know that I am a person like any other and that I am far from perfect. But I tried to be a good wife and I wanted to do my best. But Lord, did I do something specific that caused Kirk to leave me? I am so grieved as I think about this."

I bared my heart before the Lord.

I discerned that God then asked me a question: *"Janice, what was your motive in your marriage?"*

"Well," I said, "to love and to serve my husband."

After this, I felt a new freedom to not analyze myself or to give in to condemnation. I realized that even though I was not perfect, my heart had been in the right place – and that God knew that.

~~~

Friday, October 15, 1999

It was the next evening after the girls had gone with Kirk, that Pamela, an old friend of Kirk's, phoned.

While Kirk had been in the ministry for the two years before we were married, a family had 'adopted' him and had him over for weekly dinners and prayer fellowship. The couple and their children all admired Kirk and missed him. On occasion, Pamela phoned to keep in touch. It had been several months since we'd last heard from them.

"Hi Janice!" Pamela's sing-song voice greeted me when I picked up the phone. "How's it all going? Is Kirk around?" she asked, oblivious.

"Well," I began, sitting on the couch, "Kirk is not here because Kirk left me."

There was a long pause. "What?" she asked, alarm sounding in her tightened voice.

"Kirk left me," I repeated, "after our third baby was born, just over three months ago. He's been involved with another woman.

"But Pamela," I continued, while she remained in shocked silence, "every time my prayer partners and I pray, we get the idea that there is something more that we should know about. And we get the idea that pornography is at the root of it all. But I've never seen any evidence of this," I informed her, while hugging a pillow on the couch.

"Well, Janice," Pamela said, serious, "I'm going to tell you something that I think you now need to know. One night, when Kirk came over for dinner at our house, he cried and shared with my husband that he had a pornography addiction."

"You're kidding?!" I said, astonished to hear this.

"Not at all," she said. "My husband and I prayed with him and thought that took care of it."

"Oh," I said. I could tell immediately in my spirit that this was the missing piece of information that God had wanted us to uncover. Pamela's eyewitness account was a full confirmation of the word of knowledge He'd already given.

~~~

I pushed the off button on the telephone and laid it beside me on the floor where I'd shrunk. Taking a deep breath, I exhaled slowly.

Time stood still for me as a single remembrance lit up my memory:

The mail had arrived several years ago when we'd been living in North Carolina. With that bundle of mail had come an unwanted magazine, one of a lewd nature.

It sported a white jacket cover with the words, 'Our apologies if you did not order this magazine and you received it by mistake.'

I'd fumed about its delivery later that night on a date with Kirk, while our neighbor babysat our new daughter, our firstborn. 'That sort of surprise mail could tear a family apart!' I'd exclaimed.

In Kirk's silence, I'd assumed his agreement with me. But then, I remembered... he'd asked me where I'd put it.

~~~

Sorrow filled my heart for Kirk. Compassion wept at his bondage. I grieved for him.

If only I'd known about this addiction that had crept into his heart long before I'd ever met him.

If only the friends whom he'd trusted with his confession had directed him to reveal his struggle to me and to others.

If only we'd stayed in one place long enough to put down roots, make longtime friends, and have accountability. Then Kirk could have received their help.

If only his father, or his brothers, or his growing-up friends would've asked him those hard questions and offered him counsel.

If only...

However, I could not help but see that God's sovereign revelation of the true root immediately became a shelter for me against the lies of the enemy.

~~~

"Blessed is the man
who does not walk in the counsel of the wicked"
Psalm 1:1

~~~

I didn't feel like attending any celebrations. But it was my friend from Bible study whose teenage children were throwing a surprise party for her. Everyone had been invited from the church and from their neighborhood.

I had free babysitting for a couple of hours and so I wanted to show my support.

However, perhaps I would've stayed home if I'd known the confrontation I would encounter there.

"But, honestly," the well-meaning friend pled with me while we talked near the corner of the crowded living room at the party, "you had to have done something to have made your husband just up and leave you like that." She shifted her glass to her other hand and her weight to her other foot. "Fault lies with both parties, not just with one. After all, we're all sinners."

I looked at her silent, stunned, and wondering what to say next because these were troubling words that needed a response, instead of a reaction.

"You need to realize what you did wrong," my friend continued, "so that if you do ever get married again, you won't make the same mistake," she counseled further, her long and curly black hair hanging down past her shoulders.

I thought of the mistake of my simple naïveté and the trust I'd had for the husband whom I'd loved so much. If only I'd been more suspicious about his past and his activities before he'd become a Christian. If only I'd been more suspecting about all those hours he'd lied and told me that he was working late. Would I have been able to stop him if I'd been questioning him at every turn?

I caught my breath and kept silent. Her words penetrated like knives making more marks in the underlying tenderness of my heart, already charred with burnt emotions.

I continued to just stand there, looking back at her, unblinking, feeling the sting of her unintentional slap. Certainly I had asked the question myself. *But she had not lived my marriage.*

"Ugh," I thought and even said it aloud to my friend as she waited for me to answer. On top of feeling the cutting pain of my husband's betrayal once again, on top of the humiliation that it was to have to explain the situation again – now I also stared into the assuming eyes of a dear friend trying to be helpful.

What flashed into my mind were the faces of faithful spouses who had endured extreme challenges of terminal sickness, financial devastation, mental illness, or depression in their marriage. Yet, those affected spouses had kept their vows in the midst of the most difficult of circumstances.

What grievance had my husband suffered with me? I had supported him in every way I knew how. He had not communicated, or given me a chance to answer, or change, or address any problems.

It was during that silence that an unfamiliar, older face stepped into our circle, having overheard our exchange. "It takes two to agree to get married," the man with kind, understanding eyes interrupted, "but it only takes one unwilling, rebellious spouse to choose to divorce."

The man continued, "Sure, there are times when couples 'fight like cats and dogs' and end up calling it quits together. But in most of the divorces I have known of, there is usually just one person in the marriage who decides on the divorce, and our legal system accepts and supports that."

"The state of California makes it especially easy for that one spouse to get their divorce," I added, speaking softly.

"Yes," the man agreed, "and handcuffing your mate to you is not permitted." He looked at my friend who then looked at me.

I tried to smile at his weak joke, amidst the background chatter of people socializing.

"In addition," the stranger added, "there is the matter of the children. At some point, the children grow up and need to have some answers. They need to know the truth. Not in a destructive way, but in an informative, helpful way.

"The fault could lie mainly with one parent or another, and it is good for them to have some honest answers to their questions and to not be left out in the dark."

All three of us temporarily ignored the annoucement that dessert was now available at the table in the dining room.

"For example," the man said, "if the children are just told that 'both parents had their faults and so they just got divorced,' then some kids are going to have trouble with that.

"An unexplained message about something so significant to their lives will make them feel like no one loved them enough to fight for them to be a family. Kids eventually need to know what happened at the appropriate age so that they do not wrongly blame themselves."

My friend nodded at us, then excused herself to get some more fruit punch and a piece of cake. The stranger with the kind eyes patted my shoulder and joined a woman with a matching jacket where she chatted with some others on the couch.

I was left on the edge of the room with my thoughts. Each marriage here on earth is composed of two imperfect people, I reflected. Naturally, every marriage has its own challenges, frustrations, and two people with great differences. But when one spouse leads a hidden, double life, concealing active sin – with no accountability or willingness to receive help or counsel, they are walking down a pathway of destruction leading to eventual disaster.

God saw the choices that my husband was making in his secret life. God gave many opportunities for my husband to turn around, repent, and to receive forgiveness and healing.

God loved my husband and showed it to him in numerous ways. But with my husband's heart becoming harder and harder with each step that he took when he made yet another sinful decision, I believed that God had a plan in place to provide for me and my children, long before I knew that I would have the need.

~~~

Thursday, October 21, 1999

For the most part, it was only Nicole, at a 'grown-up' five and a half years of age, who was able to comprehend some of the seriousness of what was taking place in our lives. In my prayer time with Miriam, we had specifically asked the Lord to send some help for her as she tried to process the major changes.

So when Pearl, who worked on the ministry team at the church, approached me to offer to meet with Nicole once a week and use a little study guide to talk with her about what was happening in our lives, I was grateful for the extra support and saw it as a direct answer to prayer.

Nicole met with Pearl for about thirty minutes at the church to talk and seemed to benefit from this outlet and care that God provided.

~~~

"He tends his flock like a shepherd:
He gathers the lambs in his arms
and carries them close to his heart;
He gently leads those that have young."
Isaiah 40:11

~~~

37

The Agreement

Friday, October 22, 1999

I wondered how long it would be before Kirk and I might reach a settlement in our discussions. I wondered if we would end up back in court because I was not willing to agree with his ideas of joint custody and shared Christmases.

A different homeschool family had asked to watch the girls today while I readied for yet another garage sale the next day to sell some of our things before the move.

"Lord," I prayed again, standing on His Word from Isaiah 59:1, *"Surely the arm of the LORD is not too short to save, nor (Your) ear too dull to hear."*

I also continued to lean on the verse in Proverbs 21:1, which said, *"The king's heart is in the hand of the LORD; he directs it like a watercourse wherever he pleases."* I prayed that Kirk's heart would be directed by the Lord and that he would make the decisions that God wanted him to make.

It was about time for Kirk to arrive to pick up the girls. I made sure they'd had some fruit, and that they had their shoes and coats by the door. Only a moment later, Kirk knocked and I let him into the foyer.

He stood there, waiting, while I put shoes on Meaghan's feet.

"I'll agree to everything," he announced, standing in front of us.

"What?" I asked, not thinking I'd heard him correctly.

"I'll agree to everything," he stated again, not moving.

"You mean, even Christmas? And paying half of my lawyer fees like the courts would require you to do anyhow?" I asked of him, looking up.

"Yes," he said, and he turned away to take the girls with him out to his truck.

"Okay," I called after him from the porch, "I'll call the lawyer and see how long it will take to draw up the papers."

Shaking, I returned inside the house, closed the door, and sank to the floor – relieved, and excited, and thankful, and wanting to get those papers signed as soon as possible.

~~~

Tuesday, October 26, 1999

Our follow-up mediation was on the schedule and Suzy took the girls while I attended the 9:00 AM appointment.

However, Kirk was a no-show and so the meeting was a short one.

~~~

Friday, October 29, 1999

Enter Angela. Angela who attended Hillside Community Church with me and who lived down the street on Strawberry Lane, also had a burden on her heart for our family.

Her two children, a boy and a girl, were further along the road of homeschool education than we and others were, and so it was that Angela had founded our church homeschool support group.

Angela used her God-given vision and managerial skills to institute the group. She articulated and planned with thoughtfulness and care. She could assess a situation and see where she might fill in a hole or two.

Today, she and her children babysat for me while I prepared for the next garage sale. She began to play an active role in our childcare and she would also fill an important position in the enormous job of packing our things and securing them to be shipped to Maryland.

~~~

Monday, November 1, 1999

Mr. Maxwell's law office phoned to cancel the appointment they had given me. Disappointed, I declared aloud scripture that reminded me of God's control over the whole situation.

I wanted badly to get the papers drawn up before Kirk could change his mind about settling out of court and 'agreeing to everything.' Again, I reminded myself that God was in control and that whatever delay would be for my benefit.

So I worked more on the wording of the contract myself and went to Ginny's apartment to use her computer for research.

~~~

Friday, November 5, 1999

Another outward setback: The lawyer's office phoned again to cancel the papers being signed. It was hard not to feel discouraged, or like I was on a rollercoaster ride. What if Kirk had second thoughts, changed his mind, or we ended up back in lengthy discussions, or even in court?

However, did I mention again how God was intervening in our lives? While Angela watched the girls and I ran errands, the words, *But God,* rang throughout my being.

"The devil meant for me to go down into the pit and to stay there when Kirk left — *But God!* Satan intended to ruin God's call on my life — *But God!* Satan meant evil and destruction for me and my children — *But God!* Instead, God gave grace and abundant provision. *But God! But God! But God!*"

I was shouting His praises by the end of my errands. I was dripping in His glorious Presence and the waves of goodness that overflowed from His wonderful Biblical truths.

"*But God!!! But God!!! But God!!!*"

~~~

That night I made a phone call. I decided that in the delay I would phone little Melanie's dad from the girls' Sunday School class. His wife, unfortunately, had also left him for somebody else. I wanted to see what more he knew that could help me.

"Make sure to put in the contract that he is responsible for doing the driving," Melanie's dad suggested. "They are the ones who chose to leave, and you shouldn't have to be running all over creation as a result."

I thanked him for his helpful advice, and got off the phone. With my ink pen in hand, I added that provision into the contract and would phone the statement into my lawyer before the signing day.

Maybe this was one more provision that had to be accomplished before the contract was signed. I had no idea how important this would be in the future. All delays, I discovered, would amazingly be for my benefit.

~~~

Sunday, November 14, 1999

Joni Eareckson Tada was a woman whom I had heard about from the time I had been a little girl. One night at my church growing up, my family and I had watched a movie about how she'd dived into the Chesapeake Bay into shallow water, broken her neck, and become a quadriplegic.

Joni was speaking locally in California all these years later. Hannah had cared for Meaghan the night before so that Nicole and I could attend a special presentation given by this woman, one who had triumphed over extreme hardship.

Now, this morning, at five months old, David Michael was to be dedicated to the Lord in a service at church. But in the rush of being out late the night before and up early this morning, Nicole could not find her dress shoes, and neither could I.

It was the Sunday School hour, but I wandered outside on the sidewalks between the different buildings of classrooms, pacing. What would I do about Nicole's shoes? How could our little family stand up in the front when Nicole had her tennis shoes on with her fancy dress?

The service would begin soon. It was an important service – one that Kirk should be here for, one where I would promise to bring David Michael up in the Christian faith, one that Kirk should be at making the same promise. How was it that Kirk could not be here with me?

It was Della who did not pass by but instead paused on the sidewalk to talk with me. Della, the music minister's wife, shoulder-length blonde hair, who had a daughter about the same age as Nicole. "What's wrong?" she asked.

"It's the shoes!" I cried, and tears began streaming down my face as I stood there. "David is going to be dedicated in thirty minutes and Nicole has lost her dress shoes. She's wearing tennis shoes with her dress!"

"Why don't I run home, Janice? I'll find a pair of my own daughter's dress shoes. You sit down here on the bench." Della volunteered.

Comforted, I nodded, trying to blink back all the tears. That is when Paula came along and stayed beside me to wait for Della's return.

"It's the shoes," I confided to Paula, still crying, "Nicole doesn't have dress shoes to wear to the dedication."

"I know, I understand," said Paula, staying by my side.

~~~

It was a beautiful service, and Pastor Logan lingered for pictures and to talk to each of the children. Paula and Hannah came close to the front to ask if they could take us out to lunch with their families to celebrate the occasion.

So it was that I found myself with my children, surrounded by a group of friends and their children, sitting around a long table at the Village Green Café to commemorate David Michael being dedicated to the Lord.

Again I felt encompassed by God's arms of love.

And it turned out that the shoes which Della had been unable to locate, had not even mattered at all.

~~~

"The LORD your God is with you,
He is mighty to save.
He will take great delight in you,
He will quiet you with his love,
He will rejoice over you with singing."
Zephaniah 3:17

~~~

Monday, November 15, 1999
Dreading another call to the lawyer's office because of how they'd cancelled the previous appointments, I phoned them anyway. Surprised, I took a deep breath because they actually had an opening for the next day at a time that both Kirk and I could make.

~~~

Tuesday, November 16, 1999
Dropping the girls off at Angela's, I drove outside of town to the lawyer's office. Would Kirk show up? I wondered.

He did. He entered the office, read, and signed the papers, although he crossed out my new ideas about him paying for half of their college education and continuing their child support until they were the age of 21. He left all else intact.

I watched from my chair far in the back of the room as he scribbled his signature on the papers. Then I thanked the secretaries for staying late, and walked out the door.

The delay, it turned out, had worked again to my benefit, as it would mean more time that I would receive alimony.

After I'd signed the papers myself and left the office, I sat in my car in the parking lot at dusk, daring to breathe.

I was free. Free to list the house, free to sell all the rest of my belongings, free to move back to Maryland, and free to homeschool if I could make it financially.

I looked down at my wedding ring which I would not take off until the sad date was official, six months later. Just in case.

The ring had been handmade especially for me from a design that Kirk had drawn up himself with the help of a family jeweler. The centered, larger heart-shaped diamond caught some lingering rays of sunshine, and shone brightly. This middle brilliant heart that connected to the two ordinary ones on either side stood for Jesus, who would never leave my side.

38

More Angels Sent by Him

Thursday, November 18, 1999

"Can I clean your toaster oven?" Cynthia, a new friend, asked. "I just love to clean up dirty old toaster ovens," she continued. "It just gives me such a feeling of accomplishment!"

"Really?" I said, wondering if I should believe this vivacious person, who I was just beginning to know. "Well, okay," I consented, skeptical.

Cynthia began the task with vim and vigor and sang a song while she did so. I nursed the baby and watched her, not knowing quite what to make of my new friend.

A few hours before, I'd received her unusual phone call. "Janice," the woman at the other end of the line had begun, "you don't know me, but I've heard about you. God has placed it on my heart to come over and to clean your house.

"And if it is alright with you, I am going to come over and clean your house today, and I will clean it tomorrow, and I will clean it every day until you go back to Maryland. So you needn't worry about that anymore!"

I didn't really know what to think about her offer, but I sure did need the help. In only three short weeks, I would leave with the children to move back East.

So, enter Cynthia, most often accompanied by her homeschooled son, Chad, a ten-year-old.

Cynthia was a member of my homeschool support group, though I'd not met her yet. Cynthia was trained as a nurse and wasn't afraid of a little mess. She was funny, and made me belly laugh at my outdated prescriptions which I'd carted around the country for several previous moves.

And, Cynthia generously kept me fed from then on by taking me out for meals of pot roast and salad at Mimi's Café, and bringing freshly-baked chocolate croissants to my door.

Extravagant blessings. That is what God poured out on me time and time again!

How could I be experiencing so much joy and fun, I wondered, in the midst of such heartbreak?

~~~

"You prepare a table before me
in the presence of my enemies.
You anoint my head with oil;
my cup overflows."
Psalm 23:5

~~~

Friday, November 19, 1999

In all, I had nine garage sales. The purpose of selling my things was because it would cost too much to transport them back across the country to Maryland.

Every Saturday was a garage sale. And, every Saturday God provided workers to help me. Hannah first encouraged me to part with my precious belongings, and came to help me to price them. Then Ginny joined in the adventure. Sometimes Frankie came. I was never by myself.

One day, someone sent an e-mail around to the homeschool groups in the area. Before I knew it, homeschool moms began dropping off vanloads of additional items to be sold at my garage sales so that I could earn even more money.

Handfuls of ladies volunteered to come and help me to sell at the Saturday morning events, and other ladies came over to purchase the items available for sale.

One by one, my favorite TV walked out the door, and then my lovely, green, wrought-iron, canopy bed frame. Teenagers from across the street purchased our round country kitchen table and chair set for $150 as a gift for their mother, and then many of my kitchen appliances ran away.

On Friday afternoon, I sat with the baby on the old, blue couch. An assortment of volunteers, never solicited, but eager to help, carried boxes to me filled with my belongings. "What do you want done with this?"

They posed the question as they pulled one item at a time up and held it for me to see.

It was my job to decide if it should be kept, considered, or tagged immediately for the next day's garage sale.

I felt exposed and vulnerable as all my possessions were displayed, but my friends made me laugh. I felt weak watching all my property disappear, but my friends made me money. I felt sentimental handling the items because there was a story behind each one. My friends listened with attentiveness and took interest.

I don't know what I would have done if they had asked me to do anything other than sit there on my old, blue couch, holding my baby and answering their questions. They were His hands and His feet.

~~~

> *"But the eyes of the LORD are on those who fear him,*
> *on those whose hope is in his unfailing love,"*
> Psalm 33:18

~~~

Tuesday, November 23, 1999

Another friend from church, Doris, came by to take the girls out while another group of us continued the hard work at the house.

"What about these canned goods?" Cynthia asked, opening up the pantry. "You've got a lot here. Where did you buy it all?"

"Oh, at the Safeway around the corner," I answered. Cynthia bagged cans of green beans, boxes of cake mixes, containers of frosting, and other goods. Before I knew it, she and another homeschool mom put it all in her van and drove away.

It wasn't more than an hour before they returned shouting about what God had done this time. "Janice! Janice! Even though almost everything was already out of date, the manager closed his eyes and took back every single item for you!!! Isn't that AMAZING?!"

They handed me an envelope full of cash.

~~~

Thursday, November 25, 1999

I struggled to keep my feelings in check as I dressed the girls. Soon, Kirk would pick them up for their first Thanksgiving away from me.

I knew that he intended to take them back to the new family he had created without me. I knew that they would have a special, memorable day, recording it with what was once our own family's video camera, the one I had researched and picked out with Kirk.

It stung.

When Kirk entered our foyer, I stood aside as he walked past me. He greeted the girls enthusiastically and then walked away with them outside, hand-in-hand.

Again, I wondered if I were invisible.

I wanted to scream at him for doing this to me and somehow make him know my pain. But instead, I watched him buckle each of my daughters into their carseats in 'his friend's SUV,' and drive away.

I remembered that God's Word says *"Vengeance is Mine, declares the Lord,"* (Romans 12:19 KJV), and I knew for certain that God could take care of things much better than I could as long as I let Him handle it.

I knew that my job was to forgive Kirk and to pray for him, and that, honestly, I really did want Kirk to come to repentance and to receive the love that the Lord had for him. I knew that it was between the Lord and him now, and that God would forgive him if he asked.

I stood alone, hands at my side. "Oh, God," I said, looking up toward heaven, "You see this." I spread out my hands, "You see all things."

And then I began to list aloud who I was in Christ. "Thank You, God, that I am Your beloved child. Thank You, God, that You died for me and saved me from hell so that I could know You.

"Thank You, God, that You have good plans for me and my family. Thank You, that I am not alone and that You will never leave me nor forsake me. Thank You, God, that You provide for me. Thank You, God, for all that You have already done."

Then I began to list the specific ways in which God had taken care of me and shown me His love, and I felt refreshed, strengthened, and encouraged.

Hearing David awakening, I ran to pick up my sweet bundle of comfort. How grateful I was to hold this warm body once again and to have him there with me. It was hard to imagine him growing up past this helpless little babe of waving arms and legs and smiling coos.

The phone rang. It was Cynthia who said she'd be over to spend the morning with me before I went out later that afternoon. Grateful for her company, we talked and laughed and went through the bathroom drawers emptying and sorting.

~~~

It was 2:00 PM and Rosalyn had invited me and another woman who was also alone to celebrate Thanksgiving. Her family was out of town, so she'd invited us to come and visit with her and then to accompany her to a luxurious meal at their country club. It was perfect.

Rosalyn and Sylvia and I sat together around a stylish round table in elegant surroundings. Served by tuxedoed waiters, who flourished our table with champagne and delicious salads and steak, we shared and we giggled. I thoroughly enjoyed myself.

Again, how strange it was to be having so much fun and to be so well taken care of, I thought, in spite of such a terrible situation.

It was a special Thanksgiving, as the Lord again made His love known to me.

~~~

"Surely goodness and love will follow me
all the days of my life,
and I will dwell in the house of the LORD forever."
Psalm 23:6

~~~

Saturday, November 27, 1999

It was the last of nine garage sales and for awhile I stayed inside, resting on Nicole's bottom bunk where I could peek out the window as I wanted. I didn't know which was worse: having my husband leave me? Or having to part with all my belongings? I knew that losing the husband was worse, of course, but this also felt pretty bad.

Didn't people know how precious each item was? But it didn't make sense to pay to have those things shipped back East.

Ginny entered the house, laughing as she came, and raced down the hallway to the bedroom where I lay. "Janice!" she yelled, "You'll never guess what?!"

"What?" I asked, sitting up in the bed.

"Do you know that old grill that you had that you insisted be sold? The one that we put in the trash because we said it was just plain junk?" she asked.

"Yes," I answered, leaning back on the pillows.

"Well, you'll never believe what happened!" she said. "This man just came up, pulled it out of the garbage, and paid for it! I just can't believe the favor you have, Janice!"

Before she finished, Cynthia entered the room. "Well," she said. "I just sold your glue gun."

"You mean the low-melt blue one?" I asked, suddenly feeling great distress. I had used that precious glue gun to make hundreds of Christmas ornaments for the Jesse Advent Tree calendars I'd made. I hoped it wasn't that one.

"Yes, that one," Cynthia said. "We got $2.50."

I blinked back tears as I thought of my precious glue gun walking down the street in the pocket of someone who did not even know it's significance – the hours that I had used it. It had provided me with such faithful service – and sold for only $2.50!

I really did so appreciate everyone's help, so I lay there without saying a word. But I really did feel dizzy over what felt now like an enormous loss, an obscure and precious link to my past, one that could never be retrieved.

It was then that Nancy, one of the other moms from our homeschool co-op came into the bedroom. She handed me an envelope. I thanked her, took the envelope, and opened it.

Many people had handed me checks of $50 and $100, and even $200 over the last couple of months. But, I was not expecting what I saw written on this check: $3000.

I could hardly believe that what my eyes read was accurate.

"I thought this might help," she said, standing by me.

Overwhelmed, I blinked back more tears. "Do you know, Nancy," I said. "People have been so good to me. Just so good to me."

Looking at her, I continued, "One day I am going to write a book in order to show all that God has done. You just wait," I said. "I am going to write a book," I vowed. "I will share with others how the Lord takes care of those who believe and trust in Him."

~~~

Tuesday, November 30, 1999

The work parties continued each day with three-four different ladies coming over at one time, never coordinated or planned by anyone other than the Holy Spirit. The girls were cared for by different families and others took me out to eat at night in restaurants.

The laughter and the fun and the giggling were contagious. The praise and worship music played and we talked again and again about all that God had done.

The fridge was cleaned by a few ladies, and the car was meticulously vacuumed and detailed by a handful of homeschooled kids. Dads painted and repaired. The house was a busy hub.

In fact, sixty families came and went and helped and served from all the various groups in which I'd been involved. Every need was met by someone having it on their heart at just the right time, and people changed places arriving and leaving without a schedule. Yet it was coordinated perfectly, as only God could do.

~~~

My departure was approaching in just under two weeks and there was still much to be done.

Angela approached me and spoke softly, "Janice, normally I don't have time like this, but I do right now. It is so strong on my heart that I just want to ask you this question: Could I be in charge of boxing and shipping all your things back to your parents' home?"

I hadn't even thought about that chore and all that it encompassed, or how much work would have to be done after we'd left.

I'd narrowed my belongings down to 1100 pounds and it would cost $1/pound to ship. Mostly, the load consisted of clothes and photo albums and books. And I had held onto a few odd items, like the remarkable toaster oven which my brother had purchased for me one Christmas.

Before I had time to answer Angela, Cynthia sprang down the hallway and into the room where we worked, interrupting. Cynthia had taken a call in the kitchen and she exclaimed, shouting, "How much do you love your church?! How much do you love your church?!" She grinned ear-to-ear and still held the receiver where she jiggled, dancing in the doorway, beaming.

"A lot, of course! What are you saying?!" I wanted to know, moving toward her.

"Well, your church just phoned to say that they are going to pay for all your belongings to be shipped to Maryland!!!"

The three of us jumped up and down as only a group of excited ladies can do when they see God at work.

"And," Angela inserted into the festivities, "I'll manage all the boxing left to do and the weighing and the addressing and the getting it there!"

39

A Chapter Closing

Wednesday, December 1, 1999

In the meantime, I had Kirk to face and the continual conflicts, awkwardness, and discomfort that came with it. Issues arose about the use of baby formula, proper medications for the children, and even a disagreement about the transportation of my childhood furniture, handmade by my father, which was broken in carelessness.

The choice to forgive and to release him and his new partner to God's Hands was a constant opportunity requiring action.

~~~

Here are other questions people would ask me: "Janice, why aren't you angrier at Kirk? And why aren't you mad at God?"

The answer was simple: Neither one made logical sense.

Sad to say, but Kirk had made his decision to leave me, first through pornography, and then through adultery, long before I'd known about it. Then he refused to enter into any discussion with me. It was like Kirk was not even there.

I've heard that if you fight with someone, it's because you both care about the outcome. But Kirk had only one ambition by the time I'd made my discovery – to divorce me because his heart belonged to another.

There was nobody present to fight with over our marriage. He had abandoned it.

Because God made the root of pornography in the situation so amazingly clear and because God intervened and showed this fact without a doubt, it was hard to get angry at Kirk. I had heartfelt pity and compassion for him and for his choice of slavery for both now and in the future.

Now it was God's problem to work out whatever He needed to with Kirk. But I belonged to God and I could trust Him (Proverbs 3:5-6).

I understood that if I forgave Kirk and released him into God's hands, then God could deal with Kirk in a much more effective way. My job would be to pray for Kirk as He led me to do so.

And why didn't I get angry at God? Because God loved me! And God promised to take up the role of a husband for me – to provide and to protect me (Isaiah 54:5).

I had known and experienced God's amazing kindnesses and generosity during this season as I'd never known before (Job 42:5). I felt His closeness and I saw His care in clear, visible ways.

I didn't blame God for what Kirk did. And I knew that God hated the actions of husbands who treat their wives in the way that Kirk had treated me.

~~~

Friday, December 3, 1999

Angela had the girls again and had taken them to the park with her children, who seemed to delight in helping to babysit. It was almost time for them to return home so that they could be here before for their overnight with Kirk.

I pulled out the silverware from the drawer and put it in the to-be-packed-pile. As I did, I paused, remembering, "You know, God," I said aloud, "You've always shown me a rainbow in the sky each time before when You've ordered our steps and we've made a big move."

I thought of the three or four major relocations we'd had, and how funny it was that each time before leaving, I'd seen a rainbow in the sky. After it had happened a couple of times, I'd started to take note of it as a special lovegift from the Lord. I wondered if maybe God had not shown me one this time because it was such a sad reason to relocate.

Soon I forgot my musings and began to sort through the drawer that held the pens and pencils.

Within a few moments, I heard Angela's van pull into our driveway and the voices of the children outside. Nicole and Meaghan flew to the door before I reached it and as they pushed inside, they talked all at once.

"Mommy! Mommy!" they both cried.

I looked up as Angela and her 12-year-old son, Nate, and her 9-year-old daughter, Becky, joined us inside, all smiles and grins.

"We saw a rainbow!" exclaimed Nicole.

"Yes, Mommy! It was a BIG rainbow!" Meaghan chimed in, still jumping up and down.

Angela stood smiling, nodding, and confirming, "It was the biggest and brightest looking one I think I've seen."

I marveled at what I'd just been thinking about in the kitchen, and my heart filled with thankfulness.

God had not forgotten His rainbow of promise.

~~~

After our last AWANA Club, I hugged Beatrice and Barbara and Marlene and the others goodbye. It was only the beginning of special-friend goodbyes. One by one over the next week, I would have a few precious moments with so many and grieve over my significant loss of them as well.

This chapter of my life was coming to an end.

~~~

"There is a time for everything,
and a season for every activity under heaven:"
Ecclesiastes 3:1

~~~

Saturday, December 4, 1999

Mostly, Paula and Hannah and Angela took turns having the girls this week. It was the final countdown which included getting the car to the company which would transport it back to Maryland, visiting the library to print out the airline tickets, and the last-minute cleaning and packing at the house.

However, I was not alone. I had lots of help.

It was on Saturday evening that all the ladies took a break and left early.

I bundled up the children and we walked the few blocks over to enjoy the splendor of downtown Hillside decked out in Christmas lights and old-fashioned, dressed-up carolers.

It was the date of the annual *Lighting of the Christmas Tree*.

I pushed David in his stroller and the girls skipped along beside me. We sampled free appetizers provided by the little shops along the main street.

It was hard to believe that I would not be a part of this small, fanciful, California town much longer. The place had grown to have a special place in my heart. I would miss it very much.

~~~

Sunday, December 5, 1999

It was my last Sunday at Hillside Community Church.

At the conclusion of the service, Pastor Logan called me up in front of the congregation and asked if I'd like to say a few words. I thanked everyone for all the ways that God had used them to support me during this time. I told them how grateful I was, and how I would miss them.

After my short speech, Pastor Logan added that all were invited to a farewell reception for me and the kids in a large room located on the second floor of the Sunday School building.

I picked up Nicole and Meaghan from their classes and we wheeled David on the sidewalk in his stroller over to the building where the reception was being held. Entering the large room with the children, I found decorations and a long table with a huge spread of food laid out.

Inside, my friends began to gather with their spouses and families, even those from outside of our church. Prayer partners Ginny and Kayla from Aglow were there, as well as Lacey from Glamour Shots, who had dressed me up for the court date.

I saw Cynthia, once a stranger only belonging to the same homeschool support group, who had come alongside me to pack and to laugh and to take me to dinner. And there was Frankie, from our homeschool co-op, who had ridden the waves with me the first days when I had made the discovery of Kirk's adultery.

My secret sister, Emilie, and Detective Hannah, and Paula from playgroup. Ladies from the church Bible study, the pastors and their wives. Suzy, who had also come alongside to pray with me daily.

Rosalyn and Rhoda and Ida and Teri and Sherri and Diane and Marlene and Donna and Jennifer and Sandra. And Angela, who was taking over the shipping and handling of all my leftover personal belongings.

Other friends stood there, who had helped for a day or in an on-going way, with garage sales and cleaning. And some from the two different Promise Keepers men's work groups.

We ate and the kids played and laughed. I wondered, how could I be having such a special, wonderful time in a crisis such as this? Truly, it appeared more like a festive celebration. There was cake and there were cards and there were hugs and there were many, many, many heartfelt goodbyes – one by one.

How I would miss these dear people, these precious, precious friends.

These people were instruments – each playing their part to create a beautiful song, a symphony of love. The Lord alone had conducted it.

The last gift the group handed me was a painted woodcarving of Hillside Community Church with their names signed on the back, praying for me and sending me off with more blessings.

~~~

Tuesday, December 7, 1999

It was the last MOPS meeting. Again, I was asked to come to the front and to share a few words for the group of about fifty moms. I looked out over the strangers who had become friends because they had joined me in my journey.

Again I thanked them for all their prayer support and help during my time of need. And again I said, "I am going to write a book about this someday!"

I'd run into Faye, our hairdresser, out shopping one day at Safeway. "My husband left me," I'd announced.

Her Asian face grew red with anger and she said, "I also just discovered that my husband was unfaithful."

Another member of the unspoken club. We looked at one another feeling the same pain.

"Please come," she implored me, "for free haircuts today." And we did, and we visited, and we both understood, and we embraced, and we said goodbye.

Frankie phoned and set aside time in her home for us in the afternoon, before the girls had their last visit with Kirk that evening before we moved. "Don't worry," she promised. "We'll stay in touch."

You really get to know someone when you lose everything and they climb down into the trenches with you in order to walk it out together.

Then my prayer partners, Kayla and Ginny, came to the house. I walked outside with each of them, leaving a handful of others still inside working. We held one another and I could not imagine my life without these dear sisters whom God had provided since first moving to Hillside. They had journeyed with me in prayer and experienced God with me. It was so hard to say goodbye.

Kirk returned with the girls at 9:00 PM and came inside the foyer to say goodbye to the baby.

My friends and I stepped to the background, praying and watching Kirk with our children, wishing that he would even now come to his senses and see that what he was doing was wrong. We held our breaths, but it was not to be.

"Goodbye," he said as he held each daughter individually and squeezed her tight. Then he took baby David into his arms and held him up high, and then kissed him on the forehead. A tear glimmered in his eye. "See you right after Christmas," he said. "I'll come to visit."

He handed the baby back to me without saying anything more, and he walked outside the house. He did not turn around, and he did not look back.

It was 9:00 PM when the phone rang. Hannah asked, "Can Hailey come over and say goodbye just one last time?" So 4-year-old Hailey came and hugged the necks of 5-year-old Nicole and 3-year-old Meaghan. And Nicole sobbed, not even fully understanding why.

It was late and we had to stop our work. Angela reassured me not to worry as we parted because she would oversee the packing, and Cynthia would manage the cleaning. The children went home with her family to spend the night again, so that I could focus on packing for the plane trip.

Cynthia called her son, Chad, to help, and he gathered our suitcases. I went home with her to finish the packing and to spend the night there. Her husband was out of town so she gave up her bedroom for me, with a private luxury bath to enjoy.

The next day, our flight was scheduled to leave midday to return us to Maryland.

~~~

Thursday, December 8, 1999

Angela dropped the girls off in the morning at Cynthia's and I had my final moments of goodbye with her. I was so grateful for all her help with the children and the packing and the sharing.

Paula picked our family up in her SUV, and along with Cynthia, drove us to the airport. I looked out the window as we passed the familiar sights of the Golden Gate Bridge and 'The City.' I blinked back tears. I wondered which was the worst – my husband leaving me, or losing almost all of my possessions, or saying goodbye to so many dear, special friends?

"Embrace the pain," Cynthia spoke when she saw me out of the corner of her eye. "It's good to feel the pain," she repeated. "Don't forget to embrace and feel the pain." It seemed like only a few moments before we arrived at the crowded airport.

Checked in, we waited in the lounge chairs, looking at one another, speaking softly. Time sped by inside the busy hub, and the plane's storage compartments were soon filled with the luggage of many passengers.

Before long, families with small children were called over the loud-speaker to board the plane first. I wished for a few more moments, even minutes, to spend with my friends and to say final goodbyes to Paula, Cynthia, and to California. But the time had come. I had not been able to will time to slow down for me in these final precious minutes.

Holding each friend close for one last moment, not knowing if I would ever see them again, then waiting as each one had a few words with the children, I turned to take those first few awkward steps while holding a little hand, a stroller, and a carry-on bag, toward my new life, toward the good plans that God had for me on the East Coast.

~~~

I sat still on that plane headed back East toward Maryland, surrounded by my small family on my lap and by my side. I made a mental list and took time to thank God for one gift after another that He had lavished upon me.

As our plane took off, driving us into the realms above the clouds, the girls' eyes slowly grew heavy, and they began to doze with their heads leaning over their armrests on top of their favorite blankies. I noted the new backpacks in their laps and on the floor, filled with brand new cassette players and other puzzles, toys, and snacks that Jennifer had provided for each girl for the long trip home.

My past of being a happily married wife and having an ideal traditional family was over.

My future gaped with huge, unanswered questions and I leaned heavily into God's promises, calling to mind Bible verses to whisper aloud.

Nestled safely in His arms of love, I began to comprehend, for the first time, the danger I'd been in. It was like I'd been on a tightrope walking over Niagara Falls, hundreds of feet high above ferocious waters, crashing wildly down into the huge drop.

How had I not seen that I'd been up so high, in such a perilous and precarious place? Why, I could have fallen at any moment and been carried away to my death.

But instead, all I'd seen was Jesus beckoning me forward. His face, His encouragement, His words, His breath.

I hadn't even realized the deep, dark danger I'd been through. Instead, I'd feasted on His love, His joy, His peace, His face.

~~~

"My ears had heard of You
but now my eyes have seen You."
Job 42:5

~~~

"Don't be afraid. Am I in the place of God?
You intended to harm me, but God intended it for good
to accomplish what is now being done,
the saving of many lives."
Genesis 50:19

~~~

"For I am convinced that neither death nor life,
neither angels nor demons,
neither the present nor the future, nor any powers,
neither height nor depth,
nor anything else in all creation,
will be able to separate us from the love of God
that is in Christ Jesus our Lord."
Romans 8: 38, 39

~~~

"And we know that in all things
God works for the good of those who love him,
who have been called according to his purpose."
Romans 8:28

~~~

~~~

Believe

The Work of God… is to believe in Him.
The Work of God… is to believe in Him.
The Work of God… is to believe in Him.
And this is what you do:

When you face trials… choose to believe in Him.
When there are no smiles… only believe in Him.
Across the miles… you can believe in Him.
And this will work for you.

Song from my Quiet Time in 1996

~~~

God is looking for someone
who will believe Him.
Will you soften your heart,
and be that one?

Seven Keys To Victory
Over Any Crisis

1. Belonging to God

Since childhood, I'd believed from the Bible that Jesus had died on the cross for my sins and had saved me from hell.

"If we confess our sins,
he is faithful and just
and will forgive us our sins
and purify us from all unrighteousness."
I John 1:9

I knew that He had done this because God loved me and wanted a relationship with me.

"God, who has called you into fellowship
with his Son Jesus Christ our Lord,
is faithful."
I Corinthians 1:9

As a teenager, I'd also been filled with the Holy Spirit (see Pentecost, Acts 2). As a result, I prayed in tongues daily. Frequently using this gift kept my heart closer to God and helped me to love Him and His Word more.

~~~~~~~~~

2. The Choice to Forgive

The question about forgiveness had been settled back in my senior year of high school. Our Bible study leader, a charismatic woman near my grandmother's age named Marjorie Horton, had conducted a full year of study centering on God's reasons for us to forgive, always.

She had challenged me to make a vow all those years ago about what I would do if someone hurt me. With God's help, I'd decided, I would forgive. No matter what.

But Why Forgive?

The first reason I knew to forgive Kirk was that I, too, desperately needed God's forgiveness. So I could not withhold it from him.

~~~

"And when you stand praying,
if you hold anything against anyone,
forgive him,
so that your Father in heaven
may forgive you your sins."
Mark 11:25

~~~

Second, I believed that if Kirk really understood what he was doing, he would not be doing it. Sin keeps one in darkness.

~~~

"Jesus said,
'Father, forgive them,
for they do not know what they are doing.'"
Luke 23:34a

~~~

Third, I knew that if I held unforgiveness, it would hurt only me. I reflected on Matthew 18:21-35.

Fourth, I knew that God's Word proclaimed that *'Vengeance is Mine.'* This means that it is God's job, not mine, to execute justice. My job, on the other hand, was to pray for him.

~~~

> *"Do not take revenge, my friends,*
> *but leave room for God's wrath,*
> *for it is written:*
> *'It is mine to avenge;*
> *I will repay,' says the Lord."*
> Romans 12:19

~~~

I knew that God Himself could do a much better job at handling what Kirk had done than I could. The sooner that I stepped out of the way, the more that God could move into Kirk's heart and life. So I handed Kirk over to God by making the choice, aloud, to forgive him.

It was simply a choice to forgive Kirk, having nothing to do with my feelings which would change back and forth with a thought or a memory.

Forgiveness did not mean that I agreed with what Kirk had done. It just meant that I was willing to allow God to handle Kirk in His way and in His time.

It was a choice that I would have to make repeatedly, but one that I had already settled in my heart, so I did not need to use up energy wondering whether I would or would not do it. I simply did it again, aloud, every time I noticed that I felt offended.

Sometimes when it was hard, I'd pray, "Lord, I am willing, please help me to forgive." And when I opened my heart to God, He was faithful to fill it with the grace and strength I needed to forgive Kirk.

I also knew that it did not mean I was fully healed from the wound that had been inflicted. It just was a first step in the journey I would travel toward healing, keeping me close to God, and allowing God's good plan to unfold in my life.

~~~~~~~~

3. Surrendering My Whole Life to God
and Trusting Him

~~~

"Therefore, I urge you, brothers,
in view of God's mercy,
to offer your bodies as living sacrifices,
holy and pleasing to God—
this is your spiritual act of worship."
Romans 12:1

~~~

One of the most important decisions that I made was to put myself wholly in God's Hands and to trust Him.

I could not control Kirk. Everything he was doing was out of my sight anyway. But God could see, and God loved both of us, and God had the power to help.

I knew that my job was to praise God for His active and loving care and to pray for Kirk.

~~~

"Submit yourselves, then, to God.
Resist the devil, and he will flee from you."
James 4:7

~~~

"Trust in the LORD with all your heart
and lean not on your own understanding;
In all your ways acknowledge Him,
and he will make your paths straight."
Proverbs 3:5-6

~~~

~~~~~~~~~

4. Speaking God's Word Aloud

Speaking God's Word and God's promises aloud frames and defines one's thoughts.

Please hear me: This is SO important.

Doing this keeps one focused and on the right track.

Do it first in the morning, last at night, during the silent moments, during the errands, and whenever else you can.

~~~

"So then faith cometh by hearing,
and hearing by the word of God."
Romans 10:17 (KJV)

~~~

~~~~~~~~~

5. Meditate on a Specific Truth
From God's Word Each Day

Each day, I read the Bible. Each day, I'd find a Bible verse that spoke to my heart and that I could carry around in my thoughts.

The Word of God is like a seed. We plant it by meditating on it and thinking about it. Then God does what only He can do: He makes it alive in us and it produces results.

It's an amazing thing, but God produces fruit in our lives when we just simply plant the seed of His words in our hearts.

~~~~~~~~~

6. Thanksgiving

~~~

*"...give thanks in all circumstances,
for this is God's will for you in Christ Jesus."*
I Thessalonians 5:18

~~~

Say it. Sing it. Do it. Don't stop. Keep busy by praising Him.

- Praise Him *first* because your first reactions count the most to help you to head in the right direction.
- Praise Him because it magnifies God's greatness and puts your enemy in the correct perspective.
- Praise Him because it is actually a powerful weapon of spiritual warfare. (Psalm 149 and II Chronicles 20:22).
- Praise Him for the victory in whatever way He chooses. Because you are in Him, your victory will happen.

~~~

*"for everyone born of God
overcomes the world.
This is the victory
that has overcome the world,
even our faith."*
I John 5:4

~~~

Make a vow to praise God no matter what.

~~~~~~~~~~

7. Build a Faith-Filled Environment

~~~

"But they laughed at him.
After he put them all out,
he took the child's father and mother
and the disciples who were with him,
and went in where the child was."
Mark 5:40

~~~

- Surround yourself with others who are believing God.
- Limit media such as TV, movies, secular songs, surfing the Internet, and other avenues that do not feed your faith.
- Play praise and worship music 24/7 quietly in the background so that you hear it when there is nothing else happening.
- Make a prayer tape by recording your prayers aloud with a heart of faith, a voice of belief and strength, and prayers grounded on Bible verses. Then play it at night or during other quiet times in order to keep your mind focused on God's truths.

J anice Lynch has a driving passion to spread stories of God's faithfulness and has been published in Guideposts, Crosswalk.com and Homeschool Enrichment Magazine. Recipient of a Cec Murphey scholarship, Janice is a graduate of the Proverbs 31 Ministries' 2010 She Speaks, speakers and writers conference.

Over the years, she has served as a church youth director, a campus leader for InterVarsity Christian Fellowship, and a social worker for emotionally disturbed children. As a participant of Aglow International, Janice has spoken for women about God's care and His exciting answers to prayer. Janice also enjoys serving in her local church's Single Parents Ministry.

Janice embraces the call to raise and homeschool her three children and relies on the Lord every day for His help.

The Lord impacted her life at the age of 15 when He rescued her with the truth from the Bible and changed her life forever.

Visit the author website at www.WhenGodisFaithful.com for additional free resources and help.

Printed in the USA
CPSIA information can be obtained
at www.ICGtesting.com
BVHW041324270723
667886BV00005B/24